CHANGING TRAINS

STEVEN NORRIS

CHANGING TRAINS

An Autobiography

HUTCHINSON
LONDON

This edition first published in 1996 by
Hutchinson

Random House UK Ltd
20 Vauxhall Bridge Road, London SW1V 2SA

Random House Australia (Pty) Limited
20 Alfred Street, Milsons Point
Sydney, New South Wales 2061, Australia

Random House New Zealand Limited
18 Poland Road, Glenfield, Auckland 10, New Zealand

Random House South Africa (Pty) Limited
Box 2263, Rosebank 2121, South Africa

A CiP record for this book is available from the British Library

Papers used by Random House UK Limited are natural,
recyclable products made from wood grown in sustainable forests.
The manufacturing processes conform to the environmental
regulations of the country of origin.

Cole Porter lyrics reprinted by permission of International Music
Publications Ltd, © 1934 Harms Inc., U.S.A. Warner/Chappell Music Ltd.

Set in Plantin by Deltatype Ltd, Birkenhead, Merseyside
Printed and bound in Great Britain by
Mackays of Chatham PLC

ISBN 0 09 180212 1

For Tony and Edward
with love

Contents

1 Scouse for Starters   6
2 'Put Him in for the Law, Mrs Norris'   16
3 Make a Million, Lose a Million   28
4 Blessed Margaret   42
5 Backbencher   62
6 Lobby Fodder   81
7 Margaret in Her Stride   94
8 A Foot on the Ladder   103
9 Out and In   113
10 Second Maidenhood   133
11 That Bloody Woman   146
12 Annus Horribilis   158
13 Yes, Minister   172
14 Mind the Gap   185
15 Too Much Too Soon   200
16 Never Complain, Never Explain   207
17 Taking the Tabloids   219
18 Transport of Delight   224
19 First Among Equals?   235
20 Ersatz Tories   245
21 It Was Just One of Those Things   254

Index   267

Illustrations

John Norris, 1943
Eileen Norris with Steven and Richard, 1951
Steve as a cub, 1954
'The one that got away'
Worcester College Second VIII
Steve with Margaret Thatcher, 1983
Wylie, 1987 – a family group
Epping Forest By-election, 1988 © Solo Syndications Ltd
Campaigning in Epping Forest for the dog-loving vote © Ian
    Swift, *Guardian*
With Simon Burns
William Waldegrave © Srdja Djukanovic, Camera Press
Nicholas Ridley © Richard Open, Camera Press
Kenneth Baker © Richard Open, Camera Press
Daily Mail article © *Daily Mail*
Mahood cartoon ©Mahood, *Daily Mail*
Edwina Currie © Stewart Mark, Camera Press
Digging with John Marshall © National Pictures
The Tardis in Westminster
With Glenda Jackson © Stratford Development Partnership
Selling London Transport Bus Companies, 1994 © Solo
    Syndications Ltd
Starting Bike Week, 1994 © Solo Syndications Ltd
With Emma, 1995
John MacGregor © Richard Open, Camera Press
Brian Mawhinney © Richard Open, Camera Press
Sir George Young © Richard Open, Camera Press
Tony Blair © Sue Adler, Camera Press
John Prescott © Sue Adler, Camera Press
Clare Short © Richard Open, Camera Press
Steve with John Major

Michael Heseltine © Rex Features
Michael Portillo © Richard Open, Camera Press, and ©
  Stewart Mark, Camera Press
William Hague © John Wildgoose, Camera Press, and ©
  Stewart Mark, Camera Press

Unless otherwise attributed, all the photos are from Steve Norris's collection.

Acknowledgements

There are two people without whom this book would never have been written: Tony Austin, whose phone call the day I announced my retirement from Parliament sparked the original idea and who has worked with me throughout the project, and Tony Whittome, my editor at Hutchinson, whose tireless good humour never faltered despite considerable provocation. I owe them both enormous thanks. I had tremendous help from my private office staff at the Department of Transport, Stephen Heard, Rachel England, Heather Pilley and Angela Marlow, who found the time for me in an impossible diary and gently bullied me to make sure I used it. Finally, Emma Courtney not only looked after me wonderfully well at home, but typed almost every word of the manuscript. Without her this book, and a great many other good things in my life, would simply not have happened. The words are mine, but the credit is theirs.

Steve Norris
September 1996

Prologue

Alarm Bells

I was at New Scotland Yard, talking with Sir Paul Condon, the Metropolitan Police Commissioner, in my role as Minister for Transport in London. We were well into our meeting, one of a regular series to discuss policing traffic in the capital, when the telephone on his desk rang. Not for him, but, unexpectedly, for me.

The bizarre thought that my driver had parked on a double yellow line and gone off for a cup of tea flashed through my mind. That would be hardly the easiest thing to explain to the Chief of Police when we were considering how to keep the traffic flowing. But no, the call was from John Nicholls, my private secretary at the Department of Transport. I was unaware of any impending crises at the office and took the call cheerfully.

John dropped his voice reverentially. He had, Minister, a personal matter to, er, mention. John thought I should know urgently that a gossip columnist had telephoned requesting a comment on a piece to be published the next day saying that I was in a relationship with Jennifer Sharp while a married man.

John was not surprised to hear Jennifer's name mentioned. My meetings with her were hardly clandestine. They were public knowledge in the sense that we would go to a restaurant, or an exhibition, together. In the office I made no secret of who I was seeing or where I could be contacted. Indeed, they needed to know where I was if some emergency arose.

The impending publication was at least mischievous, inevitably embarrassing, possibly potentially dangerous though, as far as I could judge, far from lethal. I turned back to Paul and we continued our discussion. But, unknown to me the touch paper had been lit for an almighty explosion which had nothing at all to do with Jennifer.

The essence of the story was true. Jennifer was one of my

oldest friends, someone whom I admired intensely for her looks and her good company. I had been passionately in love with her years before, but it was a friendship that did not lead to marriage. We went our different ways, and lost touch.

Jennifer married David Sharp, a painter. I had married Vicky, a relationship destined not to be as happy as we had hoped. Nevertheless our marriage was pragmatically sustainable because Vicky was a Catholic and would not put divorce on the agenda while, more importantly, we had two young sons to consider. We remained on good terms. Neither of us found it too difficult to put on a united front, so it was in everyone's best interests for us to stay together as far as the rest of the world was concerned, including the constituency. When we were together with the boys we were a family unit.

The reality was that during most of my parliamentary career I spent the week in my London flat and Vicky lived with the boys in our houses, variously in Berkshire and Wiltshire and Epping. I usually went to the constituency on a Friday and was home with Vicky and my sons for weekends. Otherwise we lived independent lives. The rest of the week, once ministerial and constituency duties were completed, was my own.

The situation was not unique at Westminster and Vicky, being an intelligent and worldly-wise woman, was not entirely innocent of the situation. She never wanted the detail. She accepted the situation without approving of it. I had had several relationships and was now living with Emma Courtney, a wonderful girl who was secretary to another MP, Henry Bellingham.

Then Jennifer had come into my life again. Not so long before I had bumped into a mutual friend, Grant McIntyre, and as we gossiped he told me that Jennifer was no longer married and had subsequently been in a relationship which had not led to a second marriage. Only half jokingly I told Grant that it would be a wonderful idea to have a reunion dinner party. Grant took up the idea and invited Hugh Homan, another old university friend, and Jennifer and myself to join him and his wife, and also his first wife, for a meal. Grant was nothing if not progressive. Jennifer and I soon caught up on the intervening years.

As I continued talking with Paul Condon about policing the metropolis, damage limitation possibilities whirled around my head. My concerns at that stage were personal rather than political. It was an open secret in Westminster political circles that I was living with Emma and none of the lobby journalists had blown the whistle on that. What was so different about Jennifer? It was not as if we were living together.

Yet tabloids were hungry for juicy snippets. Even when they nominally supported the Conservative Government, editors did not mind embarrassing the party, indeed some revelled in it. I knew enough about journalistic methods to be aware that many a story was published because the targets lost their cool. They fell for the old journalistic line that they 'could put the record straight' if only they would talk to a sympathetic reporter. Often, without that comment which served to confirm the story, publication could not be justified. Why the *Daily Mail* had decided to go for me at that time I had no idea. If there was a funny side to it, it was that they had got the wrong girl. Nevertheless I had two somewhat delicate telephone calls to make. I rang Jennifer and warned her and I rang Emma, who was none too pleased but more understanding than I had any reason to expect.

I did not have a comfortable night. I knew I could withstand any ribald comments from colleagues in the House. I hoped that if the Chief Whip deigned to summon me he would be understanding and say something about the frailties of human nature and that the Prime Minister, even though he had been buffeted by the Mellor affair with Antonia de Sancha, would have weightier things on his mind. If I had known that the following week John Major was due to make his Back to Basics speech about family values at the Tory Party Conference I doubt if I would have slept at all.

Next morning the item appeared with an innocent enough picture of Jennifer, with me, walking along a street. We were not holding hands – just walking. The picture explained an incident a few weeks before, when, returning to Westminster after lunch, out of the blue a lone girl photographer had snapped our picture. She had not spoken to us. I didn't know whether she was a staff press photographer, or a freelance commissioned to take it, or just a freelance on the make. At the time I had not thought too much about it.

And then all hell broke loose. According to the reports, mistresses came creeping out of the woodwork at every turn. I was a once, twice, three, four, even five times cheat – readers

3

nearly ran out of fingers to count on – as the editions rolled through that week. On the basis of the physical stamina with which I was credited I was a sexual superman, bonking from bed to bed, yet who cared about the details? And would it actually help to 'put the record straight'? Whether I said something or nothing I was uncertain I could ride the storm.

My constituency party in Epping Forest had assumed that Vicky and I were happily married because that was the image we presented. Would they feel deceived and want me out? Would Conservative Central Office pontificate that I had one mistress too many? Was the Chairman of the Party already tearing his hair out? A bald Sir Norman Fowler was one consequence I had not foreseen. Would I have forever earned the journalistic epithet 'disgraced'? Worse, would I be made aware that the Prime Minister disapproved, in which case I might as well clear my desk?

I plead guilty to temptation but not to hypocrisy and there are other chapters detailing these events in greater detail, but at that moment, I reflected on what I had achieved, and what I might now lose.

At one time I had been relatively rich. I had owned a Georgian stone farmhouse in the Wylye Valley, a beautiful part of Wiltshire with a river at the bottom of the garden, a flat in Westminster, a house in Provence, and drove a Bentley turbo. I had run a growing business, spending upwards of £10,000 a year on entertainment alone. True, many of those material manifestations of success had disappeared in the rollercoaster economy when Margaret Thatcher was at the wheel. You can earn money and lose it, you can also invest it well and you can invest it badly. I had lost a million or so at one point. But if you've made it once you could surely do it again, or so I believe.

I had become an MP in 1983 in a cliff-hanger of an election, had soon become a parliamentary private secretary to three stimulating Cabinet Ministers in turn, so I suppose however high the mortgage and the school fees, however appalling the current bank balance, I could always feel I had achieved something.

I was now a Junior Minister to whom, usefully, the media would turn for a soundbite. Whatever people might say about politicians behind one's back they were respectful to one's face. The opportunity to eat well was a hazard to the waistline but, in

4

the company of many varied companions, provided a civilised oasis in what was a busy, fulfilling, life.

There was no resentment about the long hours. Many a day simply wasn't long enough. Life was good. I was enjoying politics. I was on the greasy pole which, with luck and hard work, could take me much higher. I was confident. Having a hand in government was invigorating. And now I risked the lot, including the congenial club that is the House of Commons, packed with the camaraderie and egos of clever and ambitious men and women, even if, at moments, I wondered increasingly whether half of my colleagues were not actually barking mad.

I had got there by luck – mainly luck, but also work, and via a wonderful school, fine university, and business career, all of which had shaped my attitudes to life. My young days, brought up in a terraced house which looked like something out of the credits for *Coronation Street*, were neither poor nor privileged. My background made me appreciate where I had arrived at from a standing start. Not quite from rags to riches but certainly from a very modest upbringing which did not, in fact, breed much modesty into me. But then no one accuses Liverpudlians of being slow in coming forward.

1

Scouse for Starters

On 24 May 1945 the London *Evening News* carried the banner headline 'Young Tories may get chance'. 'Mr. Churchill, I understand,' announced their political correspondent, 'is determined to give several of the young Tories their big chance in his caretaker Government.' The same front page told of the biggest-ever fire blitz on Tokyo, the admission by General Jodl that the Germans had planned their own D-Day for 2 July in 1940, the timetable for the forthcoming general election, with polling day due on 5 July and declaration of results three weeks later on the 27th, and, because this was Britain, the equally momentous news that buses on Routes 21 (Moorgate–Farningham) and 94 (Crystal Palace–Southborough) were diverted by a burst water main in Lewisham. Trams were also affected. Hitler, no doubt aware of my impending arrival, had committed suicide a few weeks earlier. My poor mother had been in labour for forty-eight hours when I, having ascertained that V.E. Day was a fortnight past, made a typically leisurely entrance to this brave new world a few minutes before midnight. My father was away on active service in Belgium, so my mother was first dispatched to Southport to recuperate and then to our home. 25 Burdett Street is in the typical working class area of Aigburth, not more than a stone's throw from the Mersey. There were two rooms downstairs with a hall and kitchen, and upstairs, three bedrooms and a recently-installed bathroom. The outside toilet was still in the tiny paved yard at the back with the luxury of a wooden seat to give less of a shock on a bleak winter morning. The house is there now, although these days it rather incongruously sports a large red burglar alarm. In 1945 there was precious little to steal.

I, of course, had no notion of poverty or deprivation in those early years. I was clothed, fed and loved as much as any child of

6

working class parents trying to build a new life from nothing after the war. If there was a weariness as Liverpool came round from the awful conflict that had brought the Blitz to the docks, I did not notice it. Only later did I become aware that in fact the damage was all around me. The city was a patchwork of bomb-sites which might have been marvellous playgrounds for children, but were stark reminders for many years afterwards of the horrors of that war.

Shortly before my third birthday I ceased to be an only child. I distinctly remember my mother telling me she was 'just going shopping', as she made elaborate arrangements for her brief stay in the maternity wing of a local Salvation Army home. I was unconvinced. Asked if I liked the idea of a baby brother I said I would sooner have a fire engine. Richard duly appeared two days later and my father and I went to collect them. Our family was complete.

Ours was not a distinguished inheritance. My paternal grandfather was an army riding instructor who had lived at the riding school a few yards away. He had died long before the war, leaving a widow who was my only surviving grandparent. My mother's family came from Ireland in the late nineteenth century. Her grandfather, Willie Walsh, was a night superintendent at the Mount Pleasant GPO sorting office in London. His shift finished at six in the morning when, a born entrepreneur, he began a second job collecting rents on the Duke of Westminster's East End estates. As he started so early he was often knocking on doors before the tenants were out of bed and caught them before they could disappear. He did so well that he became a minor landlord in his own right, owning several streets of houses. He had sixteen children on whom his wealth was sadly dissipated, of whom my grandfather was the youngest.

When my mother was two, her mother died. She was a nurse and probably contracted her TB from a patient. In any event, she passed it on to her husband. When my mother was four her father died. She dimly remembers sitting on his knee. He called her 'Copperknob', after her beautiful auburn hair. My mother had an elder sister, and the orphaned girls were taken under the wing of one or other of their many maiden aunts, and packed off to board at Notre Dame Convent School in Southwark. The school overlooks what was then Bedlam Hospital where she recalled for me, seventy years later, how she and her friends

7

used to find great amusement in the antics of the poor unfortunates who were confined there. The school is still there, although now, perhaps appropriately, it solemnly proclaims its grant-maintained status. The magnificent building which was old Bedlam now houses the Imperial War Museum. I pass both each day, and as I do so think constantly of my mother, and the extraordinarily tough life she endured during those early years. The nuns who were her guardians may have had faith and hope, but they knew little of charity. She told me once, quite without rancour, of how at Christmas she was given a doll. It was her only present. It was taken back in the New Year to be a present for another child the following Christmas. Despite an almost total absence of affection and kindness in her own early life, she is the most generous and warm-hearted person I have ever known. She bears no grudges and I have never once heard her utter a word of complaint at the way she and her sister were treated. A bright student, she survived Notre Dame and eventually trained as a teacher. When war came her school was evacuated to St Agnes in Cornwall, but not before one last private tragedy. When my mother was twenty, her sister too, succumbed to the same dreadful tuberculosis that had claimed both her parents.

My father was the youngest of five. His education was unremarkable, although the manner of its termination was less conventional. He fused the school bell by inserting a screwdriver into the wiring system. The bell rang and the entire school left early. It was a popular move among pupils and staff but not with Jack Edwards, the Headmaster of the Liverpool Institute, from which he was promptly expelled. It was the school I later attended, though without similar distinction. He was taken on as a clerk in a milling company and then, pretending he was a year older than he was, joined the army in 1938. He rose to the rank of Battery Sergeant Major and spent most of his war as a gunnery instructor. He has the kind of brain that enabled him to do trigonometry in his head. Formidably bright, he had little formal education, but, as for so many young men, the war gave him a real opportunity to shine. Fate took him too to St Agnes, running a gunnery course for senior officers. He was six foot three inches tall, dark and undoubtedly handsome. My mother says she fell for him straightaway. Theirs was a typical wartime courtship. They were married in London in 1942. He was on a forty-eight hour pass and in uniform. The witnesses were the taxi driver who took them to Ealing Registry Office and the office cleaning lady. Dad gave them a tip and they both duly obliged. Their wedding breakfast consisted of a shared jam sandwich cake bought in the ABC café next door. Gold was in short supply during the war and they searched high and low for a wedding ring. They seriously contemplated using a curtain ring instead, when the genuine article turned up in one of the few jewellers still in business. It was all normal enough in wartime.

When he was demobbed in 1945, my father took his new wife to Liverpool to live with his mother. An unexceptional arrangement was marred by my grandmother's intense but entirely predictable Liverpool Protestant prejudices. My mother had the misfortune to be a Catholic and my grandmother bluntly detested Catholics. They did not get on. I suspect my mother put up with a very great deal in those early days, and certainly she felt lonely for a very long time. The situation was only relieved after I was born when grandmother moved to live with her elder daughter, happily married to a respectable Protestant in Taunton. She stayed there until she died ten years later.

When I was five I went to St Michael's in the Hamlet County Primary School. The building was a typical redbrick single-storey pre-war construction, and so close to home that I could see it from our front door. When the school bell rang, I could run and be in my place before half the other kids had finished their playground games.

Mine was not an auspicious beginning. For a reason no one in my family can now remember, I did not start on the first day of term but a couple of weeks later. On my first day it was clear that the other children were part of a mystical routine. It began each time with us all being told to stand in a line. The teacher then read out everyone's name and as each was called they shouted 'present'. I did not have a present so I did not say anything. Nobody took a blind bit of notice. I was deeply puzzled but judged silence the best course of action. This ritual repeated itself for several weeks until it dawned on me that no one ever gave anyone a present so if you said 'present' it didn't mean anything. It was years later that I worked out that 'present' meant I'm here. On that first day Mrs Pritchard asked us to get a pencil. I promptly walked out of the class, and the school,

9

went back to 25 Burdett Street and asked for one. My astonished mother quickly obliged. When I went home at lunchtime, it was my turn to be surprised. As she cleared our plates, she led me to the front door.

'Off you go then,' she said.

'Do I really have to go back again?' As the truth dawned, shades of the workhouse closed upon the growing boy.

At St Michael's I was generally and fairly effortlessly top of the class. At the age of ten I had no difficulty in passing the eleven-plus and my parents agreed that I should apply to the best school in the city which was still the Liverpool Institute. It was an extraordinary place, and the generation of boys I joined were among its most remarkable. I have school photographs from which I can pick out the young Paul McCartney and George Harrison, all fresh faces and quiffs. They were a couple of years older than me, but they were minor heroes in school even then. Paul was more outgoing than George and hugely popular. Quite apart from his musical talent he was also a creative painter. Art in those days was taught by Stanley Reed, a distinguished Royal Academician, no less. On one occasion when my mother toured an exhibition of school work she, no mean amateur artist herself, remarked that one particular line drawing was quite the best she had seen in years and outstandingly superior to anything else in the show. It was a Paul McCartney rendition of an old boot.

Also on that school picture would have been Peter Sissons, now a household name as one of Britain's top TV news presenters, and the young Bill Kenwright, who went on to star in *Coronation Street*, marry or walk out with every beautiful actress in Britain, and became the most prolific and successful West End impresario after Sir Cameron Macintosh. He is also a director of Everton Football Club. Bill and I share a lifelong passion for the Toffeemen, one of Liverpool's two great football teams. The other, of course, is Everton Reserves.

The Liverpool Institute had started life as the Mechanics Institute, out of which the University of Liverpool also grew. It was a benevolent Victorian charity founded to teach young men engineering, in a fine neo-classical building with pillared frontage and oak-lined entrance hall. It was situated on the appropriately named Hope Street, which ran from Paddy's Wigwam, the modern concrete Roman Catholic Cathedral, at one end, via the magnificent art deco Philharmonic Hall, to one of the finest buildings of the twentieth century – the great Liverpool Anglican Cathedral. The Institute directly overlooks the Cathedral site and my father told me that he watched it being built every day while he was there. They were still building it in my day, completing the monumental west front.

The 'Inney', as the Liverpool Institute High School for Boys was universally known, had been brilliantly led for thirty years by its Headmaster, Jack Edwards. He had earned the nickname of 'The Baz', although I never discovered why. He was a small, dapper and pugnacious man with sleek black hair immaculately oiled. He invariably wore a dark three-piece suit with an impressive watch chain across his expansive belly. He was ruthless with pupils and staff alike, but ruthless too about his pursuit of success for the Institute. Under his leadership at least half a dozen pupils every year would go to Oxbridge on open scholarships, and another half dozen earned places. He made the school the finest in the city. He retired to Southport, just as I was about to enter the sixth form, but insisted on keeping in touch with the staff and the school. He generally beat his target of finishing the *Telegraph* crossword each day in six minutes flat. He died only recently, well into his nineties.

It was a tough school both physically and intellectually. Its whole ethos was to take in children from every walk of life, not to mention every colour, race or creed, provided they were amongst the brightest one hundred and eighty of their year in the city of Liverpool. The building was intended for 650, but by the time I arrived, housed 1150. You had to be fairly fast-footed to survive in that eclectic mixture of sons of dockers and doctors, architects and bricklayers, and a fair sprinkling of boys who had no idea who their father was. I suspect it was rather tougher for the staff than for the pupils. Many of them suffered cruelly at the hands of lads like Mike McCartney, Paul's brother, whom I remember once leaping into one poor unfortunate's class unannounced, sticking a steel bar into the light socket and fusing the entire classroom. 'Weedy' Plant was locked in a cupboard in his own form room with lighted cigarettes stuck under the door for good measure.

But if some failed, then others succeeded triumphantly. I had many quite brilliant teachers. Tudor Jones, an excitable little Welshman who loved the English language, knew Shakespeare

11

and most other respectable literature backwards and, more to the point, could communicate his enthusiasm, took me under his wing. He gave me a love of books which I have never lost. Jack Sweeney, who had himself been a pupil at the school, taught me French and later Spanish. He had studied Russian at Cambridge and helped introduce it into the school curriculum. We must have been one of the first schools in the country to offer the subject at A-level. Jack too was a superb tutor and became a lifelong friend. Now retired, he still lives in Liverpool and, on the all too rare occasions I see him, we can still convulse each other with laughter remembering the old days. Gareth 'Jolly' Rogers was my form master and history tutor and later Headmaster of the school. He treated every young boy as an adult. He never patronised, and, as a result, no one ever took advantage of him. It may be an appalling cliché, but he made history live for me in a way that few others could.

Alan Durband was head of English and much more, as his long and respectful obituary in the *Guardian* attested. He was a founder of Liverpool's Everyman theatre, and a particularly gifted drama producer. The standard of our school plays was high. Both Peter Sissons and Bill Kenwright performed brilliantly under his direction, but so did others. A year ago I was sent out of the blue, by someone from Liverpool who kindly remembered me, a copy of a cast list for Bernard Shaw's *St Joan*. Page to the Duke, about the smallest speaking part, was played by Steven Norris. Among the Assessors (confined to the occasional 'rhubarb' during the trial scene) was one Paul McCartney. One evening Macca decided to liven up his performance, at least for the cast, by smoking a Woodbine throughout. He secreted himself behind a hollow stage pillar from which wisps of smoke emerged during the most dramatic moments of Joan's titanic struggle with her destiny. As far as I know, the whole episode was undetected by the audience, but it convulsed the small boys watching from the wings. Paul could pull an audience even then.

Incidentally, the Militant Liverpool Council in one of its periodic fits of cultural revolution closed down the Institute. They saw it as elitist, and thus to be destroyed. It was an act of sheer vandalism for which they should never be forgiven, for they put nothing whatever in its place. More than a decade later, it was Paul who was shocked to see how badly the fine old buildings had deteriorated and promptly put up a million pounds of his own money to found the Liverpool Institute for the Performing Arts, arguably the finest facility of its kind in Europe for young talented contemporary artists, which, thanks to Mark Featherstone-Witty and his team, now occupies a brilliantly refurbished and extended Institute building. I've heard people say Paul is tight with money; I know differently.

After my effortless success at St Michael's, life at the Institute was a more formidable proposition. A quick mind and a quicker tongue were no longer enough. It was clear a little application was needed. I was content to work just as hard as was absolutely necessary to avoid coming in the bottom half-dozen of the class of thirty, but I certainly had no particular ambition to be in the top ten. The school did in fact divide after a year into two streams: those who were due to take O-levels in four years and those regarded as less able who would take five. I scraped into the fast stream and in due course sat the usual clutch of exams. I recall Jack Edwards writing in my final end of term report that year, 'I seriously doubt this boy's ability to get into the sixth form'. Thankfully, he was wrong. I passed in six subjects which I later parleyed into eight. I went into the sixth form, dropping the subjects which had bored me to tears along the way, including all of the maths and sciences. I took French, English and History at A-level and given the opportunity to concentrate on subjects which I actually enjoyed, was able to do well. After two years I was astonished to find myself selected as Head Boy of the school, the first anyone could remember who had not been awarded his colours for some sport or other, for I had no interest whatsoever in games and no talent for them either. Being Head Boy at the Institute was marvellously good fun, although one of my particular duties was peculiar to the early sixties in Liverpool. Several times a week I rounded up recalcitrant pupils who lingered overlong at the lunchtime sessions in the Cavern. The Beatles, Gerry and the Pacemakers, Stu James and the Mojos, Farron's Flamingoes, The Mersey Beats, The Big Three, there was no end to the stream of young raw talent that tumbled onto that makeshift stage immortalising the Mersey sound. I heard them all, but only for the last five minutes of every gig. As I arrived a substantial section of the audience departed. It was amazing the bouncers ever let me in.

Opposite the school was Blackburne House, formally the

13

Liverpool Institute High School for Girls. There was little
contact between the two, but some sixth-form girls were allowed
to attend our Literary and Debating Society meetings run by
Donald Bentliffe, a classicist whose head was so bald and face so
gaunt that his classroom was known as Golgotha. Donald was
an elderly bachelor who lived alone in a large flat in Sefton Park.
He would invite three or four pupils at a time home to tea, at
which he always served the same meal of Polish ham and
coleslaw purchased from Coopers in Lord Street. He was
solicitous, interested, friendly and concerned. He never married, and we were sufficiently innocent never to question his
lifestyle. Sadly that relationship would be almost unthinkable
these days without someone pointing the finger of suspicion.

It was at one of Donald's joint debates that I first met Edwina
Cohen. I never thought of her as particularly good looking, at
least in any conventional sense, but Edwina at fifteen was
sparky, interesting and vivacious. Her interest in politics was
much more developed than mine, and I hugely enjoyed her
company. We were sufficiently close to go to the pictures
together a few times, but no more. For reasons best known to
herself, Edwina has since chosen to suggest that our relationship
was rather more developed. She may, I suppose, have imagined
a brief fumble under her school blouse behind St George's Hall
to be an orgasmic experience, but I fear I was less impressed.
She went up to Oxford a year before me, and although we were
in the same university for two years at least, I cannot recall ever
seeing her. She apparently frequented the Union. I found the
very few debates I ever attended there unutterably childish and
tedious. The next time I saw her was at my first Tory
Conference in Blackpool, when a girl I thought I recognised was
standing at the podium, waving a pair of handcuffs and
declaiming loudly and at length. The enunciator board referred
to her as Edwina Currie and she was a dead ringer for the girl I
knew. We did not meet then, but on the day we were both first
elected to Parliament I saw her in the Central Lobby where we
exchanged a single sentence. She said, 'I won't say anything if
you don't.' Neither of us appear to have kept our word
particularly well.

Soon after I started at the Institute, the family moved from
Burdett Street to a newly-built, semi-detached house in Cyril
Grove, a small development of twelve homes in a much more

salubrious part of south Liverpool known as Mossley Hill. My parents had saved hard for the £560 which it cost in 1955. Although our new home seems tiny to me now, it was an extraordinary escape from the endless rows of drab terraced houses and back jiggers, street after street of which we now left behind. We had a garden to both front and rear. We backed onto a spacious detached house. We grew a tiny lawn and, wonder of wonders, we inherited a large chestnut tree. We were literally breathing a different kind of air. From the rear bedroom window, whilst you couldn't see the Mersey itself, you looked over it and the Wirral, to the shadowy mountains of north Wales beyond. It was my first Great Leap Forward.

2

'Put Him in for the Law, Mrs Norris'

I concentrated on the subjects I enjoyed, and my sixth-form years slipped by agreeably enough. Having added General Studies to my other three, I was able to produce a clean sweep of A grades in all four A-levels. In September of 1962, Gareth Rogers suggested I sit the Oxbridge scholarships. I knew nothing whatever of universities generally, and certainly had no idea which colleges might be the right ones for me to apply to. Gareth who, like virtually all other members of staff at the Institute, was an Oxbridge man himself, shrewdly advised me firstly to take the social studies or PPE scholarship, for which he correctly assumed I had exactly the right sort of butterfly mind, and second to apply to Queen's, Worcester and Wadham at Oxford in that order. I arrived on a dark November afternoon at Queen's – well known, I later discovered, for its links with Northern grammar schools – and was told the examinations were to be held in Trinity college. I was directed to a room which was far larger than my own at home, and settled in. In Trinity's hall, we scribbled two three-hour papers each day for three days, and then waited to see whether we would be selected for interview by interested colleges. I was invited to four – all of my first three choices, plus St Catherine's. In those days everyone who could manage to walk and chew gum got an interview at St Catherine's, largely because it was not yet entirely built, and my interview room was reached by jumping between duckboards on what amounted to a very large and ugly building site. Inevitably, they offered me an Exhibition, but as it happened, so did Worcester, and as that was my second choice (Queen's, my first, only deigned to offer me a place) I accepted. I had hardly any idea of what my prospective *alma mater* actually looked like, as my interview with the Senior Economics don, John (later Lord) Vaizey took place at around seven in the

16

evening, and the place was literally pitch black. All Oxford colleges were. It was actually during my time there that the process of cleaning began which transformed Worcester College from a dull and undistinguished hulk into a magnificent honey-yellow triumph. Other colleges rapidly followed suit.

As I returned to Liverpool I looked forward to finishing my year at school as Head Boy and to the prospect of going up to Oxford in the autumn of 1963, but in August the tutor for admissions at Worcester cruelly jolted my idyll by writing to point out that it was, in fact, an ancient requirement of the university that one possessed at least an O-level in Latin if one wished to enter into an undergraduate course, and where was my certificate?

I didn't have one. I had failed Latin dismally at O-level. It had always seemed sterile and irrelevant and I had not been helped by four indifferent Latin teachers in as many years. The college was understanding, and kindly confirmed that I would be welcome the following year, provided I had the Latin qualifications. My mother immediately found a private tutor and in a few weeks I produced the necessary pass. Amazing what you can do when you have to. I had at last secured my presence at Oxford, but now faced the unexpected prospect of a year with nothing specific to do and more to the point, no money to do it with either.

The obvious solution was a temporary job. I scoured the *Liverpool Echo*, and in due course, admitting to only four O-levels and omitting any reference to an Exhibition at an Oxford college, I got a job at £4.10s a week at the Ogdens factory in Anfield where they manufactured St Bruno, an appallingly pungent pipe tobacco, the aroma of which hung over the whole area. I was deemed presentable enough for clerical work, and was set on marking up ledger cards in the company of two other young men and about fifty girls, not one of whom had a single academic qualification to their name. It nonetheless became clear to me that, while they knew what they were doing, I didn't. I simply could not get the hang of the tedious ledger cards and endless order forms which dominated our office lives, and soon degenerated into an idle, bored and unbelievably incompetent employee who wreaked unimaginable havoc on the tobacconists of Scotland whose orders I was charged with processing. I doubt if they or the firm ever fully recovered.

Only nanoseconds before I suspect I would have been fired, the *Echo* threw up what sounded like a much more amusing opportunity, almost next door to Ogdens. John Relph, the Guinness brewers and bottlers, were looking for a van driver. It was just before Christmas, which was Relph's busiest time, and Micky Stewart, who managed the old brewery, was beside himself. He pointed to a battered minivan, got in beside me, and we drove round the block. In ten minutes I had a job for £7 a week. In an hour I was making my first delivery: twenty extra cases of bottled Guinness for Our Lady of Sorrows Community and Social, Edge Hill. The barman greeted me as if I were a St Bernard in a snowstorm and pressed a pint in my hand. I was hooked. This was definitely the life for me. The work was hard, the hours were long, but the money was fantastic. Within days, the ability to do joined-up writing catapulted me to the dizzy heights of Mickey's assistant, on £14 a week, as much as some men elsewhere got to bring up their families.

Relph's was definitely Scouse life in the raw. I discovered that the pint at every drop was a drayman's automatic prerogative, and I certainly wasn't going to frustrate tradition. Having been Road Safety Minister for several years pointing out the danger of even a single swig, I hardly dare recall how thoroughly ratted we inevitably were by nightfall. But at the time it didn't seem to matter, either to me or anyone else. And I do remember how much easier it was to reverse the lorry on full lock at twenty miles an hour into its parking space each evening than it was to extract it stone cold sober the next morning.

Of course a drayman has to have a mate. Mine was a tragic mistake called Eric, who had glasses like bottle bottoms and should never have been smacked at birth. He once managed to fall into Salthouse Dock fully clothed, while attempting the relatively simple task of rolling a beer barrel up the gangplank to an old barge called The Landfall, a drinking club for seafarers which was moored alongside the quay. Wisely, none of the old salts gave a damn about Eric and expended all their efforts on rescuing the barrel. I eventually fished him out with a boathook.

During all this time my indulgent parents never asked me to contribute to their household expenses and the brewery money was sufficient for me to buy a battered but rather stylish old Wolseley 444. It had one of those dreadful sloppy column gear changes and, I assumed, three gears. One night, driving home from my mate, Paul Lennon's, I was so well-oiled that I pushed the gear lever forward rather than down and found I had a fourth. It was not a model of reliability, but at least I was mobile.

The rest of that year at Relph's was an education and a revelation. Liverpool has produced more than its fair share of comics and characters, and most of them seemed to work for Relph's at one time or another. Alongside Mad Eric was Fat Ruby, with muscles like a stevedore and thighs to match. She stood five foot four and weighed eighteen stone. She had the noisiest, dirtiest laugh I've ever heard, and spent her entire working day in flirtatious banter with all the drivers, who rated Ruby a right goer. I reckoned I was too young to die and declined her raucous offers. One false move between those massive thighs and Charles Atlas would have expired. Entirely in character, she had a heart of gold. They all did. Their humour was so droll and original, I laughed until I nearly cried. They say you have to have a sense of humour to live in Liverpool. You certainly need one to enjoy it. I worked at Relph's every spring, summer and winter vacation for the next three years. I always looked forward to it, and was never disappointed. I felt I had graduated from the School of Life *summa cum laude* when I finally left.

All this was in marked contrast to Worcester College. I forget which wag on his way down Oxford's Beaumont Street said of Worcester, *'C'est magnifique, mais ce n'est pas la gare.'* In any event, the College was a short walk from the station and I duly pitched up there in September of 1964. As I arrived, I watched a callow youth emerging from a gigantic Rolls Royce, complete with chauffeur, who proceeded to disgorge the young master's possessions from the boot. The Louis Vuitton cases alone were worth more than 2 Cyril Grove. From that moment on I knew my life would never, ever be quite the same. I knew instantly that whatever the charms of Fat Ruby or Mad Eric, my future plans would be unlikely to include a permanent return to Liverpool.

Worcester College was also some contrast to the *Coronation Street* of 25 Burdett Street, or Cyril Grove with its one-tree garden. Worcester dates from the eleventh century and a Benedictine foundation known as Gloucester Hall, built round a quadrangle that is both one of the oldest and smallest in Oxford. The newer eighteenth-century buildings followed the classic

Georgian style and are quite wonderful. Arriving this first time in daylight I was overwhelmed. Nothing prepares you for the magic of Oxford's most beautiful college as you step through the large wooden gates. Immediately in front of its narrow lodge entrance is a large, elegant lawn, with college buildings on left and right and the exquisite Provost's garden beyond. The gardens and its own large lake are the jewels in Worcester's crown, but the Dining Hall, Chapel and Upper Library are among Oxford's finest. I had never seen anything quite so enchanting, and over the last thirty years it has lost none of its charm for me. The private park was home to all sorts of interesting wildlife, particularly rare species of duck, and on one occasion, even a pair of wallabies, though I gather they were not a great success, bounding off spectacularly up Oxford High Street on one legendary occasion. The lake was the setting for many a college play: Malvolio expounded precariously from a rickety punt during one splendid effort, but the effect, costumes and all, was quite breathtaking on a beautiful summer evening.

The Provost of Worcester was Lord Franks of Headington. Oliver Franks was a former Ambassador to Washington, and later Chairman of the commission of inquiry into the Falklands War, as well as holding a string of other government and business appointments occupying twenty lines in *Who's Who*. At one time he was chairman of two banks, although his rather unworldly and ascetic style led to him being dubbed 'No Lolly Olly' by the less deferential of city scribes. He had succeeded Sir John Masterman, allegedly the great spymaster of his time, who had run Worcester as an old-fashioned public school. Franks was in the process of modernising it, and although not naturally gregarious and clearly more at home with his papers than with the young, he was conscientious in meeting all newcomers. One made rather strained small talk in the magnificent Provost's Lodgings he and his wife occupied, and the audience inevitably ended with guests being taken to see the original John Pipers, which hung for some reason in the loo. It was said that while he was ambassador in Washington, a radio station conducted a survey asking what distinguished foreigners in the capital would wish for Christmas. The Russian Ambassador said he would like peace to reign throughout the world, the French Ambassador wanted to build an *entente cordiale* with every nation, while Oliver Franks, never a pretentious soul, said he would like a box of desiccated fruits and thank you very much. The responses were broadcast on Christmas morning. He never lived it down.

The intention was that I should study Politics, Philosophy and Economics, but among the works we were asked to study before our arrival were Samuelson's *Economics* and Susan Stebbing's *Introduction to Logic*. I could just about get along with Samuelson, but by page three of Stebbing I had come to the conclusion that this was about the most illogical, impenetrable and frustrating tome I had ever opened. If this was to be my fate for the next three years, I foresaw nothing but blood, sweat and tears. Not until reading William Waldegrave's *The Binding of Leviathan* would I come across a book that would so comprehensively bore me. In later life I never encountered anyone who had actually ever ploughed through either.

Pondering what I might do, a perfect solution presented itself very early on. 'Put him in for the law, Mrs Norris' had been my primary teacher's advice to my mother. Even at that age he knew I could talk the hind legs off a donkey. Rather fancying the idea of a wig and gown, I found myself in Hall, on my first evening at Oxford, being welcomed along with the other new students by A. B. Brown, the senior law tutor and by now also tutor for admissions. A.B. was a real character. He had been Mayor of Oxford in his day and tipped to be one of the university's MPs before that peculiarly British anachronism was rightly, if rather cruelly, abolished. He was wickedly funny, wholly irreverent, a mediocre lawyer but the best raconteur in the city. It was he who first told us of the spelling error in the notice from the Headmaster of Winchester College which advised parents that, regrettably, fees would 'have to be increased to £6,500 per anum'. Several parents wrote back to say they would sooner go on paying through the nose as usual. A.B. told us that whilst we had obtained our Scholarships, Exhibitions and entrances by various routes for the most exciting and enjoyable three years of our lives, if we had any wish to select a different course, we could do so if we saw him promptly afterwards. Diffidently I asked if I could read law instead of PPE, little knowing that this request hugely delighted him because, whether or not I was any good, he would be stealing one of John Vaizey's Exhibitioners. Vaizey, ennobled by Harold Wilson, whom he advised, was the senior tutor in PPE and he and Alan were deadly rivals in archetypal C. P. Snow mode. A.B. told me I would have to square it with Vaizey and a somewhat tense interview took place with the great man, not because he assumed I would make any worthwhile contribution to his tutorials, but because he was convinced A.B. had put me up to it.

So I joined the Worcester Lawyers – a special Mafia within the college because, uniquely, we had a separate law library at our disposal and we were naturally thrown together much more than most other faculties. My twelve colleagues in the first year were a predictable mixture but united in just one respect: they were hugely more wealthy than me. Nearly all were out of public schools like Malvern, Charterhouse, Haileybury, or Clifton. They were, of course, significantly without the advantage of twelve months working for a pipe tobacco-maker and a Guinness brewer.

That year had, in fact, been to my advantage. It meant I went up at nineteen and whilst nearly all of this new world was very strange, I at least was older and definitely more streetwise. I had learned how to keep out of trouble, even if I was unsophisticated enough to assume that ratatouille was a small rodent. Actually, my culinary ignorance was particularly striking. It was not as if I ate peas off my knife – my mother, who had been impeccably educated in the niceties of etiquette, taught me how to use utensils properly and not to say doilly – but until I went to Oxford I had not eaten fillet steak and had no idea what it actually looked like. Nor had I ever been into a restaurant other than a holiday café. And actually my mother was, and is, a lousy cook. As an orphan in an institution she had never had a mother to stand alongside. For decades her only cookbook was a ring-backed little number from the Gas Board, published in about 1941. She explained to me that every other cookbook issued instructions like 'First parboil the potatoes, and make up a white sauce'. How, for God's sake, when you were not even sure how to boil the damned things in the first place? Did you drop them into boiling water, or cold? For how long? The good old Gas Board for once must have recognised the terrible inadequacy of a generation of wartime brides, and provided the answers. It was her Bible. That is not to say that ignorance was her only handicap. I love my mother dearly, but I will never forget her arrival at table as my father, brother and I awaited one Sunday lunch at Cyril Grove. 'It's alphabet soup,' she announced, 'and if any of you find a black "o", don't eat it, because it's the rubber ring which has just blown off the pressure cooker.' Happy Days.

At Oxford I rapidly and enthusiastically began to make up for lost time. A lethally generous Midland Bank manager allowed me a small overdraft and I vowed to put my new-found wealth to good use. The overdraft, and a few pounds from Relph's were added to the twenty pounds a term I solemnly received from the college as an Exhibitioner, and, of course, a local education authority grant.

As far as I know, I was the only one of the lawyers who qualified for a grant, based, as it was, on parental income, or lack of it. In the first term, my grant failed to materialise, and I decided action was called for. In what was then broad Scouse, I harangued a beleaguered Liverpool education department from the telephone in A.B.'s outer office. No doubt other undergraduates, left without their allowance, would have telephoned their pater in the City whose secretary would have sorted it out. My approach was slightly more robust if less subtle: 'Where's me grant?' (rhymes more or less with 'ant'), said very loudly and often, was about the tenor of it, but it worked.

For all that I was an outsider at a very public-school college like Worcester, I never felt it. It was, I think, largely a tribute to my fellow students, who treated me with a mixture of puzzlement and gentle affection, as something of a mascot. Early on I recall a series of robust though never unfriendly exchanges in the Buttery Bar or Junior Common Room, when I explained that, as far as I was concerned, my fellow students were either inadequates because they were only at Oxford on account of their parents being able to afford to pay for their expensive education, or their parents were fools to spend a lot of money on sons who were bright enough to get to Oxford anyway. I confidently asserted that I thus possessed a moral and intellectual edge because no one but the taxpayer had spent a penny on my education. I could even boast that I was, in fact, one of only two entitled to a full-length academic gown in our year. The other, a mercurial redhead called Clive Anderson (now a senior partner in a Philadelphia law firm) who had the law scholarship, had been at Charterhouse.

Without exception, my colleagues were a bright and tolerant bunch, nearly all of whom have since done enormously well.

Robin Barrett is a leading planning silk, Richard Davidson earned enough money as a solicitor to retire at the age of fifty to paint. Hugh Homan, six feet five inches tall and known to all as Huge Hormone, also became a partner in a City solicitors, earning stratospheric fees in the booming eighties. Anthony Dominic Afamado Temple QC, one of the highest paid silks at the Bar arrived as plain Tony, fresh from Haileybury via Onga-Onga in New Zealand, and opened my eyes spectacularly. I particularly remember the chutzpah with which he threatened his bank manager who had unaccountably and quite unreasonably refused to extend Tony's credit, that if the manager's attitude did not improve, he, Tony, would be forced to take his overdraft elsewhere. He did so little work that at the end of his second year he pleaded religion and asked Francis Reynolds, our junior law tutor, to let him read theology. Francis may have been academic, unworldly, and generous to a fault, but even he could see that this was an extraordinarily convenient and unlikely Pauline conversion. Tony was sent packing and told to do some work. He duly got a Third – proof that a degree class is no guide to subsequent success.

One of our number did achieve something genuinely unusual at the end of his three years. Peter Baker managed to fail his degree entirely. He had inherited a great deal of money whilst at Oxford and made it quite clear he thought learning how to spend it was more important than Kelsen's Normative Theory of Jurisprudence. He did, however, manage a double blue, and subsequently joined Radio Oxford as its sports reporter. He married a lovely girl called Mary and as far as I know is there to this day.

At the end of my second term I passed Moderations relatively easily and during the second year I rowed for the second eight, enjoyed second eleven cricket, and discovered I was a half-decent squash player. I even played the occasional game of football or rugby – a far cry from my school days, when I did all I could to escape the sports ground and when that failed, stood around the freezing football field at Mersey Road or the bleak and soulless Dwerryhouse Lane, with my hands firmly inside my shorts, attempting at least some warmth if, at that age, little feeling.

But it was my social life that was flowering most spectacularly. Several of my new friends had fast cars in which, in those heady, wonderfully irresponsible days, we would frequently race down to London. Tony Temple had a TR3, and Mike Radford an ancient MG. One of my most enjoyable experiences was driving back to London with Mike after a university Law Society meeting with the delectable Nemone Lethbridge perched precariously on my knee. The nearest I got to running my own car was a deal I did with my scout, an amazingly libidinous and prolific lothario who would borrow my room to entertain his various girlfriends in return for discreet silence and the loan of his Morris Oxford. I never dared tell my mother why I arrived home in such style.

Oswald Michael John Radford, who had a room above me in the second year, read English. Now better known as Mike, he disappeared for years after Oxford only to emerge as the director of Richard Burton's last decent movie, *1984*, and then to make *White Mischief* and the BAFTA-winning, Oscar-nominated *Il Postino*. We should have known. His great claim to fame in our day was having appeared 'opposite' Candice Bergen in an utterly forgettable Michael Cacoyannis film, bafflingly entitled, *The Day The Fish Came Out*. In fact, Michael, still an undergraduate, had managed a walk-on part while in Greece on his summer vacation. About thirty of us made up half the audience when the film was premiered at the Leicester Square Odeon. Mike was visible for about six seconds in the company of at least a hundred others. It was buttock-clenchingly awful. We were hugely amused. Mike, unsurprisingly, was not.

Back in Oxford, we were all regulars at the Turl and the Turf, or the Welsh Pony at Gloucester Green. We occasionally ventured out in summer to The Trout in Wolvercote, or Dirty Dudley's at Kingston Bagpuize, renowned for the quite incredible girth of mine host and his lady. Speculation as to how bodily fluids were ever exchanged between the two was the source of a rich vein of smutty and hilarious undergraduate humour, particularly as we were all invariably heroically pissed. I developed another, more lucrative haunt. The proprietor of the Lamb and Flag in St Giles wanted a spare barman, and took me on. It helped provide some much needed ready cash and I never paid for a drink. I gathered it was against the rules for undergraduates to work during term, but none of the dons who frequented the place seemed to care.

At that age, I was really not at all political, but given the choice, I generally preferred university Labour Club meetings, listening to some of the best speakers in Harold Wilson's Government: real political heavyweights like Dick Crossman, Tony Crosland and Michael Foot, then at the height of his considerable oratorical powers. They were certainly more fun than the Tories, of whom I recall only Reginald Maudling as impressive. Even then, Quintin Hailsham struck me as enormously smug and somehow deeply silly. It is not an impression that has altered greatly over the years.

Tariq Ali was President of the Union, and I believe it was he who invited the most unusual speaker Oxford had encountered for decades. Malcolm X, the first radical black power leader seriously to challenge white domination and blatant discrimination in the United States, came to the Union. My memory of his visit is still extraordinarily vivid. He was a thin man with a neat black bow tie on a white shirt, a black suit, angular glasses and a fierce close crop. He wasted no time on polite preliminaries. From his very first sentence he spoke with passion, sincerity and inescapable logic about the plight of American blacks, the routine suppression of their civil rights, and the sheer brutality and misery facing a black person in the home of the brave and the land of the free. At this distance in time it is hard to recall just how threatening Malcolm X appeared to a largely white middle-class British audience. The press had presented him as an evil and dangerous monster, intent on annihilating the white race. But that was not his message. He spoke of injustice, violence and exploitation, even murder, but of his own people. That day, he electrified and inspired us all. His young and idealistic audience gave him a huge standing ovation. Assassinated a few years later, his message never mellowed. He remains the finest orator I have ever heard or seen.

In my third year, I managed just enough work to earn a decent second-class Honours. It was time to leave. Having done rather better than I suspect Francis Reynolds imagined, I toyed with the idea of staying on for a second degree, but recognising that I was not cut out for academic life, I came down in the summer of 1967. Apart from enjoying myself, I could boast a term's Presidency of the University Law Society, and a Harmsworth Exhibition at the Middle Temple, which excused me from the fees for Bar finals but provided no help toward the cost of studying for them for the required six months. I had been persuaded to join an Inn by Sir James Stirling, a High Court judge who was a great supporter of young lawyers at Worcester. He and other distinguished visiting judiciary all made it quite clear that serious lawyers became barristers while the less able could always be solicitors. It was about as much vocational guidance as I ever received and in my case at least, it was fatally flawed. Not being in the slightest attracted to what I quite wrongly imagined a solicitor's life to be – all stiff collars and dusty conveyancing as far as I was concerned – and quite unable to afford the Bar, I simply had no idea as to what to do next. But I was 21, an Oxford graduate and had, as northerners say, all my chairs at home. In those days it was not too difficult to find something gainful with which to occupy oneself. Only years later did Francis Reynolds confess that I was almost the first student he ever had who had not gone on to one branch or other of the legal profession. But I was probably also one of the first from a family with no professional experience or connections of any kind at all, no resources to fund six months of Bar finals, and then sixth further months of unpaid pupillage in Chambers. The Norris family experience of solicitors did not go much beyond having paid one £50 for the conveyance of Cyril Grove ten years earlier.

Whatever I did next, I knew that I was not going back to Liverpool, to Alfred Holts, or the Blue Funnel Line, or the Royal Liver Insurance Company. They were not for me. I had seen life at least in the middle, if not quite yet the fast lane. I had enjoyed the company of people who were utterly different from anyone I had ever encountered before, and who moved me a million miles away from the rough scouse grammar school boy I had been when I had arrived three years earlier. They lived a life I keenly wanted to enjoy. I knew very clearly where I wanted to go, even if I did not yet know how I was going to get there.

3

Make a Million, Lose a Million

In the event, it was easy enough to get a job. By that time I was going steady with Vicky Gibson, who had another year at Bristol University left before she took her degree, and she and I frequently met at her parents' flat in South Kensington. There I met her elder brother, Michael, who worked as a salesman for Burroughs Machines, the accounting equipment people. The company had just launched a recruitment campaign and promised employees a £50 headhunter bonus for each new recruit. Michael had no idea whether I was a good accounting equipment salesman, but he knew fifty quid when he saw it. So did I. We agreed to split the booty if I was accepted. Michael solemnly, and I suspect, rather shrewdly, insisted on deducting tax and informed me that my share would be £17.10s.

Budding salesmen or not, Burroughs not unreasonably required their employees to have some knowledge of finance and an elementary command of mathematics. This was a tough one; I was already fairly good at sums, particularly where money was concerned, and no mean darts scorer. Oxford was, after all, useful for something. But as I sat wrestling with the pathetically easy test paper in front of me, I knew in the pit of my stomach that however I tried averaging it, apportioning it, dividing it and multiplying it, I could not produce an answer that remotely represented four over seven as a decimal. Jim Power, boss of Burroughs city branch, was horrified, but he must have been even more desperate than Michael, and kindly asked if I would like to go back to their offices in Moorgate the following week and try again. I agreed and telephoned my mother for help. She knew exactly what I needed. By return of post I received *Mathematics for the Remedial Child*. Not exactly flattering for an Oxford jurisprudencialist, but just what the doctor ordered. I swatted up converting fractions into decimals all over the

28

weekend and presented myself to Jim on Monday morning. He made it as easy as he dared by giving me the same paper I had failed so pathetically the previous week. Four sevenths were duly expressed as a decimal, though goodness knows whether I could have handled four ninths.

My salary was to be a respectable £80 a month. Few of my Oxford contemporaries had broken the '£1,000 a year' barrier, but I had the added bonus of the prospect of commission on my sales – not to mention the £17.10s. Burroughs had a typically American and rather disconcerting approach to their new graduate employees. We might well imagine ourselves the bees' knees, but they knew that people like me would be quite unable to sell sophisticated machinery to a major client if they could not first persuade the average accountant to buy a simple adding machine. So we were brought down to earth with a very heavy bump as an adding machine was explained to us and then thrust into our hands. We were expelled from the office and told to sell ten before we could progress to the more serious stuff. It was a tough enough challenge to deter quite a few would-be computer tyros. At that point I had never actually had to sell anything to anyone in my life.

My 'patch' consisted of a slice of the blocks of offices, banks and insurance companies which inhabit the square mile of the City of London. Not having had any success for the first couple of days, I walked into Brits, the sandwich bar in Cannon Street. As I ordered a bun and a cup of tea, I asked the proprietor in desperation if he would like to buy an adding machine. To my total astonishment he told me he did. He looked at my sample, agreed it was exactly what he wanted, and asked the price. He was also much taken with the rather smart carrying case the machine arrived in, and asked how much that was too. I only knew that the machine itself was £87.10s, and as I reckoned the case could not possibly be worth more, I told him it cost as much again. He raised no objection, opened his till and paid cash for machine and case. I duly paid him for the bun, and returned to base. Back at the office, my new boss, Alan Cutler, asked where my machine was. I told him I had sold it. He was appalled. Apparently I was not supposed to sell it, I was just supposed to take orders from it. In the circumstances he excused me on the grounds of congenital stupidity and inexperience and asked for the order form. I said there wasn't one. Alan patiently repeated our basic training which required an order form in triplicate so the customer could be invoiced. I explained I did not need an invoice because I had the money in my pocket; I counted it out and mentioned that I had also sold the carrying case for the same price. It was apparently actually worth £5, having been made from a rather inferior plastic. Alan was, as Christopher Patten so elegantly later put it, gobsmacked. This boy was clearly one to watch.

Luck stayed with me in the next few weeks. I found at least two other customers who bought half a dozen machines each and quickly moved on to the advanced salesmanship course. I was irremediably hopeless at the electro-mechanical stuff but very good indeed at the marketing. The obvious answer was a prototype joint venture. I sold the kit, and my more scientifically inclined colleagues, who were useless at bullshit, installed it. We enjoyed an amazing array of blue-chip companies as clients, and it was a golden opportunity for a salesman on commission. Not for the first time, my timing was totally accidental and enormously fortunate. On 15 February 1971, Britain was to go decimal and every single business, large or small, was having to throw away all of its old equipment and buy brand new. Many firms which had prepared their accounts by hand up to then used the changeover as a spur to move into computers. There would never be such rich pickings again. My basic salary may have been under £1,000, but in eighteen months I was earning £2,500 a year – I suppose about £30,000 in 1996 money – pretty impressive for a twenty-two-year-old. But I was also starting to learn a vital lesson. I could see that whilst it might be profitable – particularly in the short term – to be the person who supplied data to a business, the real decision-makers were those who asked for that information in the first place. The data processing manager, a job title just gaining currency, might be at the leading edge of technology, but was always going to be second fiddle in any organisation. Management of a business involved understanding which questions to ask rather than how to provide answers and I was clear that I needed to find out just how to ask the right questions.

A Ford Motor Company advertisement pointed the way. They were looking for business management representatives whose job would be to advise Ford's franchise dealers on how to run their business. I was taken on after an interview at Ford headquarters in Brentwood, and was immediately immersed in intensive Ford business management training. It was marvellous. I learned how to read a balance sheet, how to make a business profitable, how, in short, to manage a business from top to bottom. In those days this Ford training facility was virtually unique. They were great teachers and I was a keen and fast learner. I was based at Ford's most exotic office, over the Café Royal in Regent Street. It was from there that I set off to give advice to horny-handed motor traders from Hampshire to Kent. My salary was £4,000 and I was given a huge car – in fact a series of huge cars, because every time a new model came out, all of us on the staff immediately had one. On the very first day I inherited a quite massive Ford Zodiac of billiard-table proportions, with an automatic gearbox, armchair leather seats, and all the petrol paid for. I had been expecting an Escort. I do believe my love affair with expensive motorcars began that very day.

Vicky and I were married in 1969 and bought a flat in Kensington Park Road. From there she began a post-graduate teacher's course at Goldsmith's College, whilst I looked after about eighty of Ford's dealers, ranging from public companies to 'owner driver' businesses where the accounting was still largely done by quill pen. Ford were in the process of introducing a system to persuade dealers to record their figures on a standard format, which would give them monthly accounts and which we could collate to produce a set of composite indicators of average dealer performance. We could then encourage the poor performers to improve and show the better ones how to make even more money. My Burroughs' systems experience came in useful and I felt on top of the work. My complacency was, however, to prove short-lived. Sir William Batty, then Chairman of Ford of Britain, packed me off to Gowrings of Reading to show them why their Ford main dealership was under-performing. Apparently the owners, Mike Oldland and John Fowles, were complaining that business was not good enough, and Sir William was determined to show whose fault that was. John Fowles, who had lost an eye in a shooting accident and wears a piratical black patch, was no easy touch, and I knew I had to be convincing. One of my key recommendations for improving their workshop was to tackle the issue of the service bays which were continually occupied by a company-sponsored Formula Ford racing car over which

31

hovered the tall blond driver whose activities distracted every mechanic as he constantly wheedled them into working on his machine rather than the customer's standard production-line model. Mike and John took my advice to get rid of him. He was clearly going nowhere. His name, as it happens, was James Hunt.

Another Batty assignment was at F. English Ltd, a large Ford complex in Bournemouth, where again in 1969 performance was less than sparkling. The company was owned by one of the most mercurial men in the British motor industry, Colonel Ronnie Hoare, who had bought the franchise with a partner after the war. Ronnie was larger than life. He was a scion of the Hoare banking family, had been commissioned into the army and as a young field officer attached to Montgomery's staff, served in the Western Desert and elsewhere, rising to the field rank of Brigadier. Many of his contemporaries believed he had the talent to have eventually been Chief of the Imperial General Staff, had he only wished to apply himself. But Ronnie was more concerned with the good life. He adored the fast lane. He was enormously attractive to women, good looking, dark, slim, tanned, aquiline and possessed of a quite effortless charm. He could also be as tough as anyone who had been a field commander under Montgomery. He got into the motor business when he left the army, and after his friends, Tommy Sopwith, son of the famous aviator, and the Carey Elwes brothers told him that they had quite independently bought Ford main dealerships and discovered a wonderful way of making a lot of money. And in the fifties and sixties a Ford franchise was indeed a licence to print money. Ronnie joined the gravy train and pursued his love of fast cars and even faster women. He ran a massively fast power boat called *Ultraviolet* with Lady Violet Aitken, had a girlfriend in practically every European capital, and although separated for many years from his long-suffering wife, Anne, was seldom alone. He was enormously good company. By the time I met him he had his Ford car dealership, truck dealership, two smaller Ford garages, an engineering company and (pursuing yet another rather untypical passion) an unrivalled collection of model trains, some of which later went into the Science Museum. He and John Freeman began Sabre Marine between them, out of John's

eternal tinkering in the corner of our workshop in Bournemouth, and that company went on to produce the finest diesel
marine engines in Europe. Ronnie was simply brilliant at
whatever he did. He had even turned his hand to politics for a
time and was awarded the CBE for his services as Chairman of
Finance on Dorset County Council.

Ronnie's most spectacular success was ironically born of a
real tragedy. When Mike Hawthorn died in an accident on the
Guildford bypass, the nation mourned a potential world motor
racing champion. But Mike had also been in deep negotiation
with Enzo Ferrari for the Ferrari concession in the United
Kingdom, and Ronnie, whose interest in racing had brought
him into contact with the old man, told Enzo that he would sell
four cars in the first year if he was awarded the franchise instead.
The Commendatore was impressed. In those days four was an
enormous number. Maranello Concessionaires Limited, occupying the well-known Tower Service Station at Egham in
Surrey, became the most successful Ferrari operation outside
Italy. Whether it made any profit or not, the prancing horse gave
Ronnie everything he wanted. Exotic cars, world class engineering, enormously wealthy customers and contacts, and legions of
impressionable and generally inordinately beautiful young
women. At Egham he was in his element. It was unsurprising
that he found Ford a bit of a bore by comparison.

But Ronnie was not just a playboy. He was a brilliant engineer
and manager of a highly successful racing outfit. He had formed
the United Racing Stable Formula 2 team in 1956 along with
Bob Gibson-Jarvie, and from 1961 until 1967, and one final
event in 1972, he raced Ferraris driven by the likes of Richard
Attwood, Innes Ireland, Mike Parkes and the legendary John
Surtees and Graham Hill. He recorded 24 overall wins from 92
starts. The perks of this lifestyle included a new Rolls Royce
every year, at a time when the day it was driven out of the
factory gate it was immediately worth more than the showroom
price. Sir William Lyons, who was a personal friend, also made
sure that Ronnie was supplied with every latest Jaguar.

My role in his life was clear. By the early seventies, the gilt
had worn off the Ford gingerbread, while Ronnie believed his
funds were still limitless. If he had been down to his last £10
note, he would have gone to Paris to spend it. With all the
naïveté and false confidence of a twenty-four-year-old, I told

him bluntly that his core business was a mess. I put forward a rescue strategy which impressed Ronnie, and to my complete surprise he offered me the job of group finance director at £7,000 a year. That was nearly double my Ford salary, and while Uncle Henry promised security, life with the Colonel looked to be infinitely more exciting. I already had Ronnie's taste for exquisite cars, and now I also had the wherewithal. I bought the first of a long series of elegant Bentleys. We parked it in the drive of the large house Vicky and I bought in Talbot Woods, an elegant Bournemouth suburb.

I learned a great deal from the Colonel. Ronnie was a brilliant organiser who managed his business from copious daily entries in his *Economist* diary. The key was that no item he entered was ever forgotten. They were all religiously carried forward until dealt with. It was an infallible technique and he updated that diary every night, however many miles he had travelled that day, and however much he had drunk. I have tried it for years, but never managed Ronnie's military precision and iron discipline.

The F. English business was in fact basically sound, and by the end of the first year, we had arrested the decline, and produced a respectable profit. I thought myself hugely clever and clearly destined for even greater things. I would dearly have liked that to be with Ronnie, but after only two years I was headhunted to join Kirby's of Liverpool as managing director and became, at the age of twenty-six, probably the youngest managing director of a quoted public company in England. The new job also intriguingly offered a return to Liverpool, but in markedly different style. Kirby's, the largest Chrysler dealer group in the North West, was a basket case. Mercantile Credit and Chrysler had 52 per cent between them, and their brief to me was to sort out the mess. Unfortunately, unlike Ronnie's business which was fundamentally sound but in need of a good kick, Kirby's really was in an almost terminal condition. It became clear that we were more in the business of raising Lazarus than merely tending the sick. The more I uncovered the less I liked. Had I been older, no doubt I would have carried out more due diligence and been warned off. But I was young, brash, and thought I could walk on water. If anyone could sort Kirby's out, I was sure it would be me.

By now I was extremely well paid and on the strength of that, and a low interest rate mortgage from Mercantile, I bought

Brook House at Parkgate on the Wirral from Sir John Nicholson, the shipping magnate who coincidentally then moved to
Norris Castle on the Isle of Wight. With its nine bedrooms, five
acres of garden, stream and ornamental pond it was magnificent. It cost me £25,000 and I really felt I had arrived. Brook
House was certainly the largest in the village, situated behind a
large long sandstone wall and sporting its own castle turret from
which to enjoy the superb views over the marshes of the north
bank of the river Dee over to what was then Flintshire and the
Welsh mountains. Parkgate, still famous for its shrimps and ice
creams, was a hauntingly beautiful place and I loved every
minute we were there. But Kirby's was not proving a happy
business experience. The problems were so bad that if I had sold
the surplus premises we occupied on the Dock Road in
Liverpool and other equally derelict areas of Merseyside in
order to reduce costs, the loss on the balance sheet would have
rendered the company comprehensively insolvent. I was in a
terrible bind, and after just over two years I felt I had done as
much as I could, and negotiated a handsome termination
package. Kirby's was subsequently sold to Cowies, the north
eastern motorcycle and car group, for a single pound. Ironically,
while a Transport Minister I was responsible for the privatisation of the London Bus Limited subsidiaries, and Cowies were
interested in becoming bigger players in the bus market. I had
lunch with Sir Tom Cowie at the Connaught, and he reminded
me of our deal. 'It was the dearest pound I ever spent,' he wryly
remarked.

While at Kirby's I had found a job for an old friend from my
Ford days, Fred O'Brien, who had run a franchise in Reading
but had been a casualty of reorganisation. I was glad to take
Fred on to look after a Kirby dealership in Southport and Fred
returned the favour when I was looking for work after Kirby's,
and the general economic climate was significantly less promising. Ford, he had heard, was looking for a management team to
take over a Thames Valley dealership, and was I interested in
joining him? I had no better offer, and so travelled south where
we met Sydney Wood. Sydney was twenty years my senior and
looking for a new investment opportunity. His father had started
his business during the first war, converting vans into army
ambulances, but when his father died leaving him what had
become a large Ford dealership at Highbury Corner, Sydney

had sold out. He then found it difficult to play second fiddle on the Board of the new owners, and moved on to the Board of United Dominions Trust, one of the big motor finance houses of the time, but found that equally unsatisfactory. He desperately hankered after his own business, and had the money to buy it. He wanted Fred and me to do the legwork. We got on well together, and formulated a package for Reading.

Delivering it proved less easy. By 1973, property prices were rocketing and the economic climate was not half as favourable as two or three years earlier. We were stalled until our friends at Ford put us onto a Ford industrial products franchise, based in a portakabin on a forlorn and windswept industrial estate south of Reading. It was losing money and the owners, Gowrings, the people whom I had once persuaded to sack James Hunt, wanted shot of it. We were convinced we could make a go of the business, so we formed Reading Industrial Engines of which Sydney was chairman, Fred, managing director, and I, finance director. We sold Ford products such as engines, gearboxes, wheels and tyres – in other words the thousand and one components which Ford used to make their products and which we then sold on as sub-contractors to original equipment manufacturers in the Thames Valley. The superb Sabre Marine diesels which Ronnie Hoare and I earlier helped John Freeman to produce were based on a Ford truck engine sold in just that way. The diesels that power a million generators and water pumps around the world start life as truck engines. We had a wide potential customer base to attack.

Vicky and I were sad to have to sell Brook House, particularly because the large cheap mortgage went with it, and new mortgages were rationed by the building societies to a maximum of £10,000. We were obviously going to have to lower our sights. Eventually we found a lovely cottage, part eighteenth-century and part newly-extended, in Hampstead Norris, a delightful village in the Berkshire Downs. I had only gone to see it because the address amused me, but when we moved in, I found to my intense chagrin that the locals had unwittingly decided just a few months earlier that the 'Norris' spelling was far too modern and that the village should revert to the ancient spelling of 'Norreys'. Thankfully, the local authority took forever to get round to changing the signposts. I stuck with what I asserted was the proper spelling and happily looked forward to signing myself Norris of Hampstead Norris. Our cottage was called White Hart House and was directly opposite a pub of the same name. With its three double bedrooms and two boxrooms, it was more modest in size than Brook House, but the River Pang flowed alongside. The village itself was a jewel, with a wonderfully old and characterful Norman church in its centre, and it suited our new circumstances. It remained home for thirteen years. We both became thoroughly involved in village life, and grew to love the gentle Berkshire countryside around us.

Our instincts about Reading Industrial were right and in a couple of years we were making good money and expanding. We bought a large Ford car dealership in Staines which was frankly almost moribund and set about revitalising that too. Fred O'Brien left us, and Doug Wimpress, one of the best business administrators I have ever met, and an old friend of Sydney's from his Highbury days, joined us to run the motor side while I ran Reading Industrial Engines, and Sydney kept us up to the mark with an astute eye for detail.

Within another two years, we were ready for yet another acquisition and our prey this time was the Ford dealer in Torquay. The business had been virtually run into the ground by its colourful and amusing owner, Jehenbaz Ali Khan, a latter day Imran who raced cars with Prince Michael of Kent and, exactly like Ronnie Hoare, spent money like water. Unlike Ronnie, he hadn't a clue how to make it, and his considerable fortune was rapidly dissipating. It was like taking candy from a kid. We were about the most voracious sharks in the Ford ocean at that time. Sydney and Doug had a sharp eye for a deal and both knew the value of money. 'In God we trust: everyone else is cash', was Doug's motto. 'No cash is petty' was Sydney's. Either way, we worked hard and long hours, to be sharper, quicker and more careful than the competition, and by and large we succeeded.

For myself, the more successful the engine business was, the more I knew I wanted to start one of my own. This was a time when British industry simply wasn't able to keep up with the demand for engines. Ford in particular had chronic supply difficulties and it became acutely embarrassing when one's conversations with customers were not about obtaining orders but explaining why it was impossible to fill them. I recall one extraordinary occasion when Sir Neville Bowman-Shaw, the founder of the Lancer Boss fork-lift truck empire, harangued me from a phone box in Caracas to complain of our having brought his entire production line to a halt and frustrated all his hard-won export orders. It was actually a perfectly legitimate gripe.

There was a huge gap in the market, and I found what seemed the answer. Fiat in Milan had bags of surplus engines, and although we would have to convince a sceptical British industry of their quality, I knew personally that they would fit the bill. Having set my sights on my own business, I teamed up with an engineer friend from Reading Industrial Engines, Martin Lowe, and off we went. Sydney could not have been more decent. He agreed that I could take Martin with me and even allowed us in the early days to work from the Reading premises. Then when I left, he gave me a cheque for £5,000. He was under no obligation whatever to do so. The most I had expected was lunch and a glass of champagne, but here from Sydney was my £5,000 toward the £10,000 capital that Martin and I had agreed to put up for our new business. It was an incredibly generous gesture. Martin and I formed Southern Diesels Limited, and took a lease on a small factory in Swindon – and a big pay cut. We did have some early orders and set about finding more. I ran the business and the accounts, Martin ran the workshop and provided the technical engineering know-how. We grew rapidly and along the way found what every British businessman fantasised about at the time – an import-export business with access to the inordinately wealthy Saudi market.

Eddie El Bazi and Vahe Agababian had their office over the Indian Tea Centre in Oxford Street. They found anything and everything for their rich Middle Eastern clients, and generally sold it on for a handsome profit. There are huge reserves of water under the Saudi desert, and they were looking for diesel-powered irrigation pumps to access them. Martin promptly produced a prototype which was exactly what they wanted. Their Saudi clients liked it too and our first large order followed. Soon our one factory in Swindon had become three. The four of us worked well together and the Saudis wanted as much as we could deliver. We frequently worked all night to produce the goods on time, and on occasions we went forty hours on the trot without sleep. We also played Middle Eastern rules. Everyone added their 5 per cent and everyone else knew it. It was the way the Middle East worked. Had we not done so, we would have simply lost the business.

Martin and I spent two years developing and selling prototypes of our equipment, and right up until 1981 we were optimistic that the business could be a long-term success. It takes a long time to develop this sort of business from the initial approach to a production order, and we were just getting to the point where orders were arriving in large numbers when disaster, in the unlikely form of the Chancellor of the Exchequer, Geoffrey Howe, struck. Geoffrey's economic policy sent the pound soaring and left most industrial exporters high and dry. Most of our customers either collapsed or at the very least, hugely reduced their orders. There seemed little chance of the situation improving either, and so Martin and I made the sad decision to wrap the business up before things got worse, and go our separate ways. It was the first time I realised how abruptly the Lord giveth and the Lord taketh away – especially when the Lord in question was the First Lord of the Treasury.

All of the next year I lived hand to mouth. Fortunately, a generator manufacturer in Leicester called Ali Ladak asked me to help him with a contract he was negotiating with the Algerian Electricity Board, who were big buyers of equipment for their burgeoning oil and gas industry. The deal was very simple. Ali didn't speak a word of French, and I did. French and Arabic were the only two languages ever heard in Algeria, and that made me quite a valuable commodity. I added a few extra words to my normal French vocabulary, such as fuel injector and crankshaft, and off I went. I got on well with the Algerians, and we secured a series of lucrative orders. I became used to leaving Heathrow on Thursday evening, booking into the Al-Aurassi – Algiers' best, but still indescribably incompetent, hotel – and working over the weekend to arrive back in England on Monday morning. It was a tough schedule, but it paid off. I also acquired a regular driver, Mustaphah Derbah, who eased my way around the occasional crisis with cunning and good humour. I bought him Marlboro cigarettes and forbidden whisky in exchange. In those days crises in Algiers happened regularly. The Al-Aurassi would often turn out to be full, but Mustaphah always knew that the nearest decent cockroach-free bed was sixty miles down the coast in a beautiful fishing village almost unspoilt by the Islamic-Marxist revolution.

The regime had originally nationalised everything, and the minute it did, whatever it touched stopped working. It nationalised the fishing fleet, so the sailors found reasons to stay at home rather than venture out if the weather looked a bit rough. Why not, when they were paid anyway? They even nationalised taxis, and overnight a free taxi in Algiers became as rare as a hen's tooth. Those two excesses of stupidity had been quietly but rapidly reversed, but elsewhere life was still pretty dire. The Al-Aurassi, for example, had been built in the sixties on a magnificent site overlooking the city and bay of Algiers. It goes without saying that no one actually saw the building through to completion, so none of the approach roads was ever constructed, but it was a towering thirteen stories high. Too high, unfortunately, for the Algiers Water Board to service with any regularity. I soon discovered that you might think you were lucky being allocated a suite on the tenth floor, but only until you turned on the tap. Most days the water petered out by the ninth!

Back in England one Sunday morning in 1982, I was rather unusually catching up on my beauty sleep when Sydney rang to ask me if I would be interested in buying a Volkswagen-Audi dealership in Salisbury. He explained that he was planning to buy a large dealership in Bristol from the Renwick Group, who were pulling out of car distribution in favour of the energy market. The Salisbury branch was part of the sale which he, for his own good reasons, did not want, and he thought I was the ideal person to take it off his hands. It sounded a perfect opportunity. I leapt out of bed, drove to Salisbury and found what looked like an excellent garage in a good position. I phoned Sydney and told him to count me in, although I hadn't the faintest idea at that time how I would finance the deal. I just knew I had to own it.

After a great deal of haggling, I eventually persuaded Renwick's own bankers to lend me £30,000 on the security of White Hart House, and Nick Gibson, Vicky's other brother, introduced me to Brian Cotton, a senior partner at BDO Stoy Hayward, who came in as a co-investor with Tania Mason, a friend of Brian's who had been widowed some years previously and was looking at some investment opportunities. They put up the rest of the capital and we bought the business which I modestly renamed Steve Norris Ltd. Actually, I wanted our customers to know that the business had ceased to be owned by a faceless public company which had offered indifferent service, and was now run by someone prepared to put his name on what he sold. Certainly the business performed exactly as I predicted in my business plan, started making money almost immediately having been run at a loss for years, and took me into the most lucrative period of my life.

The site was just over an acre, and the buildings were clean and modern. We had a showroom, workshop and large separate body repair shop, and we employed about thirty people. It was an ideally-sized business and Volkswagen had an excellent reputation for quality. Quite incidentally, Salisbury itself is one of the loveliest Cathedral cities in Britain. In the summer of 1982, I counted myself a very lucky man indeed.

4

Blessed Margaret

As the business at Salisbury established itself as a thriving and profitable source of income, it provided an ideal springboard for my new and rapidly expanding political career. Politics had not previously figured on my agenda, at least until we were well installed at Hampstead Norris, with one exception. In the sixth form of the Institute, Malcolm Smith, successor to the Baz, had invited me to take part in an essay competition organised by the Council of Europe. It was virtually a command and, under exam conditions and without, as I recall, much preparation, I set down my views on 'The Future of Europe' for three hours and promptly forgot all about it. Some months later Malcolm called me into his study and informed me that I had won one of the two gold medals awarded for a UK entry. My prize was to go by train to Vienna where in the Congress Zentrum I was presented with my medal by the Chancellor of Austria and then taken on a two-week tour of Italy, visiting Milan, Turin, Florence, Rome, Naples and Capri. It was all a quite superb experience for a seventeen-year-old who had never been out of Britain before. Despite this political initiation, I took little interest in the subject at Oxford, and certainly never joined a political party. But it was becoming clearer to me that there was only one political path I would ever be likely to tread. The more I listened to Labour, and particularly their backbenchers and friends in the Trade Unions, the more I found myself listening to the politics of envy. I listened to speeches in which people exactly like me, who had asked nothing of the State and paid a great deal in taxes, were treated not as being part of the solution but as part of the problem. The proposition that we make the poor richer by making the rich poorer seemed to me then, as now, absurd. There was evidently no place for initiative or enterprise in Harold Wilson's party, and thus no place for me. Having seen

how their education policy had already managed to destroy
Liverpool's fine grammar schools without erecting anything
remotely as good in their place, I needed little convincing.
Socialism seemed to me both incoherent and unworkable. Tory
pragmatism might not be expressed in terms of such high-
minded ideals as socialism, but it had the small merit of being
demonstrably right.

When the local Tory committee member called on me at
Brook House in 1971 it followed that I had paid my £5
subscription happily enough, and quite certain, in a benign sort
of way, that I was in the right party. Once we had left Parkgate
and travelled south, joining the new Abingdon constituency was
routine. Indeed in Hampstead Norris being in the Conservative
Association was rather like being in the WI or the village social
club. If anything, the one club rule that mattered was that the
less we actually talked about politics, the better the village liked
it. We raised funds with lots of jolly social activity, and that was
about the height of it. And so that might have remained for me if
circumstances had turned out even slightly differently.

Inevitably it was a trivial event that sparked off my whole
subsequent political career. Through the letterbox came a note
from the Conservative agent in Abingdon, advising us that Rear
Admiral Raymond Tribe CB was due to retire as County
Councillor for the Compton division of Berkshire County
Council at the next County Elections in May of 1977. Two
nominations had been received, from whom a successor would
need to be chosen.

I knew both the candidates he listed, and frankly I was
distinctly unimpressed. Vicky was in my line of fire when I
launched into a broadside about their pathetic inadequacies,
and she listened patiently enough to my rather unflattering
diatribe. And then she dropped her bombshell. 'I don't know
why you don't do that,' she said, 'you would be rather good at
it.'

That desperately simple and straightforward remark planted
an idea in my mind which simply refused to go away. Over the
next few days, the more I thought about it – and I thought about
it a great deal – the more I knew that this was something I had to
do, or at least try. I did not know a great deal about local
politics, and I certainly had no idea what the precise function of
a county councillor was. In that, I suppose I was no different

from the vast majority of the population. But there was something else. Many years later I came across a quotation from Plato on a leaflet published by the Industry and Parliament Trust. I never needed consciously to learn it. I knew I had understood its message right back from those days in 1977: 'the price that good men pay for not being involved in politics is to be governed by people less able than themselves.' That was it. In the end, I knew that railing at the television screen was not enough. I knew that armchair politics could never satisfy me and that in the end I would never be able to resist the challenge to put up or shut up. All this sounds rather pompous and I am enormously diffident about suggesting that this rather facile philosophy amounts to a political credo, but I can only say that over the succeeding twenty years, I have always felt that in a democracy people get the politicians they deserve. At the same time, no one was going to be able to say of me that I merely pontificated from that armchair. If there were difficult decisions to be made, either I made them or I gave up the right to be critical of those who did.

In addition to all that, I was very fond of the sound of my own voice. All politicians are a mixture of altruism and egotism and I am no exception. I knew that my most powerful weapon was an extraordinary gift for persuasion and for presenting complex messages in a simple and straightforward form. It had made me a lot of money and given me independence. Now I could see a way in which precisely that quality was also going to open up new and potentially exciting opportunities.

So, returning to the circular letter, I rang the agent and asked him whether I too could possibly be considered as a candidate. 'I don't see why not,' he said. 'All I can tell you is that you need a proposer and a seconder, and I am afraid we cannot afford to print a new leaflet, but you are more than welcome to come along on the evening if you can find your two sponsors.' I took him at his word, and signed up our branch chairman, Lady Pamela Sarrel, and Peggy Cundell, wife of Compton owner and trainer Ken, as my two champions. I spent two days on the telephone making sure that every friend I could find who was in the association – and that meant virtually every friend I had in the village – would be there to make their vote count on my behalf. When the contest finally arrived we all three addressed the packed meeting, and never the most modest of souls, I can confidently assert that if I had lost, suicide might well have been on the agenda. The other two were as dire as I had predicted and all I had to do was to avoid tripping over my own tongue and the nomination was mine. I won by a mile and was duly elected as the prospective candidate for the ward. Admiral Tribe who had never met me before was charming and friendly: 'anything I can help you with old boy, do please let me know,' and he cycled off into the night.

The next morning I thought I might as well find out what being a candidate involved and rang the county secretary at Shire Hall in Reading. 'Oh, not much,' he said, 'a council meeting once a quarter, a major committee meeting once a quarter, and a subcommittee on the same routine. That's just about it.' 'So that works out to about one meeting a month?' I asked. 'Yes, that's the formal commitment,' Clive Williams asserted, 'Best of luck, and perhaps we will see you soon.'

Sydney Wood took a very simple line: 'If the business goes on growing and profits aren't affected, I don't care what you do. But if the business slides, you know where your loyalties lie.' It was typical of Sydney, direct and to the point. I knew, though, that if all I had to do was to work harder, that would be the least of my problems. I have never minded working pretty much all the hours God sends, and I was determined that my one meeting a month could be amply compensated for.

The election in May of 1977 was a doddle. I got my first taste of canvassing, and found it as every candidate does, much less intimidating than I had feared. I discovered that I represented about 3,500 people in thirteen villages spread over the whole of the beautiful north-west corner of Berkshire, where it adjoins Oxfordshire to the north and Wiltshire to the west. Unusually, because Raymond Tribe had been unopposed for the whole of his time, a Liberal whose name I do not even remember put up against me, but he proved no threat and I was elected with a majority of over 1,000. My political career had begun.

Shortly thereafter I discovered that I could probably have sued Clive Williams for gross misrepresentation. The notion of one meeting a month was a far cry from reality. I learned too that in the land of the blind, the one-eyed man really is king. With some notable exceptions – Lewis Moss, senior partner in a firm of London surveyors, and Christopher Ward, former MP for Swindon, come particularly to mind – the rest of my colleagues did not seem to have a great deal of desperately relevant industrial or commercial experience. I found that I could offer fairly useful constructive suggestions, and that they were eagerly seized upon. All this was a heady experience and I was inexorably drawn into the local government net.

In practice I found that every major committee generated its own working parties, *ad hoc* subcommittees, *ex officio* appointments to boards and other committees and so on. Within two or three months my commitment was not one meeting a month but more like four in a week. On most days I was in County Hall for one reason or another, but more to the point, loving every minute of it as I found out firstly just how much the Council was actually spending (in the case of Berkshire in the early seventies, well over £500 million a year) and the huge responsibilities we had in areas like education, social services and structure planning. Within six months I was even given my first committee chairmanship.

My crowning achievement was as Chairman of the Waste Disposal Committee of Berkshire County Council. Fame at last. But actually, that extraordinarily mundane and almost comic title was the most wonderful introduction to serious politics. All of us are fairly adept at producing household waste, but no one wants it disposed of anywhere near their own home. In a densely populated county like Berkshire, needles in haystacks would have been considerably easier to find than waste disposal sites near Ascot, Bracknell or Newbury. Negotiating crowded and extremely angry public meetings was something I rapidly became used to, and learning how to deal with an audience to bring them on side rather than having them fight me was a useful weapon in my armoury. We actually had some success too, developing one of the very first county strategies for compacting and removing the stuff. My colleagues were delighted.

At the same time that I was finding my feet in Shire Hall, I was becoming more involved with the local Conservative organisation. My Compton division was the only part of the Abingdon constituency in Berkshire. The rest was in Oxfordshire, an anomaly created by the revision of the county boundaries on that famous occasion when the White Horse was stolen by Oxfordshire. Given the motley collection of retirees and housewives who populated the association, it was, in all honesty, difficult not to shine. I found I was generally listened to fairly attentively and was able to persuade meetings to my point of view. They increasingly looked to me as far as the business of the association was concerned, and of course as a business management specialist, the finances were unchallenging territory. By the time of the 1979 general election I was well ensconced.

Margaret Thatcher was by then Leader of Her Majesty's Official Opposition. The story of her extraordinary success in seizing the leadership in the wake of Ted Heath's disastrous U-turn and the loss of the 1974 general election has been told elsewhere, but central to her campaign, and indeed the man who is said first to have inspired the thought of the leadership in her was my own MP, Airey Neave. Airey was a complex and frankly difficult man. He was an unlikely personality among all the gladhanders and affable extroverts who are the stock of any political party. Cold and distant, he had nonetheless earned a reputation for personal bravery from his remarkable history as a Colditz internee who successfully completed a home run to Britain. Subsequently he had become deeply embroiled in the politics of Northern Ireland. Margaret had appointed him her shadow Northern Ireland Secretary, and he had made his uncompromising Unionist views clear at every turn. He was a poor public speaker, but over the years had developed a formidable respect among the activists in the constituency. A few weeks before the 1979 general election, Airey got into his unprepossessing saloon car outside his London flat and drove as slowly as he always did to the House of Commons. He carefully negotiated his way down to the underground car park and went about his work. Some short time later, he returned to his car to leave. As he negotiated the ramp leading up into the daylight, the mercury switch in the massive bomb hidden on the vehicle contacted and Airey was blown to pieces by a massive blast which was quite audible in the Chamber itself. Within half an hour his identity had been established and a sombre Chamber informed. Everyone from Margaret downwards was appalled. There have since been several atrocities committed against parliamentarians on the mainland of Britain, including the bomb blast at the Tory Conference in Brighton and later the assassination of Ian Gow. But at that time this direct attack on Parliament was a new and terrifying phenomenon and the nation was literally in shock. When I attended Airey's funeral in the beautiful church of the Oxfordshire village in which he lived, I knew the whole country was mourning too. It was our first experience of really tight security. Little did I know that I was going to spend the next twenty years of my life among the sniffer dogs and X-ray machines myself.

With inexorable inevitability, the general election moved closer, and the thoughts of the Abingdon Conservative Association were forced to turn to the grim business of electing a successor to Airey for the forthcoming contest. Although at that time I had no experience of Parliament and knew I had very little chance of winning, I decided to throw my hat into the ring. To my astonishment I got through to the penultimate round, being placed fifth behind Tim Yeo, who was far and away the front runner, and Tom Benyon, Tony Trafford and Joan Hall.

At that time, Tim was an ambitious young entrepreneur who had been involved in the Slater Walker empire. For some obscure reason it had recently been alleged that one of his deals had been shady, or some people he had worked with had not been of the highest reputation. Whatever the allegation was, and I do not pretend to remember it accurately, I do recall that Tory Central Office went into a flat spin. The order went out to the Abingdon Executive Committee that Tim should stand aside, and he decently and quietly did. The final massed meeting of the association only considered the other three candidates. Tim was able to see all his detractors off by securing an equally safe seat in Suffolk in 1983. None of his other three competitors survived into that Parliament. He definitely had the last laugh, but the circumstances of his withdrawal and subsequent vindication were to be cruelly contrasted with one other of his competitors for the nomination.

On that final selection evening, I transmuted from candidate to elector. Being a local party member I had a vote in the final selection and I listened intently to the three presentations. Tony Trafford was a doctor who had previously been MP for The Wrekin. He was clearly a thoroughly solid citizen, but he did not last long that night. In response to a fairly pointed question about the role of women in our great party, and with a portrait of Margaret Thatcher staring down over his left shoulder, he confidently asserted that without women to make the tea and

48

lick the stamps, not to mention prepare the cakes and sandwiches, none of us men would be able to get on with the serious
business of politics. That finished him that evening, although
fate took an extraordinary turn for him too. Tony happened to
be attached to one of the Brighton hospitals the night the bomb
went off, and was widely credited with having done a magnificent job, as so many did, that night. Margaret recognised his
contribution with a Knighthood and then a peerage. Although
he took his seat in the Lords he died, tragically young, shortly
thereafter.

Joan Hall was obviously quite a different proposition. She too
was an ex-Member, having been elected for the marginal
Yorkshire seat of Keighley which she lost in 1974, but her
accent was sadly out of place in deepest stockbroker Oxfordshire. She too failed to please, although she put up a feisty
performance and I know she was the choice of many of the
women present. Looking back, she was probably the best
choice, but the candidate chosen that evening in 1979 was Tom
Benyon, and on that very first occasion I met him, something in
his CV rang a very loud bell. He listed himself as a director of a
company called Rossminster and I knew I recognised the name.
As finance director of Sydney's companies, I had been introduced to them. Their business was plain, simple tax avoidance.
In those days of penal Labour company taxation, that was big
business, and most company accountants spent far more time
on mitigating tax on the profits they had earned rather than
worrying about how to create more profitable businesses in the
first place. The tax avoidance industry was just that, and anyone
with a proven scheme for beating the Revenue could expect a
path to be beaten to their door in short order.

We had run a financial and legal ruler over Rossminster in the
finest detail, and were satisfied that the scheme was entirely
above board. Ostensibly at least, we saved a great deal of tax.
But by that spring of 1979, I also knew that the Serious Fraud
Office were taking an interest in Rossminster's affairs, whether
out of deliberate spite or because there was any genuine reason
to do so, I was not sure. I had no reason whatever to think Tom
Benyon involved. His was not a name I had ever come across,
but it struck me even then as distinctly odd that whilst Tim Yeo
had been prevented from standing because of a series of totally
unproven allegations, Tom should have been allowed through

despite what I knew to be fairly serious assertions circulating about a company of which he was a director.

At the time, however, none of this mattered, and Tom was returned at the general election with a thumping majority. I decided that as I had done well enough at Abingdon, I would at least try to put my name on the Conservative candidates list. Having attended what I had been told would be a horrendously difficult weekend of scrutiny and cross-examination at a hotel near Maidenhead, I duly entered the list of accredited candidates in 1982. In all honesty I had not found the grilling or the competition particularly daunting. The young men who made up the majority of the applicants would have generally persuaded me to vote Communist, although I did meet Richard Ottaway there, and marked him down as the only other serious contender. Predictably, Central Office gave him a limited pass. He put two fingers up to them, was selected for Nottingham East and promptly won the seat. He is now a Government Whip representing rock-solid Tory Croydon. A great tribute to the forensic skill of those depressingly amateurish Tory selectors.

By then I was chairman of the Abingdon constituency for no better reason than that the bulk of it was splitting under the forthcoming boundary review into the new constituencies of Oxford West and Abingdon on the one hand, and Wantage on the other. Only the tiny bit of Berkshire in which I lived was going off to join Michael McNair Wilson in Newbury and that meant that my impartiality was guaranteed in dividing out the very substantial spoils between the two halves of the old constituency. The association owned the premises in which not only they, but the much more lucrative Conservative club on the ground floor, carried on business. My job was to arrange valuations, finance and legal transfer on a basis that would keep friends talking to each other once the deal was done. My negotiations involved meeting the officers of the old City of Oxford constituency which was also splitting in two. The more respectable half was joining with the northern half of our seat to form Oxford West and Abingdon, and the rather poorer part to the east of the Cherwell formed the new and highly marginal seat of Oxford East.

Having sent off my details to Central Office with a cheque for £20 – nothing is ever free with the Conservatives – my CV did the rounds of associations either looking to replace their

candidate or find one for a new seat. It did not, however, find
favour with any that were particularly attractive. The one
exception was at Swindon where I was invited for an interview
and terrified myself by almost being selected. I withdrew when
they were down to a choice between me and Simon Coombs,
thus handing Simon the seat on a plate. The local association
were not best pleased but by that time, events had moved on in
Abingdon in a way which I could have hardly imagined. Tom
had come under greater and greater pressure because of his
Rossminster connection. Never the easiest of men, he had also
managed to offend quite a few of the local squirearchy – a fact
which seemed not to bother him in the least. But having suffered
the indignity of having his home raided by police early one
Sunday morning whilst he and his wife were in their night attire,
he was looking increasingly vulnerable. There was a serious
prospect of his being obliged to resign or walk the plank
voluntarily. And as long as there was a chance of my being
selected in Abingdon, I did not want to commit myself to
Swindon. Tom, however, proved determined to soldier on and
face down his critics. As he simply refused to quit, I became
increasingly depressed and convinced that I had made a fatal
mistake. Tom was going to contest the new Wantage seat, and
John Patten, the incumbent in the City of Oxford, would be the
automatic choice for the other. I, meanwhile, had blown my
only real chance.

Then, out of the blue, I was asked to go to Oxford East for an
interview. I gathered afterwards it was largely because they had
been impressed with the way I had negotiated the property
transfer that persuaded them to have a look at me. I had found it
difficult enough to persuade any association of my dubious
merits when no one had the vaguest idea who I was, so the fact
that they knew what I looked like was clearly a big advantage.

Oxford East was far from hopeless. Indeed, it looked about as
winnable as Swindon. Both were predicted as red on most
psephological maps, but only on the 1979 election result, and it
was obvious that the Tories were going to improve on that. I
made the final short list, alongside Andrew Turner, an Oxford
City councillor who lived and worked locally, Robin Harris, the
director of the Conservative Research Department at Central
Office, and a short, squat and terrifyingly pugnacious lady who
was introduced to me as Ann Widdecombe.

After the final interviews, Ann was quite clear that Robin had won: a somewhat extraordinary assertion as she had heard no other presentation but her own; but I rapidly gathered that she was something of a regular on the selection circuit, and saw herself as a considerable expert. If Robin had not won, she confidently opined, then she would win. And if not she, then Andrew.

It was an exquisitely pleasurable moment for me when Mary Freeman, one of the Oxford East committee, stuck her head round the door of the small room in which we were gathered and asked me if I would care to join them. I had won, and Vicky and I spent the rest of the evening thanking our new-found friends, and commiserating with my fellow candidates. Robin, of course, remained in the party hierarchy for many years, and Andrew later joined me in the Grant-Maintained Schools Trust which he has run very successfully ever since. Ann, undaunted, eventually secured the candidacy for one of the Plymouth seats in 1983, but lost. She finally succeeded in 1987 when Sir John Wells retired as Member for Maidstone and Ann took his place. She has since proved to be a startlingly aggressive performer at the dispatch box. She is a woman of intense convictions, nearly all of which I profoundly disagree with, but she inspires fierce loyalty from a number of my colleagues and her trenchant views on religion – she joined John Gummer as a convert to Catholicism at Westminster after the Church of England decision on female ordination – brought her a new legion of admirers. For my part, it would be dishonest of me to say that I ever regarded her as outstandingly beautiful. She is indeed to pulchritude what Paul Gascoigne is to *University Challenge*.

A few short weeks later, Margaret called the 1983 general election. Confident that her fortunes were fully restored after the success of her Falklands war campaign had obliterated the painful memory of her massive unpopularity during the first two years, she was equally confident that she could beat Michael Foot. That frankly pathetic Chaplinesque shadow of a once great orator was probably the perfect example of why no political party can afford to choose a compromise candidate as leader. Although he went on to be re-elected in 1987, he was a shadow of his former self. The cadences were all there, but one had the impression listening to him that he had forgotten why it was all so important. As an eccentric and rather engaging old cove he was almost endearing, but as a prospective prime minister he was a joke. Margaret was going to walk all over him.

Meanwhile the Benyon saga was played out to its finale. His adoption meeting for the new Wantage seat should have been a formality, but such was the controversy surrounding his recent difficulties, that over 400 members flocked into Abingdon's Abbey Hall, keen to be involved in the fateful decision. I actually started the meeting off in my role as chairman of the old, and soon to be defunct, Abingdon constituency, but because I was not a constituent in the new Wantage seat, then handed over to the new chairman-elect. Almost immediately a heated debate began from which it was clear that opinions were equally divided. In due course, a vote was called on whether Tom should be automatically re-adopted and the result, almost incredibly, was a tie.

The chairman, John Flaxman, was now in the extraordinarily unenviable position of having to use his casting vote. Given that the meeting had not endorsed Tom as its candidate by any margin at all, he voted against his automatic re-adoption on the grounds that Tom would then be invited to the final round of a new selection process. Tom, of course, assumed that he was entitled to automatic re-selection and was bitterly disappointed. As the meeting broke up in uproar, I distinctly remember him turning on his heel and after very few words, leaving with his wife Jane. As far as I am aware he never said another word to the association, and nor did he have anything whatever to do with the choice of his successor. I happen to think he did the right thing in the circumstances.

The eventual choice of a new candidate lay between two men who had so far not managed to obtain a seat. One was the Euro-MP, Robert Jackson, and the other a thin, dark, angular chap with no small talk but a formidable brain, called John Redwood. Robert eventually pipped John at the post and John had to wait four more years before succeeding Bill van Straubenzee in Wokingham.

This was one of those very rare instances in which the Conservative Party effectively removed its sitting MP. And it is worth noting that it is a myth that Tories never do such terrible things. In 1996, Norman Lamont became the prospective candidate for Harrogate after the association effectively ejected their sitting Member, Robert Banks. In Robert's case his problem was that although he had represented Harrogate for nearly twenty years, no one there appeared to know either his name or his face. He badly misjudged the resentment in the local association towards an absentee landlord and paid a terrible price. George Gardiner too fell foul of his association in Reigate, but won a huge amount of sympathy when he was accused by one disgruntled member of being ugly. No doubt speaking for two thirds of the House of Commons, poor old George apologised profusely. 'I am afraid I was just born ugly,' he confessed. It was enough to ensure his survival, and given he had threatened a by-election if the result had gone the other way, the biggest sigh of relief probably came from Party Chairman Brian Mawhinney.

Whilst I had lost the chance to inherit Wantage, the consolation of Oxford East proved enormously good fun. I liked all the people there and felt at ease with them right from the start. Having been elected as the candidate in April, we were catapulted into the election campaign literally within four weeks. We had to get down to work, raise some money and fight a serious election. We did not have much to go on. My agent was a genial Scots giant, Alasdair McNutt, who had spent most of his life in the colonial police and not long after, went off to be in charge of the Sultan of Oman's personal security. Alasdair was rushed off his feet trying to handle both Oxford constituencies and so we were very much on our own.

Although far from hopeless, Oxford East still looked like hard work for a first time Tory candidate. The Labour Party offered us Andrew Smith, who was already prominent on the council and lived in one of the best Labour wards, Blackbird Leys. He and his wife, Valerie, were steeped in city politics, and confidently assumed that the seat would be theirs. The Liberal candidate was Margaret Godden, all brown rice and open-toed sandals, full of vague commitments and no specifics, but perfectly pleasant. She, of course, would play a vital role in the contest because the more anti-Tories who opted for her, the better chance I had of splitting that vote.

Right from the outset, I dealt with the potential difficulty I faced as a former Ford man who was now the owner of a Volkswagen dealership standing for an Austin Rover Constituency. The Cowley works still loomed massively over the Oxford bypass in those days. (It was incidentally, the only car plant in

Europe where the production line had to vault over a four lane highway. And we wonder why Britain was uncompetitive.) I was not prepared to wait for the questions, but came straight out and argued that my real expertise in both sides of the motor industry would be a great help in representing my car manufacturing constituents. It did the trick. I never once had the Trojan Horse allegation thrown at me, and indeed, when I met the *Oxford Mail*, they proved friendly enough, if mildly sceptical about my chances.

Vicky was the hardest working campaigner in my whole team. She has always been a brilliant organiser and threw herself into the battle with enormous energy, accompanied, to my surprise and delight, by my mother, who although in her mid-seventies proved as keen as mustard. She announced to my father that she was leaving him for the campaign, came down to Oxford and worked her socks off. Between them, the two would boldly go where no Tory had ever gone before, into all the toughest areas, and up tower blocks who had never even heard of a Tory, let alone seen one. They trudged up literally hundreds of dank, uninviting staircases, covered in graffiti and the ever present smell of urine, and to everyone's astonishment and delight, met quite a few closet supporters – particularly amongst the elderly. Many of these poor souls seriously believed that putting up a Tory poster was an open invitation to have their window smashed, and kept their political opinions fairly close to their chests. The reality, of course, is that nothing of the sort would have happened, but we were unearthing exactly the kind of support you need to dig out in a marginal, and that hard work proved crucial to our success. Vicky also badgered every friend I had in the world to come and help. Old friends I had not seen for a decade appeared to lend an evening's canvassing support and most had never tried anything like it in their lives. They all took to campaigning like ducks to water, and we had an enormously happy time together with all the hardworking locals like Mary Freeman and Zöe Kurtz, Tom Gibson and Vernon Porter, Patsy Yardley and Andrew Turner. Incidentally, Andrew was a real hero because he had, of course, been one of the losing finalists for the nomination. Far from taking his bat and ball home, Andrew threw himself into my campaign with enormous enthusiasm and endeared himself to me forever.

The staple diet of any campaign is canvassing, but it is a much misunderstood technique. The uninitiated assume it involves having to persuade people to vote for you, your party or your candidate. The reality is that that would never be practical, let alone likely. Political conversions generally require more than ninety seconds of explanation or entreaty. Doorstep conversions simply don't work, and if a canvasser is ever told that his or her honeyed words have changed a voter's mind, they would do well to count their fingers upon a farewell handshake.

All canvassers do is ask a simple question. Will the elector support our candidate in the election? If the answer is yes, the professional advice is to say 'thank you' warmly, and leave as soon as possible. Doorstep discussions of the candidate's merits, however reassuring, are simply wasting time. If the answer is no, then the only other relevant question is to try to determine who the elector might actually vote for. Often, it becomes clear that the answer is nobody. But either way, the canvasser returns with the only two pieces of information which are ever truly relevant to a campaign.

After a complete canvass you should know where your voters are. By recording them separately, you then have a chance to tick them off as they vote on the day and much more importantly, come midday, start nagging those who do not appear to have turned their promise into action. Otherwise, the only other useful steer is an indication of who the principal competition is, so that campaign publicity can be targeted accurately.

Canvassing stories are legion, but my own favourite involves the young hopeful who walked down the drive of his next call, only to see a rather large dog sitting on the doorstep. Having knocked, he was invited in and noticed that the dog followed. As he sat urging the assembled family to support him, he noticed that the dog ambled into the middle of the sitting-room and promptly peed all over the carpet. He thought it best to say nothing and the family too seemed to take little notice. Rapidly taking his leave, he shot off down the path and was nearly at the next gate when a head appeared round the door he had just left and his host shouted 'Here Mister, don't you want your dog?'

We did also have one or two public meetings, although when all of the serious political debate was on television and the radio, they tended to be fairly thinly attended. About half the audience on these occasions is likely to consist of the candidate and the candidate's wife, mother, minder, driver and agent. At least that was certainly the case in Oxford East when Douglas Hurd of all people came over from Witney to speak for me, and found himself addressing an audience of less than ten. Given that at least two of the remaining members of the throng were Labour Party spies and the *Oxford Mail* reporter had gone to the wrong venue, I doubted that we were in the business of mass conversion. Frankly, I was deeply embarrassed.

Douglas assured me later that he was perfectly well used to that sort of attendance, and over the years I too came to realise that it was far from unusual. More to the point, he told me that as he drove home that night through the sea of red and yellow posters all over East Oxford, he was convinced I hadn't an earthly. Neil MacFarlane too, came to speak for me in Horspath. Neil was a consummate professional. Having never met me in his life, he told our audience in the warmest terms of his deep and abiding regard for my talents, and his huge enthusiasm for my forthcoming election. I would be a great asset to the House of Commons, the electors of Oxford East were obviously perceptive, and so on and so on. He charmed the entire meeting, uttered warm words of encouragement, smiled alongside me as we shook hands for the *Oxford Mail* photographer, and departed. What a player.

Michael Heseltine proved a different proposition altogether. Part of my rearranged seat had previously been his, and my campaign team had arranged for me to earn some publicity by meeting the great man on some pretext or other after he had spoken to a village meeting in his massively safe Henley constituency, close to its boundary with Oxford East. We arrived outside the village hall after a hard day's canvassing and edged our campaign bus into the car park bulging with BMWs to await Michael's emergence. He did indeed burst forth from the hall shortly afterwards. He strode across the car park, would have walked straight past me if his agent had not steered him in my direction, shook my hand wordlessly, with a quite obvious lack of enthusiasm and turning on his heel, continued his royal progress. That was it. In a few seconds his limousine sped off and we were left standing there like complete lemons.

I quite forget what the press story was that we were hoping to generate out of the event, but I do remember how popular he was with my campaign team thereafter. Indeed, when we

57

relaxed after hours with the occasional game of darts in the Cowley Conservative Club, one of his campaign posters came in rather handy.

Michael, of course, could not have cared less. His support has always been based on grudging admiration rather than affection. I thought it ironic when, many years later, Emma Nicholson's patience finally snapped and she, having thrown in her lot with Hezza after failing to gain promotion under Margaret, left in a fit of pique for the Lib Dems. Whatever she told the waiting hacks at the time, we all knew that the real reason was that after years of dogged devotion, she had come to realise that Heseltine could hardly remember her Christian name.

Some Ministers look after their PPS's and make sure that they are promoted. David Young secured positions for Pat McLoughlin and Robert Atkins and Christopher Patten found a place for his PPS, Robert Key, when Patrick Nichols decided to amend the drink-drive legislation. I know very well that Ken Baker put in a kind word for me when the time came. But Richard Ottaway, who was Michael's PPS, had to wait forever until the whips were simply unable to ignore him. He had no help from his highly placed boss. Keith Hampson, who was Michael's right hand man through his leadership battle with Margaret and his tireless champion during feast and famine, remains unrewarded by the Deputy Prime Minister and First Secretary of State to this day. Only Michael Mates among his acolytes succeeded in enjoying a spell at the Northern Ireland office until his rather laboured attempt at a humorous inscription on a timepiece brought his ministerial career to a premature close.

If a week is a long time in politics, then three weeks of a campaign flashed by like lightning. In no time at all we found ourselves in Oxford's magnificent Town Hall awaiting the count. We had worked hard at the canvass and knew we had badgered, beaten and bullied virtually every ambulant Tory into the booths. But reports from the polling stations were inconclusive. It was obviously going to be a close run thing. As ever on these occasions, after the voting papers have been checked and rechecked they are laid out in lines on trestle tables in the middle of the hall. The evening began to resemble a mechanised Royal Ascot. As each line nudged in front of the other a great cheer went up from the rival bands of supporters and as the piles lengthened and the lead was blurred, the tension mounted.

At about one o'clock in the morning, the Deputy Returning Officer, who does all the work on these occasions, called the three candidates over. He told us that there were a thousand votes between the first and second places, and asked us if we wanted a recount. None of us did. What we wanted was to be told who had won, but the humourless killjoy was having none of it. We were clearly going to have to wait for the public announcement. As it happens, just as he turned away, I caught sight of a piece of paper in his hand. I could see that it contained the result, and whilst I could not see the top number, I could tell that of the two figures that followed, the middle one was the larger. It took me a split second to work out that the ballot paper would be in alphabetical order, and that my name would appear in the middle – Godden, Norris, Smith. I was as certain as I could be that I had won. As we were ushered onto the stage, I whispered to Vicky, 'I think we have got it.' She turned to me delighted and astonished, and I think that that was the first moment when it actually sank in. Barring a disaster, I was about to become a Member of Parliament.

After the usual preliminaries, 'I, the undersigned, being the Returning Officer . . .', we got to the meat of it. Margaret Godden polled respectably enough, but it was clear she was out of it. Next was me. 'Norris, Steven John, the Conservative candidate, eighteen thousand, eight hundred and eight.' A large cheer went up, but was it enough? The whole packed hall complete with regional television crews, local radio, and every teller, canvasser and supporter who could possibly be squeezed in waited breathlessly. 'Smith, Andrew David, the Labour Party candidate, seventeen . . .' The rest was simply drowned as the triumphant roar from my supporters nearly took off the roof. We punched the air, threw blue and white rosettes high, and shouted ourselves hoarse. I made a very short acceptance speech, thanking the usual people, and left the stage as quickly as I could to join my helpers. They were as thrilled as I was, the more so as it became clear that this was a wonderful night for the Conservatives. We were winning everywhere; whole swathes of Britain were turning from red to blue. Out of the corner of my eye I saw Valerie, Andrew Smith's wife, in tears. She was not the only one who was tearful that night. Labour supporters were simply stunned. They could not believe that in a city where they controlled the council by such a huge margin they could lose by over a thousand votes. And perhaps too, they simply could not bring themselves to see how strongly the tide was running against them. Andrew had been a thoroughly decent adversary. Whenever he and I had met to debate local issues, we found ourselves sharing a real dislike of personal abuse and trivialisation, and we learned to have genuine respect for one another's abilities and views. He was to be my opponent a second time in 1987 when the placings were reversed by an equally small margin and he is now destined for a Labour Cabinet.

So perhaps in the event, the better man lost, but that night was mine, and I was going to enjoy every minute of it. I gave my first interview to a television crew, went out on the balcony in St Aldate's and waved inanely at the crowd in time-honoured fashion, then kissed all the women in the hall and most of the men. I did not get much sleep that night. We went back to the Conservative club which had stayed open specially, where my reception was staggering. People turned up in their hundreds to wish me well. Even most Tories in Oxford East had not believed the Conservatives could win, and were overawed by their own success.

That night was sheer euphoria, but in the weeks to come I was treated to a rather more realistic appraisal. As Vicky and I toured the ward celebrations that were hastily arranged for the forthcoming weeks, people would constantly come up to me and offer congratulations, 'We never thought you'd do it,' they said – unfortunately in a tone of voice which implied that if they had indeed thought I would do it, they would have been a damned sight more careful picking the candidate.

Next morning I stayed late in bed recovering and taking the odd call from journalists and friends offering congratulations. I was clear we had won for two reasons. The first was that we had split that left-of-centre vote clean down the middle. Labour had polled 37 per cent and the Liberals 24 per cent. We had squeezed in with 39 per cent and that, of course, was reflected in the national vote. Despite the huge Commons majority of more than 140, Margaret Thatcher's Conservative Party polled only just over 40 per cent nationally. The same was true in 1987. It was John Major, in 1992, who achieved the highest proportion of the overall popular vote of any Conservative Government from 1979 onwards, and it was a cruel irony that all he earned from that was a majority in the 20s. The second reason I had won was Margaret Thatcher herself. I had not been the candidate. I was to all intents and purposes completely unknown. Whilst I had managed not to completely screw my chances, every single door I knocked on saw, not Steven Norris, but Margaret Thatcher's man. It was also true that whilst there were some, perhaps even a majority, who saw her as strident, uncaring, indifferent, obstinate and narrow-minded, there were also those who saw her as brave and determined, clear thinking, and standing up for and understanding ordinary people. For these quintessential Middle Englanders, her kitchen economics resonated with enormous clarity. And her stance over the Falklands had won tremendous admiration and respect, whilst giving Britain back a pride in itself which it had not felt for nearly forty years. The truth is that no one was, or is, ever equivocal about Margaret. You either love her, or loathe her. Some of us who perhaps did not love her, nonetheless enormously admired her clarity and will to lead. She was well on the way to being the defining political figure of my lifetime, and I was to have the extraordinary privilege of serving with her in Parliament.

My immediate problem was rather more prosaic. I had only a rough idea of where the Palace of Westminster was, and none as to which entrance I should use to get into the House of Commons. I had literally only visited it twice, once with Vicky when she was an undergraduate at Bristol and I went with her to meet the Bristol MP, Sir Clive Bossom, Bt, (of whom Winston Churchill had once waspishly remarked that he was neither one thing nor the other). The second occasion was when Tom Benyon invited me to sit in the public gallery to listen to an Adjournment Debate which he had secured and in which I was vaguely involved as a Berkshire councillor. Tom shrewdly managed to work my name into his speech, and I have never forgotten how enormously impressed I was at seeing my name in Hansard the next day. It was a technique which I later shamelessly repeated and for which I am extremely grateful.

I was thirty-eight years old. Having by then been in business for fifteen years, I came to realise that I was actually far from the youngest of the new intake, but I am fairly clear that few were less experienced. I was about to embark upon the biggest and most exciting learning curve of my life.

5

Backbencher

Ask MPs about the first day they arrived at the Palace of Westminster and the comparison they offer is always the same. It is exactly like turning up on the first day of term at a new and rather forbidding boarding school. Like every newcomer, I received my joining instructions from the Serjeant At Arms within a day or two of the election. Apart from advising me when the new Parliament was to meet, the principal request was to bring with me two dozen copies of my election manifesto in order, as I later discovered, for the security attendants to pin our various mugshots on the wall near their security post so that we might be allowed access to the Palace with the minimum of embarrassment. As I approached Westminster on 15 June 1983, I realised how, in company with millions of Londoners, I had taken one of our finest buildings for granted. I had never really looked before at the magnificent Pugin creation now beginning to emerge from its industrial-revolution coating of black into the same warm soft, almost orange tones as the Oxford colleges. Now, it is my favourite building in the whole of London – graceful, sedate and imperious.

For security reasons, there is only one pedestrian entrance, St Stephens. I approached a friendly policeman, one of the band especially selected for their diplomatic skills and enormous patience, showed him my mugshot and letter of invitation, and walked through into the Great Central Lobby. To my right was the House of Lords, straight ahead the dining-rooms, smoking-room and library, and to my left, a short high corridor with massive nineteenth-century portraits of incidents in the English Civil War which, rather ironically, seemed to portray the losing royalists with some sympathy, which I followed into the Members' Lobby. This is the hall immediately outside the chamber of the House of Commons itself, where MPs congregate and gossip with specially selected journalists before, during and after attendance in the Chamber itself.

After a few minutes looking around desperately for a friendly face on that first day, I saw Michael McNair Wilson approach through the crowd. Michael was now my own MP since the Compton division had moved into his Newbury seat, and I knew him well. He was the quintessential backbench Member in what even then was an almost forgotten mould. If he had ever sought ministerial office, then he had certainly never done so openly. He had been Parliamentary Private Secretary to Peter Walker at MAFF [the Ministry of Agriculture, Fisheries and Food] for some years, but one sensed that that was entirely based on friendship rather than any aspiration for preferment. He was incorruptible, totally fair-minded and even-handed in the assiduous way he dealt with every constituent, and thoroughly liked by everyone in Newbury who came into contact with him. Although he worked hard enough on his constituency cases never to be out of a single edition of the *Newbury Weekly News*, he never courted the media, and therefore rather frustrated some of his more impatient constituents who would have preferred their Member to have had a higher profile. I doubt he cared greatly for a concept like 'profile'. He and his brother Patrick were both Members in the best traditions of what was, and to a lesser degree still is the backbone of our Parliament. I imagine it is obvious that I too admired him hugely.

Tragically, he suffered later in the Parliament from what proved to be a fatal kidney disease, although he fought his illness with immense courage and for quite a time worked on as a backbencher despite needing dialysis treatment twice a week.

Michael showed me the ropes. He took me to the tea room a few yards away from the Chamber and introduced me to the friendly girls who ran it. They were utterly unimpressed at meeting Members of Parliament. After all, they served soup and toast to Cabinet Ministers all day long and it was not unknown for Margaret Thatcher to drop in for a cuppa when the occasion demanded. Michael showed me the letter board on which every MP's name, already including the newcomers, was displayed above their pigeon hole, and a similar arrangement on the other side of the Members Lobby for telephone messages. There is a post office nearby where Members can retrieve their huge daily bundle, and all of this is supervised by the badge messengers, ex-Royal Marines with over twenty years' service, whose job it is to recognise all Members, seek out those for whom messages or mail have arrived, and generally bring order out of chaos. They are incidentally also useful for strong-arming the occasional vocal protester who tries it on from the Public Gallery. Suprisingly few do. And those who succeed seldom impress their audience. On one rare occasion when a malcontent emptied a sack of horse manure over the balcony, at least one wag below was heard to cry 'Ordure, ordure!'

Having got the feel of the place, we filed in for the first great event of any Parliament, which is the election of the Speaker. George Thomas had announced his intention of retiring and the way was open for the unopposed election of Bernard Weatherill. 'Jack' (his sister was called Jill) had been a leading light in the Savile Row firm of the same name before entering Parliament for one of the Croydon seats. He had spent most of his life in the Conservative Whips' office, and was almost unknown to the outside world. Margaret Thatcher proposed him from the Government front bench, and Michael Foot seconded for the Opposition. Jack responded with a witty speech in which he thanked the House for the honour it had done him, promised to be fair to all sides and to protect the rights of backbenchers, vainly pleaded for concord and harmony, and told one delicious story.

Sympathising with those of us who were there for the first time, he recounted his own arrival when, terrified of the whole business, he had sought sanctuary in the gents and locked himself into a cubicle. Hearing footsteps approach the urinal he told of the conversation which followed: 'I don't know what this place is coming to. I do think standards are slipping,' one Tory knight observed. 'I should say so,' said his companion, 'They've even got my tailor in here now.'

Although Jack was genial enough, he was never a great Speaker. Ultimately, the Speaker is a school teacher controlling a class. And just as in that profession, it is not shouting loudly or occasional shows of force which produce discipline and order, but rather that combination of self-confidence, intelligence, good humour, and lightness of touch which turns anger into laughter, defuses dangerous disputes and spears the errant dissenter effectively, whilst enabling order to be restored

without ever giving the appearance of losing control. The House
of Commons is never going to be an easy beast to ride, but it
seemed to me he often misread its mood, and to be quite
incapable on most occasions of imposing his personality on it.

He was an unusual man in many ways. He was a practising
Buddhist, and with John Biggs Davison, whom I succeeded at
Epping Forest in 1988, one of the few Urdu speakers in the
House, having learned the language during his days with the
Indian army (Enoch Powell was another). He used it during
John's memorial service, and I understand that afterwards a
journalist approached the Indian Ambassador to ask him what
he thought of the Speaker's pronunciation. 'It was so elegant,
and so precisely redolent of medieval linguistics, that I fear I did
not understand a word of it,' was the less than diplomatic
response.

Jack was also, as perhaps the Buddhism suggests, occasionally
simply rather eccentric. I remember on one occasion an old
school friend of his from Malvern College days who was married
to a mutual friend of ours had asked me if I could arrange for
them to meet. I wrote to Jack who generously invited us all to
lunch and Jack's charming wife, Lynn, joined him for what I
anticipated would be a jolly and rather interesting occasion. In
fact Jack spent the whole meal with headphones on, claiming
that if he were not able to listen to the World At One, he would
be dangerously unsighted for Prime Minister's Question Time
at 3.15 that afternoon. His old friend was quite nonplussed, and
in all honesty a little put out. When the lunch was over Jack had
hardly said a word and yet he waved his old friend away affably
enough and with a broad smile. He obviously saw nothing
peculiar in his behaviour.

As all Speakers do, he would also gather around him a
collection of Members for dinner in his wonderful state rooms
in the Palace of Westminster from time to time. Nothing
unusual about that, except that he insisted on concluding the
evening by making us all sing. He would produce a song sheet
and off we would go, buttocks clenched with embarrassment,
bumbling our way through various appalling cockney ditties and
traditional English songs. Jack saw this as breaking down
barriers and all good clean innocent fun. None of his guests was,
as far as I know, ever rude enough to refuse to take part, but

invitations to Speaker's House were not quite as assiduously sought after as they otherwise might have been.

Over the next few weeks leading up to the long recess I settled into the office which Lesley Reece had found for me in the Abbey Gardens building, overlooking the back of Westminster Abbey. Lesley was an old friend of Vicky's parents and already worked part-time for John Hannam, the MP for Exeter. She decided that I would be a useful additional earner, and informed me that I would employ her as my secretary. I had the overwhelming impression that it was she who was employing me, and the arrangement did not last very long. In any event, it seemed to me more sensible to combine the Steve Norris business with Parliament by employing my secretary in Salisbury, and I hired an obviously competent and friendly girl called Debbie Day to take on my correspondence and diary.

Having a splendidly professional girl like Debbie made my triangular lifestyle infinitely more convenient. I needed to spend part of each week at Salisbury, part in the constituency, and yet had to be on hand to vote at Westminster from Monday to Thursday until late in the evening. On some days I would need to be in all three places at once. Sunday was about the only full day I ever had at home with Vicky and our young son, Tony, who by then was nine years old. Tony was fairly used to my not being around most of the time, so took my sudden elevation in his stride. He has been remarkably good at tolerating my eccentricities ever since.

As far as the business is concerned, I more and more came to rely on my managing director, Anthony Ince. Anthony had been at the business when I arrived and was clearly extremely competent. He was far better at actually running the business than I was. My speciality might have been understanding the balance sheet and persuading bankers to provide the necessary finance, but Anthony was a consummate salesman. Every month turned in a profit of several thousand pounds and as far as I was concerned, I concluded that my interference was more likely to make things worse than better.

Many years later I came bitterly to regret having almost unconsciously taken so little subsequent interest in the business. I gather that an old agricultural adage is that the best fertiliser is the farmer's boot. That is certainly true in a business where profit or loss so much depends on individual deals either done well or badly. In the end, running a dealership like mine needs real hands-on commitment and I fear I simply was not up to it. I enjoyed putting the deal together to buy the business, and I was certainly extraordinarily creative about how to spend the proceeds, but the day-to-day detail of Mrs Bloggs' gearbox and our attempt to sell her a new Volkswagen Polo simply failed to excite. Fortunately, in the mid-eighties none of this mattered. The business powered away as the new car market grew and grew, and any problems I might have foreseen were convincingly postponed for a long time to come.

I found my new political career much more interesting. I would be in the constituency three or four times a week, trying to meet as many people as possible and getting to know my way round the city. Just for the record, no one teaches a new MP how to provide a service for constituents. It is an expertise one is expected to acquire by a combination of enquiry, painful experience and osmosis. It means having to understand the niceties of the council house allocation points system, having some vestigial comprehension of the 30,000 paragraphs of social security legislation with which you are expected to be intimately familiar, and in short being an expert on just about every subject under the sun. Constituents will approach you because the ring on their cooker is not working and they want you to chase up their rights under the guarantee, they will ask you to sort out their love lives, their squabbles with their neighbours and friends, their frustrated holiday arrangements, their arguments with their employers and even, on occasions, the arrangements for their own funerals. The overwhelming majority have nothing whatever to do with the constitutional function or authority of a Member of Parliament, but as MPs have unwisely presented themselves as the founts of all wisdom over generations, it is not perhaps entirely surprising that we have now been firmly gifted the role of surrogate social worker. For what it is worth, it is the individual MP who decides how conscientiously to fulfil his or her obligations. There is no contractual obligation to make oneself available, indeed no statutory requirement to attend Parliament at all, although until one swears the Oath of Allegiance, the Fees Office will not commence the payment of salary. Despite occasional calls in the media for MPs to be subject to performance-related pay, the only sanction available for the crime of indolence or indifference is the theoretical chance of being ejected at the next election. The depressing truth is that individual performance has almost no impact on the outcome of elections. It is an extraordinary tribute to the overwhelming majority of MPs of all parties that faced with that cruel reality, they still plough on.

I became used to the fifty items of mail each day which thumped onto my desk, bound up with string by the House post office, half of it consisting of glossy and impenetrably boring circulars. Generations of public relations consultants do not appear to have understood that information from the Taiwanese Embassy, the Palestine Liberation Organisation, the Engineering Employers Federation, the respective sides in the Cyprus dispute, the Brewers Society or the Patriotic Front for the freedom of whichever African state might be flavour of the month, are simply not going to earn themselves a great deal of a Member's attention unless that Member has a very peculiar interest in that subject. My own favourite of the circular genre was the no doubt brilliantly edited *Concrete Quarterly* which fortunately arrived elegantly shrink wrapped, and therefore allowed me to pass it straight into the waste-paper basket with a minimum of effort. I no doubt missed great stories of passion and intrigue, but the vast range of material sent to Members does suggest a breathtaking assumption on behalf of the public relations industry that Members' interests are infinitely broader than even the tabloid press might imagine. There is a fortune to be made, and a large Brazilian rainforest to be protected from extinction, by the person who impresses on the Parliamentary and governmental relations industry that MPs are generally unwilling, unable or both, to take in more than one or two simples messages expressed on a maximum of two sides of A4. Photographs help, as do monosyllables.

But mixed in with all the junk will be the missives from your own electors, and they of course, are all far more important. Some will simply attempt to bend your ear, protesting at whatever great injustice or stupidity the government of the day happens to be perpetrating. Those are answered promptly, either by the composition of a pithy paragraph or two summarising one's own views, or increasingly these days, whisking off a quick acknowledgement to the constituent and passing the message on to the appropriate Government Minister who then has the unenviable task of composing a reply. I am quite clear that it does not in fact matter what the reply says. Most people are simply happy to know that their point of view has been acknowledged and I have never forgotten how many electors one visited at election time who would drag out from behind the clock on the mantelpiece a ten-year-old acknowledgement of unbelievable banality, but printed on that distinctive cream paper with the dark green portcullis logo and House of Commons, London, SW1A 0AA, as the address.

Then there are the smaller letters, invariably badly written on cheap lined notepads pouring out endless stories of real human tragedy, distress or ignorance. I might try the credence of my reader if I suggested that dealing with these cases is one of the most satisfying aspects of life as an MP, but it is true. Often these people are at their wits end, simply because they have no idea which agency of the state or local government they should approach or how. They inevitably write incoherently, and often manage to leave out the only vital piece of information one needs to help them. Sometimes there is nothing that can be done, however, worthy the case, but just sometimes, a simple letter to the housing manager or the local DSS chief unlocks a door that has been tightly barred for weeks or months. That, believe me, is genuinely satisfying. Quite often, one simply has to invite the author to the weekly or fortnightly advice centres – or surgeries, as they are popularly known – which virtually every MP holds. The analogy with the medical profession is accurate. Unlike many of my colleagues who allocate about ten minutes per constituent, I always found it necessary to leave around twenty minutes for each case, and I tried to offer each person their own timed slots so that they were not kept waiting. Some cases, of course, can be dealt with briskly, either by a single word of advice, or the provision of an address and telephone number. But in a huge number of cases, by the time the patient has begun their story in the middle, moved back and forth over decades and generations, touched on the beginning and per-haps, if one is very lucky, finally got to the end, one is in a position to offer some help. Not only do most of these people have only an indirect connection with the English language, many of them simply cannot write at all. They desperately need a way into an increasingly impenetrable system, and if all that one does is simply express their concern or complaint in a form which the local Director of Housing can understand, that is an enormous service as far as they are concerned. In my case, I also decided that I should bring the mountain to Mohammed, and hold my surgery each week in a local village hall. In practice this laudable proposition meant turning up in Wood Farm, Rose Hill, Cowley, Blackbird Leys and several other equally salubrious locations, in some of the scruffiest, dustiest, dankest and draughtiest rooms that I have ever come across, bereft of any heating especially on cold winter Saturday mornings. I would arrive mostly on my own, but occasionally if she was feeling extremely generous, with Debbie or another volunteer, pull a trestle table into the centre of the room, find one chair with four stout legs and, if I was really lucky, back and arms intact, make sure that I was safely ensconced on it, and then engage in the rather more difficult business of assembling three or four more in front of me. Everyone else waited in the hallway, whilst the poor unfortunates filed in. 'Now,' I would briskly begin in my best Dr Kildare manner, 'what seems to be the problem?' I never actually asked them to cough or say 'aaah', but it was certainly useful to have some paracetamol handy – even if it was invariably me who needed them at the end of a three-hour session.

I did of course have some clients who were simply insane. One of the disadvantages of Oxford's having so many admirable medical facilities is that a number of voluntary patients lived nearby and treated me as part of their occupational therapy. I remember the Cisco Kid terrifying Debbie one Saturday morning, as he arrived firing off imaginary six-guns and convinced he was being chased by Apaches. Fortunately, Fiona Miller, who had been married to Hal Miller, the MP for Bromsgrove and now lived in Oxford East, was on hand to calm him down. She had seen it all before. But I can honestly say, without a word of exaggeration, that I had one chap who insisted on not saying a word, pulled a notebook out of his pocket and scribbled hastily on it, turned the pad to me and pointed to a message which read, 'They're listening to us, so I must write this down.' I nodded, winked, nodded again, smiled and waited. He then informed me in writing that the Russians were tailing him, that his life was being made a misery, and that I should use my influence to call off the KGB and indeed the CIA and MI6. He further informed me that his previous letters to Her Majesty and the Prime Minister had drawn a blank. By this time I had sized him up. First resting my forefinger on my left eye and pulling down the lower lid knowledgeably, I then drew my finger to my pursed lips. 'Leave it all to me,' I mouthed silently, and rising, shook him firmly by the hand, and guided him to the emergency exit. As he went I noticed the faint smell of urine that so often seemed to accompany such troubled souls. It was all in a day's work in Oxford East.

But life is not all such drudgery for a Member of Parliament. When I began in Oxford East, most of my new patch was inherited from John Patten, who had been Member for the City before the boundary review, and was now my immediate neighbour. John knew Oxford like the back of his hand. He had been a don at Hertford, had been on Oxford City Council and had then been elected as MP in 1979. He was the first of his generation to be given office, in Northern Ireland, after only two years, and was clearly on his way to great things. He had a unique way of dealing with the elderly ladies who thronged the various city Conservative clubs, and for whom we both occasionally provided a mild form of free cabaret after they had enjoyed their cream teas. Early on, I made the mistake of occasionally being political on these occasions, but John never did. I remember him once devoting his entire speech to a dissertation on the frock the Queen had worn at some recent event . . . Not only did he fail to relate this undoubtedly vital issue to any political topic whatever, it was obvious that his audience were deeply appreciative and impressed. He was greeted, as ever, by loud and prolonged applause. I was never quite able to attain such commanding heights of sheer unadulterated cynicism, but then that possibly explains why I was never Secretary of State for Education. Incidentally, John's later career defies comprehension. He was a competent and well-regarded Minister of State right through to 1992, including a long spell in the Home Office when I was there with Ken Baker. He was clearly on the ball, well briefed and knowledgeable. He was particularly good at cultivating the press. There are very few lobby correspondents who do not have fond memories of John's inevitable call after Sunday lunch gently suggesting a line that might be useful for a 'Sunday for Monday' story. As such it was no surprise when he finally made it to the Cabinet, except, ironically, that it had taken him so long. By then quite a few of his contemporaries had overtaken him.

What went wrong is, I suspect even for John, very difficult to explain, but go wrong it certainly did. The most noticeable change was that according to several journalists I talked to, the Sunday phone calls simply ceased. And then a man previously noted for his liberal sympathies appeared to change overnight into a champion of the far right, managing to offend virtually every teacher in the land, whilst more depressingly, failing to attract any new support from elsewhere on the political spectrum. He was clearly working on the basis that his message would be popular with grass-roots Conservatives, and yet, surprisingly for one previously so politically adept, he missed his target entirely. Tragically for John, it was no surprise when John Major removed him from the Cabinet a year later. He has since announced his intention to leave Parliament at the age of 51. Given that his wife, Louise, is one of the best paid management consultants in the city, this can hardly be for the same financial reason that I chose to quit. I suspect I am not alone in concluding that whilst he might feel let down, the Prime Minister had little option.

John bequeathed me three Conservative clubs, all very different in character. East Club is just off the Cowley Plain in a large redbrick building on the corner of streets of red terraced houses now almost exclusively occupied by Asian families. Inside, however, there is not a brown face to be seen. The club was quite literally a haven to which the older generation retreated. Outside, the corner shop would be staffed by a sari-clad young woman speaking little English, the high-pitched chatter of Bangladeshi extended families filled the air, and the smell of curry appeared to hang there permanently. There was no violence, nor indeed even animosity, but the gulf between the two communities was vast, and resentments flickered into life often enough in conversation and jokes in poor taste around the club bar. It survived on a diet of bingo and cheap beer as all Conservative clubs everywhere in the country do, and woe betide the young political hopeful who presumed to interrupt a game of bingo. If the Third World War broke out, the ladies of Oxford East Club would wait until after the caller called 'House' before running for the shelter. Headington Club, the venue for the Annual Constituency Dinner, was the only one at the time to accept women members, and was more genteel than Oxford East. Headington is a delightful part of Oxford anyway, and this translated into the clientele. The basic diet was the same, but with more gin and tonic, and less Babycham.

Although I enjoyed both, my favourite was the Cowley Club – a vast barn of a place where the car factory workers were able to relax over a pint and discuss the parentage of the line supervisor or the indolence and general incompetence of senior management. They were, of course, all required to be members of the Conservative Party and had duly paid their membership fee, but I suspect it was the price of the drinks that impressed them rather more than my oratory. They accepted me with enormous good humour, and I enjoyed their company hugely. I would invariably call in for a couple of hours on a Friday or Saturday evening and sit down with families or chew the fat with Alex, the steward, whilst a constant stream of banter went on around me. I would nearly always gravitate toward Aggro Corner, where Glyn Newlands and Tom Jones together with Gary, Peter and half a dozen others enjoyed trying to get the better of me in fierce political debate in which I always finally conceded their superiority in return for a steady supply of free drinks. I remember telling the Epping Forest Selection Committee that the one quality one really needs to be a Member of Parliament is to enjoy meeting people. Quite a few of my collegues would treat evenings like these as the most awful imposition, and bear them with fortitude and courage when they have to. I had a whale of a time. Perhaps I never did stray too far away from 25 Burdett Street, but I felt truly at home with these people. We did very different jobs, and I mixed most of the week in very different circles, but on Friday evenings there was nothing between us. We were friends rather than MP and constituents, and I still see many of them now a decade after leaving Oxford East and think of them with great fondness.

I did practise one affectation. Although when times were hard after Southern Diesels was wrapped up, I was down to a battered blue Peugeot, I rapidly acquired a handsome Rolls Royce once Salisbury had settled down to a steady stream of profit. I always took it with me when I visited the clubs. This is supposed to be the kiss of death for any MP, who is obliged to plead poverty – real or manufactured at all times. There is at least anecdotal evidence of one wealthy Labour Member who parks his limousine in a layby outside the city he represents and swaps into a Morris Minor for constituency engagements. I always felt this rather missed the point. Apart from anything else, people are not stupid, and they are perfectly capable of working out early on whether one is or is not well-heeled. My constituents knew that I was successful in business, and in a sense, whilst I was never otherwise particularly profligate, I was quite content for the message to be that if you wanted to know whether Steve Norris could help you, it might be useful to note that he was certainly capable of succeeding at what he wanted to achieve.

I always remember the story of poor old Peter Tatchell, attempting to gain the solid Labour seat of Bermondsey at the by-election deliberately caused by Bob Mellish in protest at the way the Labour Party was going in the late eighties. Peter was the Labour candidate, although Michael Foot never seemed to be entirely certain about this, and having fought a miserable campaign, he was roundly beaten by Simon Hughes for the Liberals. Peter, whether one agrees with everything he says or not, is actually a very genuine person, and he had apparently conscientiously chosen to live in one of the worst council estates in the Borough of Southwark as a mark of solidarity with his fellow electors. When, after his humiliating defeat, a television crew turned up to conduct the inevitable post-mortem, they talked to several elderly voters about why they had withheld their support. 'Was it because he is Australian?' they asked. 'Nah, I thought he sounded cockney anyway.' 'Was it because he's gay?' 'Nah, anyway, he always seemed a bit of a gloomy geezer to me.' Finally in frustration, 'Well why was it that you did not vote for him?' 'Well, if the silly sod couldn't get himself off the Rockingham estate, how the hell was he ever going to get me off!' My own advice to any young aspirant is clear. Be who you are. The punters can spot a poser a mile off.

Oxford East was dominated by three industries. The car plant at Cowley was famous, but more people were employed in the health service, given the presence of the huge new John Radcliffe Hospital, together with the Warneford, the Slade, the Nuffield, and innumerable other clinics and special units. Although most of the university buildings were west of the Cherwell, a huge number of academic staff also lived east of the river and the Polytechnic at Headington was firmly in my patch. Each generated a steady stream of work and interest, but the motor industry in particular was going through a period of profound change and I found myself at the centre of it.

Making motorcars in Britain had been a fairly depressing experience for several decades. By 1983, however, Margaret had achieved one of her most significant and long-lasting successes by ridding British Leyland, or Austin Rover as it became, of the scourge of Red Robbo and appointing Michael Edwardes to sort out the company once and for all. She also made it plain that government ought not to run car businesses, and that the whole operation should move as swiftly as possible into the private sector. She was dead right, if only because, by then, Austin Rover was in serious difficulties. Not least of these was that the cars simply did not work very well. Out of misguided loyalty I had decided that I ought to buy one of the factory products, and had acquired an Austin Maestro. It was a dreadful embarrassment, breaking down half a dozen times in the first month and it particularly upset me to see it alongside the new Golfs which Volkswagen had just produced and which were running like sewing machines. Something desperately had to be done, and that something arrived in the form of Graham Day, the bearded Canadian who took over as chairman when Michael Edwardes left and who had recently been enormously successful in restructuring the British shipbuilding industry. Graham is one of the few men I have encountered who is not only good at business, but is also capable of talking to government. He lost no time in negotiating a mutual share exchange with Honda, and Cowley witnessed what only a few years ago would have been unthinkable – parties of Japanese executives coming round to see their new partner in operation. The link with Honda proved a revelation. It was not that the Japanese ran faster, or broke more sweat (although as it happened, they did) but rather that the Japanese designed cars that could actually be built easily by the teams of men who would put wheels on, and axles and seats inside body frames. In our time-honoured British way, once a man was promoted to the drawing office, he put aside his overalls forever, and literally never ate in the same canteen as his former linemates. Draughtsmen were proud of being allowed to wear a jacket and would never think of consulting the men who would actually have to build the car when they came to produce some new and lavish design. The Japanese, on the other hand, created a genuine team approach in which everyone from the

75

managing director down ate, talked and worked together. This was not abstract industrial politics. It was simple commonsense, and the results were embarrassingly obvious. The minute Cowley started to use those new Honda techniques, the difference in reliability was amazing, and these days Rover, now owned by BMW, makes cars which stand comparison with the best in the world.

Early on in this process, Graham invited me to go with Roger King who represented Longbridge, and Simon Coombs who represented Pressed Steel Fisher at Swindon, to Japan to meet Honda's senior management. We went with Giles Shaw, the Minister for Industry at the time, and had a fascinating few days travelling down to Nagoya by bullet train and seeing the two quarter-mile-long Honda plants knocking out immaculate cars like shelled peas. One evening in Tokyo, the directors of Honda took us for a lavish evening in a geisha house. Somewhat to my disappointment, all the geisha 'girls' were in their sixties. They were obviously impressively well-versed in ancient Japanese custom, and gestured to us to remove our shoes as we sat cross-legged at the low rectangular table. Only then did I recall that I had put on a singularly garish pair of Italian silk socks purchased in Harrods' sale. Never have my toes so literally curled in embarrassment. But we enjoyed an extremely long meal of sushi and sake, washed down with a number of fine Western wines and liqueurs. We all fell into bed and I for one went sound asleep.

Turning up for breakfast next morning I saw Simon and Roger ashen-faced and haggard. They could not believe how untroubled and well I looked. 'God, last night was awful,' stammered Roger, 'I woke up at two in the morning dying for the loo, and as I got out of bed I could feel the whole room moving around me.' I knew the feeling. 'I staggered off to the bathroom,' he continued 'lifted the lid, and was just about to relieve myself of our dinner when I suddenly noticed that the water in the loo was churning around like a tiny jacuzzi. The whole room really was moving.' In fact, a substantial earthquake had just happened twenty-five miles offshore in Tokyo Bay, and the Imperial Hotel, like all Tokyo high-rise buildings, was gently rocking away on its specially constructed anti-earthquake foundations. As the small notices in our room pointed out, there was absolutely no danger, provided one did not stray too close to the windows. Roger unfortunately only read the notice after he had strayed close enough to look down at the Tokyo central railway running underneath and appearing and disappearing out of sight every twenty seconds. He swore to me he spent the rest of the night huddled in the corner of his room with a blanket. I gather the quake registered 5.6 on the Richter Scale, but apart from two or three burst water mains there seemed to be little visible after-effect on Tokyo's streets. Needless to say, I had slept through the lot.

The Oxford Polytechnic was already well-established as one of the best in the country, offering some courses that were not available at the university, and certainly attracting a very high grade of student. Victor Owen was the Deputy Director who ran the place, and he became a firm friend – not least on the strength of having invited me to become a member of the Brillat-Savarin dining club which was restricted to, if I remember, fifty members, and ate once a term in magnificent style, served by the college catering students who were quite up to the standard of the best West End restaurants. One year Victor asked me to present the degrees at the annual awards ceremony and I accepted with pleasure. I performed competently enough on the day, but not as spectacularly as the previous year's guest of honour, and my largest council house constituent, Robert Maxwell. Millions of words have already been written about him, but I record only that one of his most spectacular deals involved leasing the magnificent Headington Hall from Oxford City Council for peanuts, from where he ran his burgeoning business empire.

On his visit to the polytechnic his gargantuan ego and soaring imagination had led him to make a dramatic commitment to the expectant undergraduates. 'I promise you,' he bellowed, 'that I am so impressed by the quality of undergraduates here that I will offer a job to everyone who cannot find one elsewhere.' Predictably, they rose to a man, and cheered him to the echo. Equally predictably, there is no record of any single undergraduate ever having actually been able to take up the offer.

Maxwell also briefly owned Oxford United. That too was a mixed blessing as far as the rest of the city was concerned. The club had languished in the lower divisions for decades without unduly disturbing the residents of Headington where the club was rather embarrassingly located in a leafy upmarket suburb quite unlike the surroundings of almost every other football ground in the League. The locals were not particularly keen on the club gates getting any bigger. This, of course, meant nothing to Bob. He would turn up on Saturday afternoon in the directors' suite to which I was occasionally invited, bark instructions at the rather harassed ground staff who I suspect knew he was talking out of his hat and ignored most of his bluster, and then took his seat in the front row of the directors' box from which, like some bloated Roman Emperor, he received the plaudits of the crowd. And they seemed quite happy to play their part in his fantasy. The money he did put into the club ensured a couple of good cup runs, and at least one promotion to a higher division. The fans were happy, and Bob milked them for all he was worth. I recall him running onto the pitch at the end of the season Oxford won promotion, arms outstretched, a manic Pavarotti in a huge brown overcoat. When the trophy was finally presented, it was not the team captain or the manager, Jim Smith, who first got their hands on the silverware. It was Bob who raised the trophy over his head as if he had just won the ladies' singles at Wimbledon.

He could not have cared less about Oxford politics. He occasionally embarrassed the Oxford Labour Club by offering them vast sums of money which they, of course, were very diffident about accepting. Even in the middle eighties, Bob not only had a reputation for ruthless pursuit of wealth, but he was not a particularly convincing socialist either. His own spell as Labour Member of Parliament for Buckingham must be one of the most extraordinary in recent political history, and noted mostly for his chairmanship of the Commons Catering Committee. It was unkindly rumoured that he had arranged the auction of the House wine cellars immediately after he had extensively racked out the cellars at Headington Hall. He did seem to be the largest single purchaser at the auction, and the House then went on to enjoy wines courtesy of Grants of St James.

A less well-known aspect of my newly acquired constituency was its large immigrant community. Around 13,000 mostly Bangladeshi voters lived all over East Oxford and they certainly brought with them a large amount of constituency casework. Vicky learned to time Sunday lunch so as to avoid the arrival of the flight from Dhaka each week at Heathrow's terminal three. In those days, there was an informal parliamentary convention that allowed MPs to intervene on behalf of constituents who were about to be deported or denied access to Britain by the immigration authorities. Any Member could ring the Home Office or the hard-pressed immigration officials at the airport and effectively put a stop on any impending departures. Whilst there was some obvious rationale for the existence of the 'right to stop' in theory, the reality was a nightmare. All the immigrant communities became aware that the right existed, and made sure that whoever their Member was and whatever party he or she represented, that right was exercised to the full.

Every week the telephone would ring at White Hart House and I would be told stories of misunderstanding and bureaucratic obstruction accompanied by the inevitable request. Would I put a stop on the father, son, aunt, uncle or cousin who was about to be returned on the next flight? I felt I had no choice. To refuse would be to imply that I did not believe the caller. Worse, it would be to assume a knowledge of the facts which I patently did not possess. It was inevitable that if one was asked, one had to employ the stop and so I dutifully listened, took down all the details, and then rang the duty officer to put the story to him. He would equally wearily go through the routine and the stop was duly put in place. As the holding facilities for those arriving in such circumstances were pathetically inadequate, the newcomers were in practice allowed to go home with their hosts, and by the time their claims had been examined, the ability to follow up those who were less than convincing was substantially impaired. I would have two or three such calls every Sunday lunchtime. I was not angry because of the inconvenience, but because of the ridiculous position in which I found myself, and I was very grateful indeed when David Waddington, when he was Home Secretary, had the guts to change the rules so as to remove my alleged powers. The system works much better now than it did then.

Of course, at the other end of the spectrum, there were also occasions when I believed the authorities had come to the wrong conclusion. I often intervened on behalf of respectable law-abiding families who were well established in Oxford and who simply wanted to have their parents to stay or invited relatives from the sub-continent for a family wedding. They were outraged at being treated with such suspicion, and of course on many occasions their initial requests would be turned down flat.

I found that the only answer was to try to exercise some sensible judgement, and use a form of words with the Minister which, rather like bank references, were designed to convey my own opinions very much between the lines. Outlining the bare bones of a case and ending with 'you may wish to take these facts into account in arriving at your conclusion', indicated that I had little faith in the applicant. Whenever I wanted to impress on the Minister that I actually did believe strongly in the case, I was generally able to do so, and in most cases obtain the result that I wanted.

Given the tens of thousands of such cases each year, there will always be those where injustice unwittingly occurs, but my conclusion, having handled hundreds of examples, is that by and large, the system works remarkably well. My overriding experience is that if occasionally some cases were treated more harshly that they deserved, Britain does indeed remain an extraordinarily soft touch. A tradition of fair play and respect for individual rights means that many people have been able to arrive and stay in Britain for whatever reason who would simply have been turned round within hours, not just in other countries in the Third World, but here in Europe.

In my case, I could at least boast that the Cowley road sported twenty-eight Indian restaurants and an all-night tattooist. Many an undergraduate finished off a night's drinking with a prawn biryani in the Cowley Tandoori. 'All human life is there' proclaimed the masthead of the *News of the World*. Most of it, it seemed to me, was fairly well represented in Oxford East.

6

Lobby Fodder

Exciting as my Oxford East surgeries were, I was more interested in getting to know the House of Commons. My first task was to work out where to sit. Easy enough to establish that the government side is to the Speaker's right, flanked by the aye lobby. Easy enough too to establish the ministerial front benches on either side nearest to the Speaker's table, and the dispatch box from which the Prime Minister and Leader of the Opposition speak. The bench behind the Ministers on the government side is reserved for Parliamentary Private Secretaries, but only by convention. Technically, there is no such thing as a reserved seat in Parliament, though woe betide the youngster who tries usurp Dame Elaine Kellett-Bowman from her seat in the second row below the gangway. Squawking like a demented hen, she has seen off all intruders so far. Rather more decorously one is advised to note that Ted Heath will wish to sit in the place previously occupied by his great mentor, Winston Churchill, after he too had left the office of Prime Minister. Through television, millions are now familiar with his glowering bulk occupying the first seat below the gangway on the front bench. Enoch Powell and Jim Callaghan had their favourite spots on the opposition benches where the Official Unionists sit in unholy alliance with Labour. So too did Michael Foot and Margeret Thatcher in due course. We lesser mortals simply gravitated towards where we felt most comfortable. The Luton foghorn, David Evans, prefers the far end of the Chamber from which to harangue the entire House with his account of his long-suffering wife Janice's alleged opinions. His friend Barry Field the wealthy funeral director from the Isle of Wight, sits next to him, although in Barry's case, he asserts that his distance from the Speaker's Chair merely emphasises his constituency's semi-detached status from the rest of Britain. Dennis Skinner, the most assiduous and certainly one of the wittiest of attenders, has his favourite place on the opposition bench below the gangway. Indeed, in his case he has a favourite jacket and tie too. Dennis is a real Commons character, in great demand among the coach-loads of elderly ladies sightseeing in the Central Lobby. They clearly think him a terrific wag. He could comfortably retire to a life in television, replacing Jim Bowen on Bullseye, or Jim Davidson when the latter finally achieves his own Big Break and becomes a Tory MP. His long-time companion Bob Cryer was a master of Erskine May and could irritate the Government side endlessly with shrewd Points of Order and procedural motions. They made a great double act. Sadly, Bob died several years ago and Terry Lewis, who has taken Bob's place, is a feeble apology by comparison.

On the government benches, the Tories cohabit with Ian Paisley's Democratic Unionists. Jeremy Hanley told the House of his first meeting with the reverend doctor when finding himself unexpectedly alongside. Jeremy attempted to engage the great man in conversation, and said how pleased he was to see him on the Conservative benches. 'Never confuse sittin' on your side with bein' on your side', was the tart response. Jeremy, probably the best mimic in the House, delivered all this in a better Ulster accent that Ian actually possesses himself.

They are both in their different ways, good speakers, but the idea that all MPs speak well in public is strangely wide of the mark. There are notable examples of very mediocre public speakers who nonetheless achieved great heights. John Wakeham, who was an extremely competent Chief Whip throughout my first Parliament, hated public speaking and was quite obviously unhappy whenever he had to be at the dispatch box. He was caught out badly during the 1987 election by a television phone-in caller who seemed to flummox him completely. Several other Ministers would find it hard to win a prize for oratory. Nick Ridley and John MacGregor, Roger Freeman and David Davis, to name but a few, are all examples of competent Ministers who simply never conveyed that competence to their parliamentary audience. As a result, they often had a far more difficult time than they deserved.

Others are, or become over time, outstandingly good. The most dramatic transformation is that of Ted Heath. In his early days as Leader of the Opposition and even Prime Minister he was a very poor public speaker. I recall attending the annual conference of the Institute of Directors in 1970 when Ted, having been invited as Leader of the Opposition, arrived in triumph as our newly-elected Prime Minister. He had the entire audience at his feet, but his speech was so tedious and his delivery so stilted that the rustle of surreptitiously-opened lunch boxes must have deafened him. No one who heard his French as he welcomed our entry into the 'Marshay Commoon' can ever forget those execrable vowels and the sheer woodenness of the delivery. Over the years however, his speaking style has undergone a profound and almost miraculous change. Affected by the extraordinary path which his own career subsequently took, and spurred on by a manic desire to outlive Margaret Thatcher in the Commons, he has developed an extraordinarily relaxed style, based in part at least, on his complete indifference to the reception his remarks might have, allowing him to speak elegantly, and invariably without notes. These days Ted Heath is one of the few speakers who will cause Members to put down their work or their glass whenever they see his name on the screen and move into the Chamber to listen. He has a mordant wit, an enormous command of recent history, and inevitably an unsurpassable wealth of experience. He is a delight, and still capable of bruising the Prime Minister from time to time when Ted perceives him deviating from the true European path.

Whilst Ted is, in my view, the best speaker on either side, there are plenty of others who can perform brilliantly on their day. I remember Tony Benn making his second maiden a day or so after being returned as Member for Chesterfield. He had been the most famous casualty of the 1983 election, losing to Jonathan Sayeed in Bristol, but his enthusiasm had remained entirely undimmed, as had his passion for socialism. He stood up in a thin House, but over the next twenty minutes the Chamber filled. His theme was the historic and eternal struggle of working men against their capitalist exploiters. From the Peasants Revolt and Jack Cade via the Tolpuddle Martyrs and the Suffragettes to the noble miners so foully trampled over by a vile Tory harridan, it was a tour de force. Absurd and irrelevant perhaps, but a tour de force nonetheless.

Even in his last years as an Official Unionist, Enoch Powell too could fill the Chamber. I recall him speaking late one night on an obscure motion relating to the right of the Prime Minister to make appointments in the Church of England. It was not a subject on which the vast majority of the House had any strong opinion, but witnessing the fire in his heavily bagged, almost hypnotic eyes, the outstretched arm with the slightly dropped forefinger, and listening to his unmistakable cadences and faultless logic, one sensed an echo from another age: of oratory and learning, of classic allusion and exquisite phrasing. As he spoke you could have heard a pin drop.

I never thought Margaret Thatcher a particularly fine speaker. She clearly put a great deal of work into her set pieces, and thanks to Gordon Reece and others, she occasionally produced the memorable phrase, but the end result had a staged, manufactured feel to it which generally left me cold. Her resignation speech was the exception, 'I'm enjoying this,' she cried, and one senses that, at last, freed from the chains of office albeit involuntarily, she was. But if she was not a natural orator, she was certainly a superb parliamentarian. She routinely despatched every ball bowled at her at Question Time by Messrs Foot and Kinnock to the parliamentary boundary. Neil Kinnock on the other hand was a superb speaker. He was a real orator, who spoke best without a script or a Teleprompter. He had a reputation for prolixity, and it is true that on occasions the speech might not come off, but when all cylinders fired, Neil was among the best. I think of his extraordinary performance at the Labour Party Conference at which he faced down Militant. His speech then was passionate and brave. It is a supreme irony that the electorate are said not to have regarded him as Prime Ministerial material when faced with that prospect in 1992. I believe he would have been a first-rate Prime Minister. And it is undeniably true that without Neil Kinnock, there could have been no Tony Blair.

Of the contemporary Conservatives, only another Welshman, Michael Heseltine, can truly be described as a first-class speaker. In his magnificent heyday he was the Conference darling, but his performance at the 1995 Party Conference seemed at times redolent of John Osborne's Archie Rice; the gestures, the voice – even the occasional very good joke – were all there, but the whole performance was done by numbers. Nonetheless, anyone who witnessed his attack across the dispatch box on John Smith's campaign to lunch sympathetic City tycoons, 'Never have so many crustaceans been sacrificed in vain . . .' will understand that he was the Prime Minister that Labour would most have feared.

My own introduction to speaking in the Commons did not come until after that first summer recess in 1983. New Members cannot ask oral questions, apply for Adjournment Debates or otherwise participate in Parliament until they have made their maiden speech. By convention they use the occasion to pay a tribute to their predecessor of whichever party, paint as complimentary a picture as they can of their own constituency, make an anodyne contribution to the debate in question and subside after eight to ten minutes. It is the only occasion when a Member is not interrupted, and the Member who follows, invariably from the other side, congratulates the newcomer and assures him of a long and successful parliamentary career. My debut occurred in October on an opposition day debate on the health service. During my time on Berkshire County Council I had been persuaded to join the area health authority and I had found health management issues immensely absorbing. Following the tradition, I wrote a short note to the Speaker saying I hoped to catch his eye, and awaited my big moment. Neil Kinnock opened the debate for the Opposition. He had just taken over from Michael Foot as leader and he put on a bravura performance. He hounded the Tories for their meanness and insensitivity, their incompetence and indolence, their venality and indifference – it was splendid stuff. More to the point, after the dreadfully dispirited performances Michael Foot had put up before, during and after the general election, Labour MPs were delighted with him and waved their order papers furiously as he sat down. Norman Fowler as Secretary of State for Health replied competently and carefully as Norman always did, and then David Owen spoke. He had of course been a Labour Health Secretary although now a Social Democrat. To my astonishment, Jack Weatherill called me next. I was genuinely appreciative of John Patten, both as predecessor and friend, described my new constituency in glowing terms and then spoke for five minutes on how the health service was currently managed.

Many a distinguished autobiography has described the maiden as a moment of pure terror. I can only assume that I was in the same position as the man who walks across a twelve inch plank believing it to be nailed to the ground only to find that it was a mile high. I suspect it was simply my lack of appreciation of the status of the occasion that meant that I was able to be tolerably relaxed. I had in any event had time to gauge the atmosphere of the Commons and I had decided that speaking from the third bench back above the gangway suited me best. I had spoken on countless occasions at the Shire Hall in Reading, and to enough noisy public meetings, so I knew I could get through my time without faltering. The House of Commons is also a more intimate chamber than one might imagine. Although through television most people in Britain do now understand the layout and even something of the procedure, I can guarantee that the first thing any visitor remarks on when they stand on the floor of the Chamber during one of the morning tours, is how much smaller it is than they imagined. A huge bomb destroyed the Chamber during the last war, and Winston Churchill, although no longer Prime Minister by the time rebuilding began in 1945, was influential in advising on how the rebuilding project should be handled. There was much discussion as to whether to enlarge the Chamber but Churchill, himself one of the finest Commons performers of this century, knew that what he described as the 'cockpit' atmosphere of the old House would be destroyed if Members were more remote from each other in a much larger space. His views prevailed, and the result is that when empty, the Chamber is not intimidating and when full is still capable of generating enormous emotion and theatre. It was incidentally Churchill too who decided that the war-damaged stone entrance to the Chamber should not be repaired. To this day, the stonework is broken and rough. Believing as he did that 'Jaw jaw is always better than war war', he persuaded the House to leave a reminder to every subsequent generation of the consequence of resorting to violence rather than debate.

Performing (if that is the right word) on the floor of the House of Commons is a very small part of the life of a Member of Parliament. Apart from anything else, the limits of the time available to 651 Members means that each is only likely to have three or four opportunities to make a major contribution to a significant debate during each parliamentary year. There will still be plenty of chances for oral questions to Secretaries of State, and indeed the Prime Minister, not to mention the chance of securing half-hour Adjournment Debates at the end of Commons business, or putting down Ten Minute Rule Bills, or Standing Order 20 motions, but the truth is that what Members attend the Chamber for most often is not to speak, but to vote.

The whipping system rules every Member's life. At the end of each week, an impressive envelope arrives by special delivery from the Chief Whip detailing the next week's business. Each of the debates and motions to be considered is listed in the order they will appear on the House Order Paper, but far more important is the advice as to when votes are expected, and the infamous underlining system which indicates how important the Whips consider the votes to be. Two lines under the timing of the voting arrangements mean that party members should be available to vote for the Government, but can be excused if they register a pair with the clerks in the party whips office. A three-line whip was once succinctly defined for me by Tristan Garel-Jones, the Tory Prince of Darkness himself, as 'Dead or present'. Pairing is not allowed, and even the most senior Ministers have to cancel important engagements that have been in their diaries for months if the dreaded three lines appear.

The pairing system works because it is in both sides' interest. When one side has a majority of more than a hundred, simple mathematics dictate that there are a great many Members who are not going to be able to find anyone on the opposition benches to pair with, and needless to say newcomers tend to be at the back of the queue. I only acquired a pair in 1992. When Ken Hind lost his West Lancashire seat to Colin Pickthall I was enormously sorry for Ken – who, incidentally, now has a safe nomination under his belt, and will be back in the House for many years – but there was a distinct silver lining to that cloud as far as I was concerned. Colin agreed to pair with me, although initially, and perhaps understandably as he had just been elected, he was not entirely sure whether it was the right thing for him to do. My advice to him was simple: 'If you think that you are never going to be in government then you have no need whatever to pair with me because over the next few years, I will need you more than you will need me,' I said. 'But if you do happen to believe that one day, however remote, you might actually be in power yourselves, then the boot is going to be on the other foot.' Colin took the point, and we have paired extremely happily ever since. It is worth pointing out that the arrangement never compromises a Member on either side. If Colin feels he has to vote, he merely tells me, and I either make other arrangements if the pairing whip is in a particularly tolerant mood, or I am obliged to turn up. He in turn is always extremely generous to me in letting me know when he needs to be present and when he is due to be back in his Lancashire seat. That sort of quiet cooperation is the everyday basis on which the Commons works. There is nothing logical or hypocritical about the idea that we might bitterly oppose each other's views in debate and yet be perfectly civil in arranging our working lives together.

On one occasion two years ago, Labour's rather hapless and ineffectual Chief Whip, Derek Foster, formerly withdrew all co-operation between the parties in protest at some alleged procedural outrage, which he claimed had been perpetrated by the Government. What transpired was almost comic. The Government Whips decided that two could play at the same game, and promptly cancelled all MPs' overseas visits, and any other convivial occasions that they could think of where by convention, Labour and Conservative Members normally pair with each other. When the non-cooperation threat was with-drawn, it was not as a result of Tory entreaty. It was Foster's own backbenchers who told him to have more sense.

One other consequence of the whipping system is that, on many occasions, I have voted as the Whips directed without the vaguest idea what I am voting about. When the bell rings throughout the Palace of Westminster and in all of the surrounding restaurants and bars, one simply knows that one has eight minutes to be in one or other of the voting lobbies. Approaching the Chamber from either direction the key is to look for a friendly face. And the Whips will be on hand to guide their flock into the appropriate pen. On occasions, visitors are appalled when one describes this process in such blunt terms, but the reality is that Parliament could not function on any other basis. There is far too much detailed legislation for any Member, however assiduous, to assimilate. Every Member is elected in the name of their party. Although Edmund Burke's dictum that one is a representative and not a delegate is still as true today as ever, the reality is that one is there to support one's party in Parliament unless there is an overriding reason why one cannot do so. So on any bill there will be a number of Members who have taken a particular interest in the subject, who will have put down amendments and will have spoken at Second Reading, been a member of the committee that considers the bill upstairs in the committee rooms above the Chamber, and will know every line of the bill almost by heart. The rest of us simply take the Whip's advice. That discipline is an absolute precondition of our parliamentary democracy. Without it, and the whipping system, party management would be impossible and the House itself would be ungovernable. If one abolished political parties overnight, it would not be many days before coalitions would form, and groups would coalesce around agreed objectives. There are many extraordinary features of our system, but on balance it works well. I remember another Garel-Jones aphorism which summarised the relationship between whip and backbencher rather succinctly: 'We don't want your mind, dear boy. We only want your body.'

Some parliamentary issues do lie outside these general rules. The occasions when the buck does stop with the individual Member are those free votes on what are generally defined as 'conscience matters' – issues like capital punishment, abortion, euthanasia, experimentation on human embryos, and Sunday trading, all of which it had been felt inappropriate for political parties to take a view on. Legalisation of homosexuality or the abolition of blood sports are also issues which generate extraordinary passions amongst Members, and much more importantly, frequently set side against side. In common with many of my colleagues, I always found these issues inordinately difficult. Perhaps as a consequence, the quality of debate is appreciably better than normal.

During my first Parliament I spoke most often on a predictable range of health service, motor industry and education issues, but without ever specifically intending to do so, I developed at least one special interest that took up a lot of my time and energy. My initiation into this particular issue arose directly out of the influence of the Government Whips. Early in 1983 the ever-present Tristan Garel-Jones approached me in the Lobby with a straightforward question. 'What do you know about data protection?' he asked. 'Absolutely nothing,' I honestly replied. He nodded and that was the sum total of our conversation. I thought no more about it until a week later I received the formal note from the Committee of Selection advising me that I had been selected as a member of the committee to consider the Data Protection Bill. I had of course just encountered another classic whip's rule. Always ensure that the government representatives on standing committees of bills have no interest or knowledge whatever of the subject of the bill. All the whips want is to steer the bill as quickly through the committee stage as possible, and that means having the Government Minister speak when necessary, and ensuring that all other members on the government side get on with their correspondence, or dictate their letters on the benches outside in the corridor.

Committees are hugely time-consuming. A government bill will be examined each Tuesday and Thursday from 10.30 in the morning until 1.00 p.m., and then from 4.30 p.m. until 7.30 or 8.00 p.m. when the Members break for dinner. They frequently return at around 9.00 p.m. and – certainly in the case of the Finance Bill – often carry on well into the next morning. Attendance is heavily regulated. The committee composition reflects the Government's majority as a whole, but given that there are only around twenty members on each bill committee, even a single absence can be important.

Not knowing the ropes that first time, I instantly made a fundamental error: I read the bill. I compounded my felony by listening to the early exchanges between David Waddington, then Minister of State at the Home Office, and the Opposition Members who immediately began probing him on what was clearly very contentious territory indeed. The more I listened to the exchanges and read the bill carefully for myself, the more I became convinced that Waddington ought to accept at least some of the Opposition's amendments. My own legal training was sufficient to ensure that I was comfortable dealing with Bills and their amendment, and I was quite sure that I was right and Waddington was wrong.

In truth the whole area of data protection was as new to Parliament as it was to the civil servants who had drafted the Bill in the first place, and laying down rules which protected the rights of citizens who have information held about them on databases was never going to be easy. Nonetheless, I was horrified at some of the stories I heard of the effects of false information being held in a form that meant it could be sent

90

around the world long before anyone caught up with the fact that the information itself was wrong.

I remember a particular instance of a young man taken on by a security company who was summoned before the managing director shortly after he was employed and summarily dismissed. When he protested, he was finally told his security clearance was unsatisfactory. He was appalled and angry but that might nonetheless have been the end of the matter, had not his girlfriend been the daughter of a senior policeman at Scotland Yard, in charge, if I recall, of the fingerprint department. Using his Yard contacts, and probably against all the rules, the young man was able to obtain a copy of his confidential police national computer record. What emerged came straight out of Orwell's *1984*. The couple had travelled over on the ferry in their car to Holland. Arriving in a Dutch café very early one morning they were unaware of the fact that the previous evening the Baader-Meinhof gang had been in action and the police had put out an appeal for information on a young couple travelling by car, probably dishevelled, she blonde, he dark, and acting suspiciously. The young couple fitted the description and the Dutch bar owner, listening to the early morning radio, reported the number of their car to the local police. They passed the information to Interpol who in turn passed it to Scotland Yard to identify the owners. The relevant information was passed back up the chain, and no further action was taken. The young people came back from their holiday, but the result, incredibly, was that on the police file in the United Kingdom were the words: 'possible implication with Baader-Meinhof'. It was a horrifying story, but one which could clearly be multiplied many times over simply through errors in addresses or similarity of names on unchecked databases.

There were implications for medical records also, because too many doctors had been complacent about not allowing patients to see their own medical records. School records which were erroneously filed could damn a pupil for life, and social workers kept databases about applicants for such simple matters as housing accommodation which could effectively prevent a housing tenant ever moving, when in fact the authority was acting on a completely inaccurate basis.

I must have been a Whip's nightmare on the bill, but I did

make two friends for life: Maurice Frankel, the tireless Director of the Campaign for Freedom of Information, who attended the committee sessions each day and, sensing a willing recruit, supplied me with briefing material, and Des Wilson, who masterminded that and a number of other campaigns in collaboration with Godfrey Bradman, the wealthy philanthropist. Des was a former President of the Liberal Party, but we not only agreed on freedom of information issues, but on practically everything else as well. Over the years we have constantly found ourselves fighting the same campaigns and his energy and enthusiasm are endlessly infectious. He can inspire a team better than anyone else I know. He also provided me with my ideal role model in that at the age of fifty he decided he had spent enough of his life working for peanuts for humanity, and was going to spend the rest of it working for Des Wilson. He is now the Head of Public Relations for BAA and worth every penny of his substantial salary.

I took over from Jonathan Aitken as co-chairman of the Campaign for Freedom of Information, with Chris Smith for Labour and Archie Kirkwood for the Liberal Democrats. Even worse as far as the whips were concerned, I became a close associate of the National Council for Civil Liberties, which was regarded by most Conservatives as a haven for unspeakable Trots. It always seemed to me an extraordinary assumption that a body dedicated to individual rights should be ignored by a political party whose whole philosophy is based on the proposition that those rights are more important that the right of the state to dictate to the individual.

When I look back on my own work in Parliament before I took the Queen's strictly notional shilling and became a Parliamentary Private Secretary, I recall an almost embarrassingly Liberal agenda. The Data Protection Bill, a Breach of Confidence Bill which I introduced under the Ten Minute Rule, the Interception of Communications Bill on which I spoke extensively and, no doubt bored my collegues rigid, the Human Rights Bill, and the Personal Files Bill which again was a Private Member's measure introduced by Archie Kirkwood who had been lucky in the Private Members ballot. All of this marked me down as trouble as far as the whips were concerned.

I learned to my cost that the word the whips used to describe those Members of whom they wholly approve is 'sound'. For them, the soundest Members are those from whom no sound emanates but who maintain immaculate voting records. I would never decry that approach, but it was simply never me. I could not then and cannot now see the point of being there at all unless one is prepared on occasions to speak one's mind, to say the unsayable and to challenge the conventional orthodoxies. I learned perhaps an even crueller truth at the same time. The whips will always forgive you if you are wrong. But neither they nor your party will forgive you if you have the temerity to be right.

7

Margaret in Her Stride

As I was finding my parliamentary feet and beginning the long march of the backbench foot soldier, Margaret had taken the opportunity of the 1983 general election to reshuffle her Cabinet. These were the men and women who dominated the political headlines and whose personalities and convictions would determine the shape of Tory policy. Margaret's only Cabinet position before becoming Leader of the Conservative Party had been as Education Secretary under Ted Heath. Her election had owed much to Airey Neave's machinations behind the scenes but was also a product of a fierce reaction within the parliamentary party against what was seen as Heath's loss of direction and indeed his complete *volte-face* on key economic issues. The party felt rudderless. Margaret's appointment as the first woman Leader of the Conservative Party had originally intrigued the press, and she had spent her years in Opposition mounting an effective attack on an increasingly weak Labour Government, forced into alliance with the Liberals. As Jim Callaghan's parliamentary majority ebbed away, Margaret had taken the fight to him with a vegeance and her victory in 1979 had restored the Conservative Party's confidence in itself and its ability to govern. Nonetheless, she had not felt confident enough of her position within the party to give vent to the increasing frustration which she felt about the dampness of her patrician colleagues.

During her first term in office she had indeed finally lost patience with Norman St John Stevas, whose constant acid indiscretions finally provoked her beyond endurance, but Norman was of no account and his demise caused few ripples. She took the opportunity of the 1983 general election to stamp her own personality firmly on the Cabinet and move it decisively to the right. Out went Francis Pym, Janet Young and David

Howell. Francis in particular represented everything that Margaret disliked about the old Tory party. She thought him wringing wet, and worse, disloyal. Francis had been unwise enough during the election to refer in a television interview to the dangers of the new Government having too large a majority. I may say that was hardly appreciated in Oxford East where I was keen to be part of that very same majority and I for one shed no tears at his departure. Margaret also had to deal with the loss of Willie Whitelaw from the Commons. He had suffered a bout of illness which had persuaded him that he needed to lay down his heavy load as Deputy Prime Minister and Margaret's confidante. She had relied heavily on him. 'Every Prime Minister needs a Willie', was how she so perfectly summarised his contribution. Now Willie went to be Leader of the Lords, and Margaret could reshape the very top echelon of her Government.

She had wanted to make Cecil Parkinson Foreign Secretary, but he had been forced to tell of his affair with Sara Keays. Debating to the last whether she could still take the risk, she opted for the safer route of appointing him Secretary of State for Trade and Industry. She asked Geoffrey Howe to take over as Foreign Secretary, and promoted Nigel Lawson from Energy to be Chancellor. Leon Brittan arrived as Home Secretary.

The dwindling number of wets were led by the unshakeable Peter Walker who moved from Agriculture to take Nigel Lawson's place at Energy, while Jim Prior continued his sterling work in Northern Ireland. But they were heavily outgunned, not only by Mrs Thatcher herself, but by Keith Joseph at Education, Norman Tebbit, whom Margaret had brought in as Employment Secretary in 1981 to tackle the unions head on, and by Cecil. They were all of the true faith. They were, in Margaret's own famous words, 'one of us'.

This change in emphasis did mirror a profound change in the direction, attitudes and appeal of the Conservative Party itself. If there had been an age when the Conservative Party represented simply the landowning squirearchy, then those days had firmly gone. Ted Heath's origins were resolutely working class, as were those of Margaret herself. The shopkeeper's daughter from Grantham represented a new breed of Conservative who believed in self-help, minimal interference from the State, and also in the value of enterprise, of hard work and application whether in education, commerce or industry. The party had become a party of the middle class. This was at the core of Margaret Thatcher's appeal, and it was precisely why people like me felt so comfortable. Julian Critchley, in one of his typically limp-wristed sniffy *de haut en bas* pieces, referred to the new generation of *garagistes* and *arrivistes* who were now taking over the Tory party. I pass over the irony that Julian himself comes from the most modest of backgrounds, albeit rural rather than urban, and I might even be tempted to overlook his enormous disloyalty to the Conservative Party over many years of sustained hostility through the newspapers, but what is so laughable is that he appears incapable of understanding that a Conservative Party which was the elitist, arrogant and unrepresentative party of the St James's Club and the country seat would not only be thoroughly repellent to most people in Britain, but wholly unelectable. As just about the only newcomer who could claim to be both *garagiste* and *arriviste* combined, I found that Margaret Thatcher's brand of conservatism chimed exactly with my own.

As Margaret and Nigel embarked on the great economic boom that would ultimately return her in 1987 and then prove her eventual undoing, there was plenty going on elsewhere. Across the river from Westminster and clearly visible from the House of Commons, Ken Livingstone, the recently elected Labour leader of the GLC, had developed the extraordinary habit of festooning the roof of County Hall with great Maoist banners screaming messages of abuse literally across the rooftops at the Conservative Government. Most of us in the Commons thought this said a great deal more about Ken's loony left GLC than it did about the Tory Government, but Margaret was clearly not amused. With a sweep of her famous handbag, she determined that the GLC must go. Ken Livingstone had come to power in that infamous putsch which unseated John McIntosh within days of the Labour GLC victory. Ken's radical agenda was to set up an alternative government on the South Bank, but he was disastrously misguided. The GLC developed more policy on Nicaragua and Northern Ireland than on housing the homeless in Hackney. Not only were Ken's international political gestures themselves misguided or downright dangerous, but the GLC totally neglected domestic policy and created havoc in almost every area for which it did have some responsibility. The worst consequence of this was that Margaret became convinced that all local government was like London local government. London was indeed enduring a particularly ludicrous period of socialist senselessness. In Islington, the rich socialite, Margaret Hodge, had introduced a laughable regime of political correctness, while in Lambeth the activities of Red Ted Knight were to leave scars which have still not healed more than a decade later. Throughout the capital Labour seemed determined to create a caricature of left-wing government, with Ken as its most visible standard-bearer.

Margaret came to believe that local government could not be trusted. She saw all local councils as profligate, irresponsible and malicious, and she determined to take away what she saw as their capacity for mischief-making. In so doing, her cure was arguably worse than the disease. It is true that there were many idiotic Labour councils who were their own worst enemies, but up and down the country, councils run by all the political parties individually or in coalition were working sensibly and conscientiously to provide local services for local needs. The tragedy of Margaret's local government reforms is that it is now much more difficult to attract good quality people onto a local council than when I first arrived in 1977. Virtually all the spending decisions have already been made by the Department of the Environment, and local councillors are left to tinker at the edges of their budgets whilst at the same time being required to assume greater and greater liabilities.

Having determined that the GLC should go, Margaret Thatcher elevated Ken Livingstone to an unlikely status. Ken was handed the role of London people's champion on a plate, and he was not slow to take up the gift. Ken is an interesting man whom I find it enormously hard to dislike. He is personally brave, being prepared to argue views which he well knows are unpopular with his audience simply because he believes strongly in what he is saying. He and I have spoken several times on the same platform and I remember his articulating what was then the extremely unfashionable view that the British Government should talk direct to Sinn Fein IRA. The audience was unanimously extremely hostile, and he must have known this in advance. Nonetheless, he expounded his views with passion and sincerity. When it was my turn to speak I pointed out why in my

97

view almost everything Ken had said was fundamentally misguided, but I could not help noting in passing that what he said
was also extremely brave. It is true of Ken that he was
responsible for some very silly policies at the GLC, and he is
certainly anathema to New Labour. Since being elected as
member for Brent East in 1987, Ken has sunk without trace,
only to surface occasionally to embarrass Tony Blair.

As Margaret, like Henry II before her cast around for a
champion to rid her of this turbulent priest, her unlikely hero
was Patrick Jenkin, newly arrived from the DTI. Patrick was ill-
equipped to be a local government hatchet man. He has a fine
brain and considerable technical skill. He is patently honest and
incorruptible and a gentle and pleasant man. He is devoted to
public service. He is also without an ounce of political *nous*. He
proved quite incapable of handling Ken, particularly when they
were invited to appear together on television. One got the
impression, listening to Patrick, that he really had no idea why
the GLC needed to be abolished at all, whereas Ken Livingstone was protecting London from the blind viciousness of a
mindless Tory autocrat. I had gone to see Patrick personally
together with David Lightbown – the Enforcer as he was known
from his later years in the Government Whips office. David
weighed well over twenty stone, and was not lightly dismissed.
He and I were both well acquainted with the local government
scene. David had been leader of Staffordshire, I was deputy
leader of Berkshire and we were very concerned about the
forthcoming rate support grant settlement. We represented a
battalion of the Tory party that was under enormous pressure,
but we not only drew no sympathy from Patrick, we both came
away convinced that he had not understood anything of the
issues we discussed. I probably do him a great disservice, but the
complete absence of any personal or diplomatic skills in his
political make up meant that two loyal Conservatives left his
room angry and disillusioned. He was wreaking the same havoc
on millions of Londoners.

In due course, even Margaret Thatcher could not ignore what
was going on in London, and in September of 1984, she
brought in Kenneth Baker as Minister of State for Local
Government. He replaced Irwin Bellwin, a former Leeds City
Council leader whom Margaret had promoted to the Lords.
Although Irwin was perfectly competent, it was our Commons

performance that needed reinforcement, and Ken was ideal. He had been a PPS to Ted Heath, and although not a natural Thatcherite, he believed strongly in the value of loyalty and had had no difficulty in transferring his own to Margaret when she became Prime Minister. He had been the first of his generation to recognise the importance of the information technology revolution and he had sold Margaret on the idea so well that in January of 1981 she appointed him as Minister of Industry and Information Technology. As Ken himself has observed, it was the first time that a Minister had actually written out his own job specification before being appointed.

Ken had already worked with Patrick Jenkin at the DTI, and knew very well that this was his chance to shine. Almost immediately he showed what a forceful and adept communicator he was. Blue Ken was every bit the match for Red Ken, and Livingstone found himself on the back foot. The Tories were delighted as Baker took the battle to Ken Livingstone in London, and at the same time to Derek Hatton in Liverpool and David Blunkett in Sheffield. He lifted Tory morale everywhere. And it was no surprise when he supplanted his old boss in September of 1985, when Mrs Thatcher finally gave him the seat at the Cabinet table he had clearly deserved.

Elsewhere Margaret's Cabinet was an extraordinarily mixed bunch. Nigel Lawson had been an effective economics journalist and now had the opportunity to turn his economic analysis into reality. He was not a first-class Commons performer, and indeed gave the impression that appealing to his colleagues in Parliament was less important than appealing to his audience in the City. He may well have been right. Thankfully, whether or not the colleagues warmed to Nigel personally, they were enormously appreciative of what he was able to deliver. He handled the sterling crises of the early eighties extremely competently and his budgets always contained a few nuggets that backbenchers could applaud.

I was always a great Lawson fan, as indeed I was of the new Foreign Secretary, Geoffrey Howe. He had had a tough wicket at the Treasury where he had served Margaret loyally and effectively. Knowing that he was her second choice for the Foreign Office, he nonetheless threw himself into his new role with considerable skill. His quiet, reassuring and measured tones were exactly what was needed in the job and his thorough command of his brief, which was always Geoffrey's hallmark, reassured us that foreign policy was in safe hands.

Leon Brittan was less comfortable. He was clearly clever, and he had impressed Margaret during his time as Chief Secretary, but he was to have an unhappy time at the Home Office. He was a young man for the job, in his mid-forties and undoubtedly extremely bright. But he was seen by his colleagues as cerebral and intellectual and many of them felt that he, like Lawson, had few social graces. He had a particularly hard time over the capital punishment debate. He knew that Margaret was in favour, as indeed were the majority of the Conservative Party. His own natural liberal instincts would normally have drawn him into opposition, but he made the great mistake of attempting to reconcile these two competing forces by backing the death penalty for some forms of murder but not others. As such he pleased neither side. His advice was contrived and confused, and his reputation was considerably damaged as a consequence. He was also no match for Heseltine over the Westland affair. Although Margaret accepted his resignation in words that implied his absence from government would only be temporary, none of us believed it at the time and he is clearly more comfortable in the corridors of Brussels than he ever was in Westminster. He has gone convincingly native and I would not bank on his ever finding a comfortable home in the Conservative Party should he seek to return to Westminster.

Michael Heseltine had been promoted from Environment to Defence, where he was enjoying himself thoroughly. He clearly saw himself as a great strategic commander and set about a fundamental reorganisation of the whole department. I was a member of one of the groups of new MPs who traditionally are invited by Secretaries of State to meet them to discuss their department's objectives. This generally happens in the House of Commons whilst the PPS dispenses warm gin and tonic and new members relax in the green leather armchairs. The conversation is fairly leisurely, and newcomers are invited to contribute their views, whether or not any notice is taken of them. But that was not Heseltine's way. We were instructed to attend upon him at the Ministry where, having negotiated the various security checks, we were installed in the great man's room. He strode in and addressed us as if he were a pilot officer briefing a wartime air crew. He pulled down a massive organisation chart which occupied most of one wall and lectured us without a moment's humour on the breadth of his managerial command. He had not the slightest interest in any contribution which we might have wanted to make, and left the distinct impression that however enthusiastic he was about running his department, having to tell us about it was frankly a bore. There was no similarity with the Heseltine who exuded charm and concern on the backbenches, once the unstoppable force had met the unmoveable object over Westland. Then he was suddenly the man who helped the new boys on with their coats and ate his way through a mountain of rubber chicken on the constituency circuit. Now, once again, he was merely doing a job professionally. He would next emerge as the catalyst to Margaret's downfall, a whisker away from Downing Street himself.

Arguably Margaret's greatest weakness was her almost total inability to select the right personalities with which to surround herself. She chose mostly for ideological reasons and as such, forfeited too many men and women of genuine talent, whilst she promoted and sustained several who, however intellectually competent, were appalling communicators. Nick Ridley, whom she promoted to Cabinet in 1983, was clearly in this class, and I have more to say on him later, but perhaps her outstandingly awful mistake was to leave Keith Joseph at Education for three years of my first Parliament. Everyone who knew Keith remarked on his sensitivity, humanity and thoughtfulness. He was an intelligent, conscientious and intensely concerned individual, who simply had no appreciation whatever of the politician's art. He agonised and antagonised in equal measure. Like many extraordinarily intelligent people, he found it difficult to make straightforward decisions, forever testing out new aspects of the debate. And at Education, his uncompromising views had alienated every teacher in the land. He had become a hate figure for the teacher unions and yet his intellectual approach was too remote and inaccessible to enable him to reach over their heads to parents.

I saw him in action when I invited him to Newbury to visit the Mary Hare Grammar School for the Deaf where I was a governor. Although the school was independent, it operated as a charity and took its pupils from local education authorities who accepted that the school was able to offer gifted deaf children far more than they could provide themselves. It was a genuine centre of excellence. During his visit a number or local reporters turned up. I must have been on a thousand ministerial visits myself and I have never known one where this did not occur. But Keith appeared irritated by their arrival and promptly refused to speak to them. They in turn were perplexed and affronted – an attitude that was promptly reflected in the universally hostile pieces written the following week. What should have been a success turned out to be a disaster. His IQ may have been well into three figures, but he was worse than the most junior backbencher when it came to articulating government policy. Margaret appeared to see none of this and accepted the inevitability of his resignation with huge regret. The rest of us breathed a sigh of relief.

8

A Foot on the Ladder

Many dramatic events marked those four years of my first Parliament. I watched most of them from the wings, a detached, amused and occasionally appalled observer. But one event, arguably the most traumatic of her entire premiership, altered the lives not just of Mrs Thatcher and her Cabinet, but of every Member of Parliament. At 2.54 a.m. on 12 October 1984 an IRA bomb planted some weeks previously ripped apart the Grand Hotel at Brighton during the Conservative Party Conference. Five people died in the explosion.

I had been in the Grand the previous evening and I knew from personal experience that security was slack. Officially delegates show their conference pass at all times when they are inside the conference hall, but they are advised by the police to take it off whenever they leave. I had been out to a fringe meeting somewhere along the front and as I returned to the security cordon that had been thrown round the conference centre and the Grand Hotel, I rummaged through my pockets for my own pass. The young policeman looked up at me in my double-breasted pinstripe and tie. 'You look respectable enough,' he said, and motioned me through with a smile.

Although we were perfectly well aware of the danger of an attack from the IRA, I do not believe that any of us actually conceived of the prospect of a terrorist attack at the very heart of government, seeking not only to kill the Prime Minister, but her husband and a significant number of members of her Cabinet. If the IRA had been better informed about the workings of the Conservative Party they would have perhaps known that the most important person at Party Conference is the Chairman of the National Union. It is he who by tradition occupies the principal central suite. The Prime Minister occupies an adjacent one. Gordon Shattock died. Margaret lived.

On that evening before the bomb exploded I left to drive home to Hampstead Norris to pack a bag in preparation for a parliamentary delegation travelling to Jordan and Israel to investigate at first hand the tensions between Palestinians and Jews. As I left, colleagues cheerfully reminded me to keep out of the way of stray terrorist bullets. Next morning, leaving home at 5.00 a.m. for Heathrow, I switched on the car radio and caught the end of a report of an explosion at Brighton. I was hugely relieved right at the end of the bulletin to hear Margaret's voice, but knew nothing more. 'Farming Today' took up the next half hour, but as I checked in at the airport some of my colleagues who had travelled further were better informed. We knew that Norman Tebbit and John Wakeham had been badly injured and that some unnamed people had died. I did not hear a shot fired in anger on that visit to the Middle East. In Amman we sat in the Ambassador's garden listening to the BBC World Service and the first full report. In common with every member of the party we were utterly shocked. As the Conference, which Margaret insisted continued, my Oxford East constituency chairman, Vernon Porter, proposed a motion already on the Order Paper, congratulating the security forces and the Secretary of State for Northern Ireland on their handling of the situation in the province. Vernon told me later how strongly he felt that morning that Ireland was now part of every one of our lives. We had often talked about our willingness to face down the terrorists and to stand firm against the men of violence. These words had often been delivered by Ministers on the site of an outrage in which the casualties were innocent women and children. Somehow at Brighton, Vernon like many of us, shared the feelings which the Queen Mother expressed during the second war when Buckingham Palace was bombed. She knew from that moment that she could look the East End in the face. In some small way, so did we all. That afternoon Margaret was at her magnificent best. She gave the Leader's traditional winding up speech, hastily rewritten, declaring that the very continuation of the Conference was the clearest indication that not only had the IRA attack failed, but that all such attempts to destroy democracy by terrorism would fail.

We admired Margaret's personal bravery and shared her sentiments, but life had changed for parliamentarians that day as much as it had on the occasion of Airey Neave's assassination. The first conference I had attended at Blackpool had been enormously enjoyable not least because whenever one was bored by a speech in the main hall or simply wanted a breath of fresh air, it was a simple matter to leave by a side entrance, and be admitted a few minutes later simply by showing one's pass. These days it takes twenty minutes just to get into the hall. One passes through innumerable X-ray machines and body searches and on a wet and windy October night in Blackpool, it is hardly the prelude to a great evening. Around that time security was stepped up at Westminster and even backbenchers like me were visited by our local police and given instruction on home security. Vicky and I were issued with mirrors to check for devices under our cars. Although intended to reassure, the effect was exactly the opposite. Neither of us was terribly sure of what we were looking for, and, particularly at night, the whole proposition was impractical. I simply reassured myself that if the ignition was wired to a bomb I would probably never live long enough to know about it, but it cannot have been easy for Vicky or any of the other families of Members to have this new dimension of danger added to their daily lives. As far as the House of Commons is concerned, something like 5,000 people work there every day and hundreds of delivery vans enter and leave. As long as Parliament takes the view that electors should be able to approach their Members of Parliament without elaborate appointments there will always be risks. Airey Neave, Tony Berry and Ian Gow were all victims of IRA brutality. Every one of us knows that precisely the same fate could befall any of us on an equally random basis. We developed a wartime mentality which took the view that, like it or not, security has to be lived with. If a bomb has your name on it, then so be it.

Brighton apart, I was finding life on the backbenches very enjoyable. One evening in the summer of 1985, when I had been in the House just over two years, I took my first step up the parliamentary ladder. William Waldegrave, who was the Minister of State at the Department of Environment responsible for local government and planning, told me that his Parliamentary Private Secretary, Simon Coombs, had asked to be relieved of his duties because he was suffering from a bad back. Simon had been a fairly obvious choice for William, having been leader of Reading Borough Council, and I had not been surprised that he had been offered a job before me. I did have a fair amount of local government experience of my own, having just completed eight years on Berkshire County Council, but if I was of any value at all to William it was because we were so utterly different in almost every respect. William came from a wealthy farming family, the second son of Earl Waldegrave, and an old Etonian who had gone on to be a junior fellow at All Souls and then a member of Edward Heath's think-tank under Lord Rothschild. He lived in a grand house in the fashionable part of Notting Hill that backs onto Kensington Palace, where he and his wife, Caroline – a hugely successful cook in her own right – hosted glittering dinner parties. William was in his element on these occasions, mixing with the Pinters, the Jack Straws as well as with the Pattens (Chris and John), the Garel-Jones's and the Cecils, all of whom he understood and treated as equals.

Although a genuinely kind man, he somehow could not translate his good humour to the less cerebrally gifted of our colleagues. In short, he had no common touch. I frequently watched him come into his office in the morning without raising his eyes once as he walked past his private secretary, his two assistant private secretaries and his diary secretary. On more than one occasion I pushed him back out to the people who were his most valuable aids and told him to wish them good morning. He never intended to be discourteous. He simply lived in a different world in which there was always someone around to carry out the menial tasks which were so clearly beneath his intellect. As a businessman used to having to motivate staff, I thought it a fatal flaw. Whenever I rather diffidently mentioned his reputation for intellectual arrogance amongst my colleagues, William was genuinely concerned. I decided that the best thing was to throw him in at the deep end and arranged a lunch with Terry Dicks. It was time the cerebral met the Neanderthal. To no one's surprise, they got on famously, although Terry kindly avoided offering William his opinion on ballet (a lot of fairies prancing round in ladies tights) and opera (a bunch of fat foreign geezers singing in a foreign language) and confined himself to what for Terry was a modest ejaculation on Labour local government. William was thoroughly bemused by the whole experience and, as far as I can gather, has never forgotten it.

When he first entered the House, he was spoken of by many

as a Prime-Minister-in-waiting. His best friends would now regard this as an unlikely prospect. Margaret moved him on in due course to the Foreign Office and then to the Cabinet where he had an unhappy time as Health Secretary. John Major shuffled him into Agriculture where at last he seemed to have found himself, as Ministers occasionally do, a round peg in a round hole. He understood both the practice and the science of agriculture and was thoroughly in tune with the environmentalists as much as the producers. Unaccountably in my view, John Major then moved him to the Treasury as Chief Secretary, appointing Douglas Hogg in his place at MAFF. It was a disastrous error in man management. William would have been infinitely better able to handle the BSE crisis than Douglas, whilst Douglas is arguably sufficiently unpleasant to have been an ideal Chief Secretary.

Meanwhile the challenge at Environment was to reform local government finance. Margaret had long since committed herself to finding an alternative to the domestic rating system, and Kenneth Baker had been working with Patrick Jenkin on a replacement. The issue was to dominate the later years of her premiership, but in 1985 it was clear why many people saw the need for change. Margaret had been consumed by the inequities of a system in which local government was financed by a levy on property which took no account of the number of occupants in any dwelling, nor their ability to pay. She simply did not think it fair that a widow living off a pension should pay as much for local services as a family of four who, if they were all working, might have an income ten times as great. Not to mention that it would be that family that would own two or three cars, occupy more curb space, fill more dustbins, require more schooling, and borrow more books than their lonely neighbour. Nor was that the only injustice. The owner of a three-bedroomed detached house in Burnley might pay £100 a year in rates, whereas in Oxford the same property would attract a charge of £500, while the services they received were identical. It was also true that a great many people paid no rates at all, and when she had been Shadow Environment Spokesman at the time of the 1974 election, Margaret had promised to abolish the rates altogether. What to put in their place was less easy, but Kenneth and William between them worked hard with their advisors and officials to produce a Green Paper, entitled 'Paying for Local Government', which unveiled the Community Charge.

From a property tax the Community Charge would switch to a levy on each elector among whom the total amount the Council needed to raise would be divided equally. There was tremendous logic in the idea. Our analysis of local government spending showed that far more was spent on people than on property. Education, social services and the like consumed infinitely greater resources than street lighting and refuse collection. The Green Paper proposed a large number of exemptions for the less well off, and a long transition period from the old system to the new. It is worth recording the initial reaction to this new proposal. Our opponents in the press immediately dubbed it a Poll Tax. There was indeed an element of the decree that went out from Caesar Augustus, but the comparison was misleading. The document that Kenneth produced was carefully thought out and well presented. Those on benefit would only bear a small proportion of the new charge, and their benefits would be raised by the amount of the national average. This meant that no one on the bottom of the income scale would either be incapable of making a contribution or more importantly, immune from the effects of high spending. With Kenneth and William, I embarked on dozens of speaking engagements up and down the country to convince the local party associations of the merits of the new arrangements, and, generally speaking, succeeded. If the plans that Kenneth Baker had produced had been implemented as he designed them, the Community Charge could have fulfilled Margaret's ambitions for it. Sadly, those plans were hijacked along the way, not least by Nigel Lawson who never agreed with the original proposals, and Nick Ridley, Kenneth's successor at Environment, who never understood their political implications.

Kenneth's stay at Environment was all too short. I had enjoyed working with him but it was clear that his heart was set on persuading Margaret to let him pull an even more embarrassing iron out of the political fire. He had always been deeply interested in education and was appalled at what he saw happening under Keith Joseph. He was convinced that the whole education system needed to be overhauled as fundamentally as local government finance, and that we were losing the hearts and minds of our own natural supporters as long as Keith

was in charge. In May 1986 Margaret succumbed and somewhat reluctantly at first, appointed Kenneth to the job he
coveted. Nicholas Ridley arrived in his place at Marsham Street.

The change could not have been more marked. Kenneth was
a former Heathite from the centre of the party whilst Nick was a
Thatcherite before Thatcher. Kenneth symbolised all of the
modern presentation skills associated with modern media-
friendly politicians whereas Nick was perceived as difficult,
unsympathetic and prickly. He also smoked like a chimney. On
the first occasion I met him as he called the whole Environment
team together it was difficult to see if anyone was there on the
other side of the table. It was an unprepossessing introduction to
one of the great friendships of my political life. To understand
Nick Ridley it was important to distinguish the private man
from the public face. Publicly, he seemed to welcome discord
and criticism. Both he and Margaret occasionally expressed the
view that if everyone was against you, you were probably right.
There may even be occasional merit in that proposition. It is
certainly not given to man to tax and to please, but Nick
appeared to regard popularity as a cardinal sign of political
weakness and cultivated his image as an indifferent aristo.
Privately, he was a real gentleman and a pleasure to work with.
This did not mean that Nick was incapable of mistakes.
Crucially, he failed to spot how unjust the Community Charge
could be made to seem even before it was actually levied. Nick
advanced the perfectly logical proposition that on occasions the
rich man in his castle received exactly the same services from his
local authority as the poor man at his gate, and therefore should
pay no more. It was impeccable logic but lousy politics. At the
same time Nick failed to see how important it was to smooth the
introduction of the new tax. Whilst in Oxford and Epping
Forest the new charges would almost always result in bills
coming down, in some parts of the country some households
were facing bills ten times higher than before. The potential for
real trouble was evident to many of my backbench colleagues,
particularly those representing northern constituencies, but not,
sadly, to Nick. Nigel Lawson was also deeply sceptical about the
whole idea of the reform of local government and let it be
known in Cabinet that he was not prepared to find additional
money to smooth the transition. Whether he ever appreciated
the devastating consequences of his actions I do not know, but

between them Nick and Nigel ensured that Margaret was handed a lethal cocktail. Unfortunately, she never appreciated the strength of the poison until it was too late. Her reaction throughout the years of argument and even the explosion of violence that accompanied the introduction of the tax was to look neither to left nor right, and never to contemplate conceding defeat. It was to be another four years before her parliamentary colleagues, fearing their own political demise, decided that if she would not change the policy, then Margaret herself would have to be changed.

The irony which Margaret Thatcher herself identified in her memoirs is that by the time it was abolished under John Major, the Community Charge was working. By a delicate sleight of hand, Norman Lamont increased VAT to lard large subsidies into generous transitional arrangements and almost immediately, the Community Charge disappeared from the political agenda. At the 1990 Conservative Central Council in Southport more than one local government delegate wryly observed that if the government had put half as much money into introducing the Community Charge in its first year as it was forced to put into salvaging it in the second, there would have been no problem in the first place. In moving to the Council Tax, the Tories may well have laid the ghost of local government to rest for some time, but there are many of us who regret the re-emergence of a large number of electors who have no practical stake in the level of local government charges. Wherever significant numbers of people can vote for extra services without any responsibility for financing them, there is a potential for disaster. Had we persevered with the Community Charge, we would have achieved a great deal more in the long term than the present arrangements are ever likely to do.

As we entered 1987 the Conservatives were generally in an optimistic mood. The economy was improving, and whilst we had taken a hammering from the SDP and later the unholy Alliance, there was evidence that our electoral fortunes too were on the mend. Although she could have held out for another year, Margaret was convinced that the right time to challenge her opponents was in June. The previous November had seen the introduction of a deliberately low-key parliamentary agenda so that the decks could be cleared at a moment's notice. The last State Opening also offered me a final chance to make a tiny footnote in parliamentary history. John Wakeham, the Government Chief Whip, called me into his office one evening in late October. I had no idea what to expect. To my complete surprise he asked me if I would second the motion proposing the Loyal Address to the Queen which is the highlight of the State Opening for the Commons. Geoffrey Rippon was to be the proposer. As Andrew Mitchell remarked when he too was given the honour, the general idea is that the motion is proposed by an old buffer on his way out, and seconded by an oily young man on the make. It was a massive honour and for the first time in my life I made sure that I wrote down and timed every word. To make matters worse, the general idea is that one has to be witty rather than politically controversial. I would much sooner speak for half an hour on the exchange rate mechanism than be invited to make a witty speech for five minutes. There is nothing more difficult – especially when the audience consists of 650 fellow comedians. I began by confessing to feeling rather like Zsa-Zsa Gabor's eighth husband. I knew what was expected of me, but I was not sure I could make it that interesting any more. Thankfully, with my family in the gallery, the House laughed often enough, and I managed not to disgrace myself.

The real privilege of being asked to second a Loyal Address is to be invited to the private reading of the Queen's Speech which occurs behind closed doors at 10 Downing Street on the Eve of the State Opening. By tradition the Prime Minister invites all of his or her ministerial colleagues, together with the Speaker and the proposer and seconder of the Loyal Address to hear the words which the Queen will utter, but which of course the Prime Minister will have authored, in advance. These days, it is an occasion for a modest cocktail party after which the Prime Minister says a few words about the forthcoming legislative programme. In Margaret's day we sat down to a magnificent dinner which, because of the numbers involved, was laid out on a series of separate tables spreading over several rooms in number 10. I found myself placed opposite Geoffrey Rippon on the same table as the Prime Minister, Douglas Hurd, the Home Secretary, Geoffrey Howe, Nigel Lawson, Jack Weatherill and Quintin Hailsham, the Lord Chancellor. Conscious that I was unlikely to dine in such distinguished company again I made little conversation but listened avidly to every word. Margaret was in typical form. She had been as surprised as most of us when the Government's Bill on Sunday Trading was defeated at Second Reading. Given that the Government had a majority of more than a hundred, that was a remarkable misreading by the whips, but there were plans afoot to introduce a much more limited measure to give Sunday trading rights to, as I remember, garden centres on the grounds that this particular form of shopping was somehow less offensive than any other. It was an odd proposition which Douglas had hitherto resisted. Margaret however thought it an excellent idea and proceeded publicly to berate Douglas in the most frightful fashion. 'Why on earth not just get on with it, Douglas,' she demanded. 'You really must show a bit more backbone on these occasions.' Douglas looked at the ceiling throughout this tirade and then calmly pointed out the massive inconsistency in the Prime Minister's argument. She by then had turned to other things and was not the slightest bit interested in whatever Douglas said. Reading the faces around the table, it was obvious that this was not an uncommon experience for any of them.

9

Out and In

Margaret decided that we would seek our third term on 11 June 1987. My immediate task was to persuade the electors of Oxford East to return me as their candidate and the campaign duly began in earnest in early May. Alasdair McNutt having gone off to the Oman, we had been without a regular agent for some time, but by a stroke of good fortune, Sheila Chaplin was persuaded to join us as agent for the campaign. Sheila was no stranger to Oxford. She had been agent for the old City constituency before retiring to the west country, and she was an absolute dynamo. She smoked like a chimney, and terrified all around her including the volunteers as she barked endless instructions at them through the fog. She was a smart and attractive lady in her middle fifties, but far more to the point, she was a superb election organiser. Vicky once again headed my canvassing team and my mother bade farewell for a second time to my long-suffering father and told him he had to cook his own meals for three weeks. All my old friends were dragooned into action, and we set off on the campaign trail with a will.

The campaign certainly had its moments. On one occasion, canvassing a street of council houses, I found the door opened by an extremely attractive young blonde clad only in a black negligée. Determined to be unfazed, I introduced myself as the Conservative candidate and asked if I could count on her support. 'Oh well,' she said, 'I suppose you'd better come in.' Well, there was an invitation that was hard to resist! I walked into the front room where the ample white leather sofas were arranged on a leopard-skin carpet, only to find a second young lady, this time a brunette in an equally revealing white number and alongside her, an extremely smartly dressed African gentleman, complete with white three-piece suit, black shirt and white tie. 'What can we do for you, young man?' he asked with a smile. I repeated my usual mantra and hoped I could count on their support. 'Oh I don't think we have any problem with that, do we girls?' he laughed. 'We're all in favour of small business here.' I sensed it was time to make my excuses and, somewhat reluctantly, left.

This absolutely true story was closely followed by another. Oxford East was precisely the sort of seat where the election would be won or lost, so Peter Riddell, then political editor of the *Financial Times*, rang to ask if he could spend an afternoon with me to see how the campaign was progressing. I readily agreed and he turned up at the Cowley club where we had made our headquarters. Knowing him as well as I did, I realised that he would not be convinced if we took him to our best areas and so I offered him the chance to come with me for an hour or so to one of our most difficult housing estates. We set off as the light faded, and after an hour or so were thinking of wending our way home, when we turned a corner and ran into two of the largest and ugliest men I have ever met. They were both dressed in black T-shirts and leathers. One was black with dreadlocks down to his shoulders. The other was white with long dank black hair, a green painted tattoo on his face in the shape of a spider's web, with vertical lines running from his forehead, down his nose, across his cheeks and onto his neck. He had earrings in each ear, two more in each cheek, and a couple through his nose. Our prospects looked dire. Judging attack to be the best form of defence, I stuck out my hand. 'Hello, I'm Steve Norris, I hope you are going to be able to support me in the election.' 'Are you the Tory?' the largest of the two barked at me. Somewhat hesitantly, I nodded. 'That's all right then,' said my new friend 'I always vote Tory.' I would not be surprised to find we left a stain on the pavement, and as we hurried on I noticed Peter scribbling furiously. He duly reported that whatever else Steven Norris might do, he clearly had the biker vote in Oxford East.

During the whole of the campaign I was clear that our support was holding up. On one occasion Andrew Smith and I debated the state of the National Health Service in front of a large audience of nurses. It was not necessarily good territory for a government supporter, but I showed the increased funding that we had made available and, accepting that there was still deficiencies, pointed to the management reforms which Norman Fowler had recently introduced. I stressed that above all we remained committed to a service which was free at the point of delivery on the basis of need rather than means. Andrew delivered a conventional Labour broadside against our record, inferring that a change of government would cure the sick and the lame. When the time came for questions, the first was from a nurse in his forties who asked, 'Mr Smith, given the appalling mess your government made of funding the NHS between 1974 and 1979, including that dreadful year when Mr Healey managed to reduce expenditure in real terms, what on earth can you offer that makes us believe that Labour will do better than the Tories?' To my surprise, his question was greeted with loud applause.

My 1987 campaign team was even more professional than its predecessor. By my side throughout was Jonathan Djanogly, a student at the polytechnic who was president of the Conservative association there, and a mercurial organiser. He pulled together a terrific team of students including some incredibly attractive young girls, and they threw themselves into canvassing with great gusto. One of the campaign traditions in Oxford East is to address the car workers as their shifts change around 6.00 a.m. Andrew Smith announced the date of his meeting, and we decided to be there at the same time. Although Rover had a reputation for being heavily unionised, I knew enough of the men to know that at least half would be voting for me. Our campaign bus arrived after Andrew had started his speech. He was on a soapbox addressing a small crowd when out of the back of our bus emerged half a dozen nubile sixteen-year-olds in mini-skirts and extremely tight leotards, handing out leaflets. In five minutes, Andrew's audience had withered to two, both of whom must have been registered blind.

With education a large employer in Oxford East, I asked Kenneth Baker to come to speak for me at the Cowley club. At that time, Ken was at the centre of a furious row with the teacher unions over the proposals which later formed his great Education Reform Bill and when we arrived for the meeting, there were hundreds in the hall, and even more outside. Ken was on superb form and although there was some mild heckling, we had the majority of the hall on our side, and Ken delivered a thoroughly robust performance. He won a standing ovation, and afterwards was able to point to the unseemly spectacle of teachers prancing around waving placards in a most unteacherly way. My team were buoyed up by success that evening, but I knew that a few days later we were to have an even more interesting time when Cecil Parkinson was due to speak for me at the Oxford Polytechnic. He arrived accompanied by Ann, his wife, but we were forced to enter the building by a side door because hundreds of students were demonstrating outside. Mounted policemen were holding them back, and the atmosphere was fevered. Cecil had of course been obliged to resign as Secretary of State for Trade and Industry during the 1983 Blackpool Party Conference following the Sara Keays revelations. He was not yet back in the Cabinet, but he was a major draw and when we entered the lecture theatre where he was due to speak, the audience was literally throbbing with excitement. There were about 400 in the hall, evenly split between supporters and detractors. The noise was terrific. Suddenly the chanting started. '*Maggie, Maggie, Maggie, out, out, out!*', over and over again. And then, in a beautifully orchestrated move, '*Parky, Parky, Parky, in out, in out, in out.*' The audience convulsed in good natured laughter and I certainly found it difficult to keep a straight face. Cecil too, saw the funny side even when a hail of condoms in silver wrappings arrived from the back of the hall. Ann seemed less amused but to her great credit, she stood her ground.

It was then that Cecil began a magnificent speech. He told them how he started life as the son of a railwayman in Carnforth in Lancashire, and how ordinary and working-class his own origins were. He told how he worked his way through grammar school to qualify as an accountant. He talked about setting up his business, working seven days a week, and how he came to realise that the politics of envy were so supremely unattractive. It was a message I identified with strongly, but he spoke with enormous conviction, warmth and sincerity and was listened to with ever-increasing respect. When he sat down there was a second's silence followed by tumultuous applause. I noticed that every one of his detractors joined in. For a moment at least, he had converted them all.

Just as in 1983, the campaign flashed by and in no time we gathered to hear the result at Oxford Town Hall. I had been right about our support. I polled a thousand more votes than in

116

My father, John Norris, 1943.

My mother, Eileen Norris, SN (centre) and brother, Richard, on the beach at Gronant, North Wales, 1951.

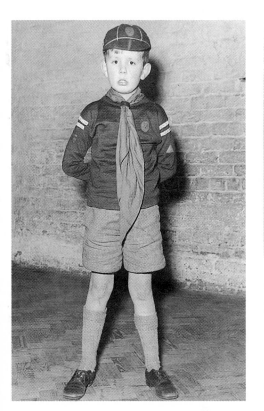

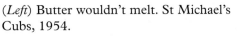

(*Above*) The one that got away. Unnamed number six, Sefton Park, Liverpool, 1949.

(*Left*) Butter wouldn't melt. St Michael's Cubs, 1954.

(*Left*) Worcester College 2nd VIII 1965. A rare sporting achievement, and enormous fun.

(*Below*) The obligatory pre-election snap with Our Leader, 1983. Hard to tell which of us is the more embarrassed.

(*Bottom*) In the garden at Wylye, 1987. Vicky, Edward, Tony (carrying Neil Kinnock, his ginger cat) and SN with Basil the corgi and Hector the labrador. Happy days - except for Edward!

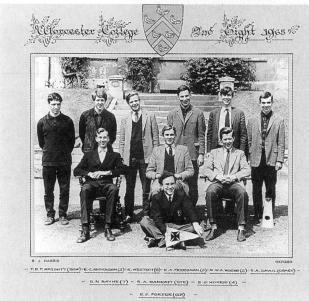

(*Below*) Epping Forest By-election, 1988. Surrounded by my campaign team some of whom had worked themselves to the bone.

(*Left*) Campaigning in the Epping Forest By-election 1988. Going for the dog-lover vote in a big way.

(*Below*) Epping Forest By-election 1988. Giving Simon Burns MP advice on his next used car.

(*Left*) My first boss, William Waldegrave, in a typically friendly gesture to Sir Richard Scott.

(*Below Left*) A rare portrait of Nicholas Ridley without a cigarette.

(*Below*) Ken Baker telling the Tory Conference we may only have won one council but in politics, one can be enough.

The minister

Norris: Sexual antics

by REBECCA HARDY

TEN years ago it was Cecil Parkinson. Today, the sexual antics of another Government Minister — albeit a junior one — is the talk of the Conservative Party Conference in Blackpool.

Transport Minister Steven Norris, it emerges, has been enjoying an unusual number of extramarital affairs — much to the chagrin of the respective mistresses, each of whom believed herself to be the only woman in his life.

First, we were told, his marriage to admiral's daughter Vicky Cecil-Gibson was over. He had finally decided to make an honest woman of his mistress of three years, Times political reporter Sheila Gunn.

Then, we discovered, Harpers & Queen promotions director Jennifer Sharp was also on intimate terms with this member of Her Majesty's Government. This revelation deeply distressed House of Commons secretary Emma Courtney, who had also been dating Norris for 12 months. No sooner had Emma dried her tears than another mistress popped up, Lynn Taylor, who enjoyed an affair with Norris for five years.

Understandably, his long-suffering wife, Vicky, has left the marital home in Norris's Epping Forest constituency and moved, with her sons Anthony, 19, and Edward, seven, to a £1,000-a-week rented house near her parents in the Berkshire hamlet of Hampstead Norris.

Since their separation some time ago, he has been living in a one-bedroomed flat in Camberwell, though even now, colleagues aren't betting on how long he will stay the lonely bachelor.

THE WIFE

Name: Vicky Norris.
Age: 45.
Marital status: married Steven Norris in 1969, currently separated.
Occupation: husband's constituency secretary.
Relationship: Vicky, the daughter of an admiral and niece of Cardinal Basil Hume, met Norris as an impressionable 22-year-old.

He was attracted by her breeding and delicate beauty; she fell in love with his energy and charm. Their early married life, say friends, was happy. Vicky remained a loyal, dutiful wife, supporting her husband throughout his political career and caring for their two sons Anthony, 19, and Edward, eight. She was by his side when he lost his Oxford East seat in the 1987 General Election and later when he fought a bitter by-election for his current seat.

But at the time of the 1988 by-election, Norris was having a relationship with Lynn Taylor. Sheila Gunn followed in 1991.

Both women claim Vicky knew about these relationships. But in Norris's constituency at least, Vicky kept up the appearance of a devoted politician's wife.

She remained supportive until the humiliating revelations of her husband's love live.

Today, she is living with her sons near her parents in a rented £1,000-a-week house in the Berkshire hamlet of Hampstead Norris.

MISTRESS No 1

Name: Lynn Taylor.
Age: 46.
Marital status: single.
Occupation: sales executive.
Relationship: Lynn met Norris at a party in a theatre near his home in Newbury, Berks, seven years ago.

'He talked about his marriage, how he loved his wife and kids but was desperately unhappy. He felt trapped. Their sex life was non-existent.

'We were very open about it. I met loads of other MPs and their floozies. It seemed most MPs were at it. He doesn't have film star looks and our relationship wasn't primarily sexual. He was very gentle and loving in bed and I was always satisfied.'

Two months into the relationship Norris produced a diamond engagement ring and proposed. But after four years of waiting, Lynn finally realised there was no future to the relationship.

She continued to see Norris until January, 1991, when he started seeing Sheila. 'I was devastated. I cried for months. I felt it was deeply ungentlemanly to promise me for years that I was the only one in his life and that we had a future and that he intended to marry me.

'Steven simply cannot help himself where women are concerned. It seemed there had never really been a time in his married life when he hadn't had a lover. He is a compulsive womaniser, who gets his kick from having relationships which massage his ego.'

---

and his mistresses

MISTRESS No 2

Name: Sheila Gunn.
Age: 45.
Marital status: divorced mother of two.
Occupation: political reporter for The Times.
Relationship: Sheila, an ambitious journalist who started her career as a secretary, met Norris at the Commons three years ago. He was then working as an aide to former Conservative chairman Kenneth Baker.

She was attracted to his charm and drive; he liked her ambition and intellect. Norris regularly spent weekends at Sheila's £400,000 West Sussex farmhouse and the couple rented a home together near Vauxhall Bridge.

Norris told Sheila he wanted to marry her but said his wife, a Roman Catholic, would not divorce him. He continued to visit his wife and sons at their Epping Forest home. Vicky was said to 'tolerate' the relationship.

Sheila issued Norris with an ultimatum to separate from his wife at the end of last year and moved into a friend's house.

They continued to see each other until August when Norris visited his wife for a weekend but stayed for longer.

When Sheila learned of his relationship with Jennifer Sharp, she was said to be shattered. 'I do not think he has behaved in either an honest or honourable way,' she said.

MISTRESS No 3

Name: Emma Courtney.
Age: 29.
Marital status: single.
Occupation: Commons secretary to MP Henry Bellingham.
Relationship: Emma, a dewy-eyed former public schoolgirl, met Norris over a year ago while working in the Commons. Norris was said to be infatuated with her innocent beauty.

An intelligent, softly-spoken woman, she was flattered by his persistence and charm. She started dating him 12 months ago and soon fell 'deeply in love'.

She spent a lot of time at his South London flat. Emma knew about Sheila and Vicky, but Norris swore the relationships were over and regularly talked to her about marriage. Emma ended the affair when she learned of Norris's involvement with Jennifer. She was said to be 'devastated'.

Friends say they had warned her not to trust Norris, but that she was convinced by him. 'She was absolutely in love with him, and still is,' said a Commons colleague. 'We all warned her not to get involved. He's far more experienced than she is, but he made a big effort to woo her and she fell for him hook, line and sinker.

'We all knew he was seeing other women. Poor Emma, she's so sweet and naive, but I'm sure she'll forgive him if he comes up with a plausible enough excuse.'

MISTRESS No 4

Name: Jennifer Sharp.
Age: 40.
Marital status: marriage to artist David Sharp dissolved 11 years ago.
Occupation: promotions director of Harpers & Queen magazine.
Relationship: Jennifer, a striking woman, has known Norris as a friend for 20 years.

Their relationship started five months ago, after, she insists, his wife moved out of his constituency to the West Country. Both Vicky and Sheila were unaware of Norris's relationship with Jennifer until it was revealed by the Mail's Nigel Dempster.

A dynamic force in publishing, Jennifer helped Tina Brown launch Tatler in 1979. Earlier this year, she ended a ten-year relationship with Vogue travel writer Andrew Powell, said to be 'terribly upset'. Soon after this, she became involved with Norris.

She makes a popular, lively companion and friends believe Norris was attracted to this fun-loving side of her personality. A colleague said: 'Jennifer has a delightfully wicked sense of humour and has him in stitches with some of the publishing stories she tells.'

Jennifer believes it is too early to speculate about marriage. 'What happened to his marriage has nothing to do with me,' she said. 'We are not living together. I have my flat in Kensington and Steven, who is an honourable, decent and hardworking man, has a home near the House of Commons.'

A cartoonist's field-day.

(*Right*) The bonk-buster novelist and dietician hard at work.

(*Below*) Clock the overcoats. Dr Who lands in Parliament Square. The Tardis examined by Cllr Robert Davis of Westminster and the Minister for Transport in London, 1994.

When in a hole... With John Marshall MP 1993.

(Left) A pair of old thespians modelling silly hats. With Glenda Jackson at the new Jubilee Line Stratford Station, 1996

(*Facing page*) Daily Mail 6 October 1993. Typical of the genre.

(*Above*) 'Wanna buya bus?' Selling the London Transport Bus Companies, 1994.

(*Left*) Note not an ounce of Lycra. Starting the annual Bike Week, 1994.

(*Right*) With Emma, 1995

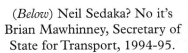

(*Below*) Neil Sedaka? No it's Brian Mawhinney, Secretary of State for Transport, 1994-95.

(*Above*) John MacGregor, my first boss at the Department of Transport, 1992-94.

(*Above*) Sir George Young, Secretary of State for Transport, 1995 – E-mail address: Cyclebart Westminster.

(*Below*) John Prescott. The Great Democratic Socialist and Deputy Leader of the New Labour Party.

(*Below*) Clare Short. The lip may curl, but she's the nicest lady in politics.

(*Above*) Tony Blair. Never mind Devil Eyes – it's the teeth that terrify me.

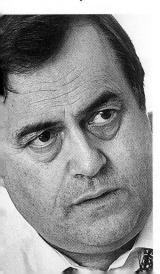

The Prime Minister advising me on my
limited career options. Opening the
Limehouse Link, May 1993.

Hezza and the bid for
the Leadership,
November 1990.

The two men most likely to.
A hair-raising proposition!

(*Left*) Michael Portillo as newly-
elected MP for Enfield Southgate,
1986.

(*Below left*) Michael Portillo as
Secretary of State for Defence, 1995.

(*Right*) William Hague aged 16.

(*Below right*) William Hague, aged
16½, Secretary of State for Wales,
1995.

1983, but once again it was the third party that was vital to the outcome. The Liberal vote collapsed, and Andrew Smith was able to take more of it than I. He won by 1,288. Andrew made a generous acceptance speech in which he thanked me for what I had done for the constituency over the previous four years and expressed the view that I might not be long out of Parliament. It was a typically generous gesture, and when I did return some eighteen months later, I was pleased but not surprised to find that the first congratulatory note in my pigeon hole was from him.

Elsewhere in the country Oxford East once more mirrored the national pattern. Although the Conservatives secured a slightly higher percentage of the vote, Margaret Thatcher's majority in the House was reduced from 144 to 101. It was still, however, an extraordinary result for a Prime Minister seeking a third term. In reality she had solidified Britain into two clear camps. Those who thought she could do no wrong, who numbered about 40 per cent of the population, and those who regarded her as the devil incarnate. Fortunately this camp could not agree on an alternative and although Neil Kinnock had put in a more powerful performance than Michael Foot, his left-leaning party was hugely unattractive to many non-Tories.

Losing is less pleasant than winning, and my supporters were understandably depressed that night. Sheila Chaplin clearly thought we could have done more, but I was convinced our team had given everything they had, and had every reason to be proud. I consoled them as best I could, and grey with tiredness, drove home. It is extraordinary how much more tiring it is to lose than to win.

As I drove home that night, I was probably the least disconsolate of all my superb election team. Like most people I hate losing, but I could never forget the plight of politicians who were infinitely more superior who were taken to the brink of disaster every election because of their wafer-thin majorities. Chris Patten never seemed to win Bath by more than a handful. It was desperately unfair, but I could see that every election would be fought on a knife edge in Oxford East and that if I were to have won, the prospects of the Conservatives winning a fourth term would be likely to be remote. Even then, I could see that this was not a bad time to look around for a safer berth, except that this time I would not be doing so as an unknown rookie but as a former MP with four years' experience including time as a PPS. Not for nothing had I assiduously trodden the rubber-chicken weekend circuit for the past four years.

The other reason why I was probably less concerned than those of my colleagues who also lost that night was that, financially at least, losing made precious little difference. In those golden years I was drawing, if not exactly earning, sufficient out of the business to have funded a beautiful new house in the Wylye valley which I fell in love with as soon as I saw it, and bought on the spot. I had done exactly the same with Brook House and fortunately, Vicky forgave me this time too. It is probably the most beautiful property I will ever occupy. It was a simple Georgian farmhouse with a vast kitchen complete with large Aga, a playroom, family room, elegant dining-room, drawing-room, in short an estate agent's dream. I had also acquired a property in France. Some years previously I had been on holiday near St Tropez in the Var, and James Scott, a friend of a friend, invited me to dinner at his small house in a village called Bargemon, a few miles up in the hills near the majestic Gorge du Verdon. We arrived in the village in the early evening and found our way to the very oldest part where the houses are actually built into the ancient walls that protected the villages from the barbary pirates in centuries past. We eventually found a tiny door in the wall with a small brass plaque in the French style and walked up a narrow flight of stone stairs to an even tinier door. But as we walked into the main room it was like walking into an Aladdin's cave. The main living-room was huge. It contained a kitchen at one end, a large and airy sitting-room and a balcony overlooking the valley below. There was no false ceiling, so the oak-beamed roof with its white plaster work was open and quite stunning. The balcony could accommodate six people for dinner. I had never forgotten that lovely place and when, completely by chance, I met someone at an adjacent table in a restaurant who told me in passing that James was thinking of selling, I rang him up and bought it then and there.

It had no garden, no pool or vineyard, but it had enormous character and was a base for innumerable idyllic holidays.

There was little attraction for me in a garage business in Salisbury and in any event it was all too easy to rationalise my lack of involvement on the basis that Anthony Ince had effectively been running the company for the last couple of years and all I was likely to do was to meddle and make things worse. We had acquired another dealership in Weston-Super-Mare along the way, but between them, Anthony and Ken Frith, who ran the Weston end, seemed to have things under control. I was wrong, of course. It is much easier to say so in retrospect, but in fact I was banking everything on the continuation of the Lawson boom. Profitability seemed effortless and my large drawings caused us no embarrassment. On the contrary, profits continued to rise year by year. If I had looked a bit more closely I would have seen that much of that profit was in stock rather than cash, but after all, I could console myself with the fact that the property I had rather shrewdly bought for £155,000 in 1983 was valued at more than three quarters of a million by 1987.

So I had money and time on my hands and was relieved and delighted when, just a few weeks after the election, John Patten called me. He was now number two in the Home Office under Douglas Hurd and he invited me to come and talk to them about a project Douglas had in mind.

I met the Home Secretary in his large room at the top of the Home Office in Queen Anne's Gate and he outlined his proposition. Up to that point I had taken no particular interest in Home Office matters. Although I could see a role for capital punishment in a very limited set of circumstances, I was always rather repelled by the Tory Conference debates that saw the death penalty as a panacea for everything from parking offences upward, and I instinctively disliked discussions about the severity of punishment necessary to assuage the blood lust of the blue-rinse brigade. Otherwise Home Office policy was a closed book to me so I listened attentively as Douglas spoke. When he had arrived at the Home Office he had asked his officials two deceptively simple questions: 'What causes crime, and what can we in government do to prevent it?' The answers were less clear. Economic deprivation, unemployment, poor housing, substandard education and peer group pressure all play their part as indeed does the notion that some people are simply more honest and decent than others. But shining through the analysis was a proposition which I still believe to be the most important of all. The most cost-effective and painless way of reducing crime is not to concentrate on punishing offenders but actually to ensure that the crime is not committed in the first place. In short, the primary duty of government is crime prevention rather than detection, conviction and sentencing. This is not to suggest that competent and adequate detection resources, a legal system which is not unduly weighted toward the interests of defendants allowing a disproportionate number to escape conviction, and tough sentencing particularly for violent crimes, are not all important. Of course they are. But they are all characterised by shutting the stable door after the horse has bolted.

It is equally obvious on any analysis that prevention is not something the police can be expected to take on in isolation. Robert Peel had established the first national police force with the primary task of preventing crime, but while the police are well aware of their technical responsibility, the public demanded more visible resources for detection and conviction and in those days in the late eighties, previous little was actually being done about prevention.

Douglas was specifically keen to get the voluntary sector and business involved in what would in practice be a business-led community initiative to encourage crime prevention. He asked me if I would be prepared to draw up a plan for how such an operation might work, and I agreed immediately. I sat down with David Faulkner, the senior official in charge of crime prevention at the Home Office, and we agreed that I would need some specialised knowledge of the crime prevention world. He suggested David Burley, a bright and enormously engaging young graduate who was on secondment from NACRO, the organisation devoted to the care and resettlement of offenders. Despite coming from different ends of the political spectrum David and I clicked and in the next few weeks we drew up a plan which identified the main players, the necessary funding, a programme of work with suggested objectives, and a draft constitution. Douglas accepted the plan and invited me to find a chairman. Whoever we appointed would have to work with business as well as with the public sector and, perhaps even more importantly, the most highly developed mafia in Britain, the Association of Chief Police Officers. The candidate would need to be able to persuade and convince and have the enthusiasm and time to coax large cheques out of corporate coffers. After exhaustive executive search, I was convinced there was only one suitable candidate and Douglas appointed me. We called the organisation the Crime Concern Trust. I invited the people that David and I had suggested might join me as fellow trustees and we cast about for a chief executive. Ralph Kantor, one of the leading lights of the security industry and a shrewd and experienced businessman, helped enormously. In a moment of unadulterated serendipity we found and appointed Nigel Whiskin and under his utterly inspired leadership the organization has since gone from strength to strength. Nigel George Lansbury Whiskin is, as his name implies, no natural Tory. But no person I have met before or since can match his concern, compassion and humanity. He is a compulsive worker who produces more results in a week than most of us – including myself – achieve in a month of Sundays. He was and is the inspiration behind an organisation that is now involved in literally hundreds of projects helping young and disadvantaged people all over the country escape that first lethal brush with the law. Crime Concern has persuaded the biggest and best of British business to contribute millions towards some of the finest community projects in Britain and the Trust is now recognised as the leading crime prevention authority in the country. In the unlikely event that Her Majesty ever invites me to compile an honours list, the first nomination for the Garter, the Order of Merit and a Companionship of Honour will be Nigel's.

Whilst Crime Concern was bringing me back to London and public life, I also took a call from Kenneth Baker. He and I had been at opposite ends of the ladder at the DoE, Ken as Secretary of State, and me as the junior PPS. But we had struck up a very happy friendship not least because Ken is one of the least stuffy, most friendly and approachable men ever to have held high office. His meetings were always constructive and enjoyable and he had been kind enough to listen to my occasional contributions with at least a semblance of respect. He too now had a job for me. He had moved into Keith Joseph's seat at Education and had spent the year prior to the general election formulating what was to be the most significant Education Act since Rab Butler's. The Great Education Reform Bill, (or 'gerbil' as it was affectionately known), was indeed a revolutionary document as far as the conventional educational wisdom of the seventies and eighties was concerned. Among its radical proposals was the novel idea that parents might actually be entitled to know how well their children were performing to a proper objective standard, and that they might prefer their children to be educated in a core curriculum centred on the three 'R's rather than on sociology and peace studies. So Ken's Bill introduced a national curriculum, attainment testing, league tables, and most radical of all, a fundamental shift toward empowering parents and school governors together with headteachers and staff at the expense of local education authority bureaucracies. This last was as fiercely resisted as indeed the whole Bill was throughout its stormy passage.

Ken proposed the creation of two new types of school. Firstly the City Technology College, devoted to producing high quality engineering and technology students and to be supported by large industry sponsorship, and secondly grant-maintained schools where parents could, if they so wished, opt for not only the DES funding, but a proportion of the local authority resources to be paid direct to the school rather than channelled via the local education authority. Whilst there was obvious merit in allowing decisions to be taken and resources spent much closer to the classroom than ever before, the concept struck at the very heart of municipal socialism. This blow against the County Hall imperialists enraged the Labour Party who vowed to frustrate the whole concept at every turn. In the early days they were having some success through a combination of crude blackmail and an ability to trade on the relative ignorance of most school governors, who were in many cases keen on the idea of controlling their own destinies, but worried about how they would fare if they dared put their heads above the parapet. Ken could see the need for an organisation which could not only promote the merits of grant-maintained status, but also take willing schools by the hand and lead them through the complexity of the process. Again, he asked me if I would take the task of setting up the organization and, more importantly, funding it. It was clear that the funding would have to come from outside Government because the Bill had not yet become an Act and under the Central Office of Information rules, Ken was not allowed to use government resources to promote a concept in a bill. Again, I readily accepted. Whilst it had taken me some time to appreciate that it matters not how rich society becomes, or how long doctors can keep us alive if we cannot walk down to the corner shop to buy a loaf of bread, my belief in what Ken was seeking to achieve was reinforced by all my own experience of St Michael's, the Institute and Oxford.

Just at the time I left, Labour's assault on the grammar schools had begun, and within a frighteningly few years the Institute had been effectively destroyed. The Liverpool City Council, increasingly under Militant control, had been quite open about their intention to destroy not only the Institute, but all the other city grammar schools which they saw as the bastions of privilege. It was Maoist cultural revolution and, as in China, whilst it comprehensively destroyed everything of value, it replaced it with nothing. The Institute had become just another inner-city comprehensive, but was so badly starved of resources that it had eventually and ignominiously closed. I suspect that its final demise gave Derek Hatton, whom I vaguely remembered as a small spotty youth when I was in the sixth form, a particular pleasure.

What angered me so much was the extraordinary proposition that selection in education was elitist. The reality is that selection in education is the greatest liberating force in a modern democratic society. It is the only effective mechanism whereby children from deprived inner-city areas, where there is little respect for formal education amongst the population at large, will ever have the chance to fulfil their own academic potential, and break out, exactly as I had done, from the confines of their birthplace. It is blindingly obvious to me that the truly dangerous notion of elitism derives from the comprehensive system in which cosy middle-class suburbs produce cosy middle-class comprehensives almost indistinguishable from the old grammar schools whilst inner-city areas invariably produce schools which decline in a spiral of neglect and under-performance. Worse, the comprehensive school offers no escape. Conservative attempts to broaden parental choice have been laudable, but produce as much frustration as satisfaction amongst parents when so many find that the popular school they want their children to attend is already full of catchment area children. It was the grammar schools that allowed millions of working-class children like me to enjoy an education which their parents could never have contemplated buying in their wildest dreams, and which would then propel them on throughout the rest of their lives – free of state support, and as contributors to, rather than recipients from the national Exchequer.

My enthusiasm for all Ken was trying to achieve was tempered only by the uncomfortable truth that Margaret

Thatcher had actually closed more grammar schools than any other Education Secretary, including Shirley Williams, and had lost all of the years between 1979 and 1988 before allowing Kenneth to introduce the one reform which was, along with her reform of industrial relations, clearly the most necessary and, not in the least coincidentally, the most enduring of her entire administration. My only regret then and now is that the Conservatives are not prepared to go far enough. There is still a diffidence about accepting the importance of selection and whilst John Major has spoken of a grammar school in every town with my applause ringing mightily in his ears, others in the Tory party appear to be uncomfortable with that notion. Their diffidence should not be heeded. Nothing would do more to restore standards of education in Britain than an open and clear commitment to allow every child the opportunity to develop their talents to the full – including those bright children who desperately need to be pushed at their own fast speed rather than to be held back by their less able classmates.

Once I had accepted, Ken packed me off to see Tim Bell. He rightly believed that no one in Britain was better connected in business, and that Tim would be able to point me towards my potential donors. I had heard of him of course. He was already a legend in the Tory party as the guru who had inspired two successful election campaigns, but I had never met him personally. From the instant I was ushered into his large Knightsbridge office I knew I liked him. He has a huge personality, ebullient, open, friendly and amusing. But he is also an enormously clear thinker. The most important quality required of any strategist is the ability to cut through the verbiage and distil a complex notion into two or three pithy sentences. Tim has that ability and within minutes of my explaining my mission, he had summarised it better than I could ever do, enthused me even more than I already was, and given me a dozen or so names who, entirely true to Tim's form, all turned out to be winners. People like John Ashcroft, the City whizz-kid then sitting on top of the Coloroll empire, and Tony Berry, the boss of the massive Blue Arrow employment business, were both typical of the successful entrepreneurs who instantly recognised what Ken Baker was trying to achieve and supported him to the hilt. They and many like them gave freely of time and money, both privately and corporately. Tony, incidentally, has remained a firm friend. I was disgusted with the way he was treated by the City establishment when their fingers were burned once the Stock Exchange bubble burst. Tony, John Ashcroft, John Gunn of British and Commonwealth and many other high flyers were darlings one day and demons the next. In America if bright people fail they are given a second chance, and frequently a third. In Britain, an entrepreneur who has the temerity to meet a recession is likely to be treated more like a criminal.

Although I was not actually able to appear as a witness on his behalf, I wrote to Michael Heseltine at the DTI when Tony Berry was under threat of being disqualified as a director following the Blue Arrow affair, telling him of the man I knew. I wrote of a man who showed concern, interest and understanding. A man who was prepared to give time and energy to a cause from which he could not possibly hope to profit himself, and a man who at all times had treated me with courtesy and consideration. I was delighted when the DTI action against him was dropped. The only tragedy is that whilst the officials who dealt with the mounting files simply shuffled a few years closer to their pensions, the cost to Tony personally in money and time, not to mention the constant pressure that he was under for several years, left a deep scar. Fortunately, and to my delight, he has bounced back magnificently. Whilst Tony and John both suffered in the recession, other supporters powered on to ever greater success. Allen Sheppard the mercurial head of Grand Metropolitan, who was also a supporter, is now rightly Lord Sheppard of Digmere and the tireless champion of his beloved capital city, London.

Only one of the names Tim gave me proved a dud. I called on Jim Prior, the former Tory Minister and Chairman of GEC, to present my case, but sitting with him in the room was Sarah Morrison, ex-wife of Charles, the MP for Devizes, and a close confidante of Ted Heath. She dominated the conversation and could see nothing good in the idea of grant-maintained status at all. Indeed, it seemed to me that she could find nothing good to say about the Tory party as a whole. Ted's defeat clearly still rankled. I told Jim that if he was not interested, thankfully there were others who were. He had the good grace to look embarrassed. I left reflecting not for the last time on how self-indulgent some alleged government supporters had already become. But whatever our internal divisions, it was clear to me that the real threat in education came from the Socialists rather than the other Tories.

I brought in Andrew Turner, my old friend from Oxford East and himself a former teacher as director of the Trust. He, like Nigel Whiskin, immediately set to work with enthusiasm and dedication. He too is still in his post at the time of writing, and the trust has grown vastly under his guidance.

As far as a return to Westminster was concerned, I had very mixed feelings. I had an office in Queen Anne's Gate while Crime Concern was being established, and I had visited Ken in Elizabeth House, that appalling sixties office block adjacent to Waterloo Station where the Secretary of State conducts conversations against the constant background of arrivals and departures. I had frequently driven past the Palace of Varieties as I made my way back to Wylye or my flat in Marsham Street, and more often than not, particularly on a nice summer evening, felt more pity for my confined colleagues than envy. There was in any event no reason for me to have to address the issue. The entire Parliamentary Conservative Party appeared to be enjoying rude health. For the whole of the first year, there were no by-elections at all. The first to induce a collective sigh of relief from the entire candidates list was sadly Brandon Rhys-Williams, the delightfully dotty Member for Kensington. Unfortunately, his majority had been around 3,000, so by-election success was by no means assured. Much to my surprise, I had several calls from Tories in the constituency asking me to stand and indicating that if I did, I was almost certain to be selected. I was flattered but cautious. As far as marginal seats were concerned, I had, in the popular vernacular, been there and got the T-shirt. I had no desire to repeat the experience. Compared to Oxford East, Kensington was the fire to its frying pan. I politely declined.

Some weeks later in his typically generous and friendly way Jim Spicer, the Dorset MP, invited me for lunch. At first I resisted. I had quietly promised myself that if I ever returned to the House it would be by the front door rather than through the security apparatus, but Jim is the kind of ex-military man who does not take no for an answer and in any event, he was a good friend and I knew I would enjoy his company. It was he who told me that John Biggs-Davison, the long-standing Member for

Epping Forest, was terminally ill. 'John hasn't long,' he said. 'Epping Forest is rock safe and it would be ideal for you.' I had never heard of the place and everything I had ever seen of Essex, including my time at Ford, appeared to confirm that I was not missing much. In any event, I thought no more about it. Then in the early autumn John died of cancer. He had represented Epping Forest for thirty-three years, first as Member for the Chigwell division, and then, after the inevitable churning of the Boundary Review, of the enlarged Epping Forest constituency. His general election majority was more than 20,000. It was indeed rock safe.

Within hours, Tania Mason had made contact. She and I had been friends since she had become an investor in the Steve Norris business, but I had not appreciated that she was also a big wheel in the Epping Forest Conservative Association. 'You've got to put your hat in the ring, Steve,' she declared. 'I've been telling everybody about you, and I am sure you have got a good chance.' Knowing that there is only one constituency fact which is of interest to any aspiring Member, and that is the size of the majority, I did so. 21,513 ought to be enough to survive even the worst the opposition could contrive.

Needless to say, I was not the only Tory interested in inheriting Sir John's mantle. 550 budding aspirants put their names forward, and the constituency party had a high old time whittling down the number to the twenty-four they interviewed, and the five who finally made the short list. To my enormous surprise, I was among them. My four rivals were Mark Robinson, who, having represented a Welsh seat during the last parliament, had actually already been a Minister, and seemed daunting opposition. Richard Hickmett who lost his Glandford and Scunthorpe seat was also in with a shout. The fourth 'retread', as we were unkindly dubbed by the newspapers, was Peter Bruinvels. I had regarded him as the greatest buffoon on the Conservative benches and was appalled that he had survived thus far. As I contemplated the prospect of his victory I knew that if they were to select him, then Epping Forest would most certainly have deserved him hugely. The last of my rivals was Howard Flight, who had made a fortune in the City with Guinness Flight, the money brokers.

We all gathered, together with our wives, in the purpose-built Conservative Association headquarters located in Meadow

Road in Loughton, a typically leafy London suburb located at the eastern end of the Central Line. We all naturally knew each other, and I was personally relaxed about the outcome. I knew both Mark and Richard to be competent performers and Mark in particular as a former Minister was bound to impress. After we had all done our respective party pieces, we went off without being told the result. The committee would communicate that the following day. I heard the result on my car phone from Tricia Gurnett, the constituency agent. 'I have got two pieces of good news,' she said. 'The first is that you are through to the next round, and the second is that because you managed to poll more votes than all the other candidates put together, you are automatically the only candidate to be put forward to the constituency general meeting. Congratulations, you've done it.'

Needless to say I was astonished and delighted. I had hoped to do well, but never in my wildest dreams had I anticipated such a clear win. Instead of the constituency meeting being a dreadful test of nerves with one other of the original five, it was the first rally of the by-election. When the time came to endorse my candidacy, every hand in the room was raised in acclamation. Well, nearly every hand. Jim Axon was a local farmer with a reputation for straight talking. Jim had decided that a single candidate was not the answer, however wonderful that candidate might be. And on a matter of principle, he voted against. Having done so, he was one of the first to shake me warmly by the hand.

Margaret Thatcher called the by-election for 15 December 1988, and we swung on to the election trail once more. The difference of course was that this was a by-election. Whereas neither of my general election campaigns had excited particular interest in the press, during a by-election – particularly one so close to London – the media interest is intense. Every day starts with a ministerial visit and a formal press conference, every nuance is reported by the nationals and the count itself is likely to justify at least an hour or two of late-night David Dimbleby. One tradition on such occasions is that the candidate should be accorded a 'minder'. Normally, an experienced Member holds the new candidate's hand and makes sure that he or she commits no irreparable gaffe. On this occasion Central Office concluded that I could probably look after myself, but asked Simon Burns, the new Member for Chelmsford who had rescued the seat from Norman St John Stevas' consummate neglect, to do the honours. Simon was the source of much good humour and stuck by me loyally throughout the campaign. He developed a remarkable talent for pulling me off doorsteps when I all too frequently found myself enticed into fierce argument, thus breaking every law in the canvassing manual. Vicky and my mother once again joined the canvassing team, although this time Vicky had to look after our three-year-old Edward, but Tania Mason let us stay at her vast palazzo in Alderton Hill and we were wonderfully well looked after. Simon and Tony Garrett, the Central Office Campaigns Director, also ensured that regular posses of MPs arrived from the House each evening, all of whom did sterling work. Patrick Thompson distinguished himself by having the backside taken out of his trousers, by a rottweiller in Chigwell. Patrick had forgotten that in Chigwell it always pays to believe the notices about dangerous guard dogs.

I managed not to blot my copy-book unduly in the three weeks of the campaign. The regular political reporters became almost friends, including the doyen of the genre, Robert Carvell, who reported each day for the *Evening Standard*. Most of the lobby correspondents were there at least once. Colin Brown from the *Independent* was particularly taken by my complaint that apathy amongst voters so near to Christmas was likely to be my biggest threat. 'My main opposition at this election is Santa Claus,' I quipped, 'Santa never wore a Rolex,' was Colin's pithy rejoinder. It was he, too, who reported my rather indiscreet observation that this was the constituency that fell off the back of a lorry. Thank goodness he did not actually attribute the remark directly to me during the campaign, although it was a perfect description of a certain type of gentrified East London resident with whom I was rapidly becoming familiar. Victor Smart described me in the *Observer* as 'bluff, matey and a touch condescending'. That was far too near the truth on all counts for my liking, but he was kind enough to say I was the best of the losing Tories and would probably win. Sheila Gunn from *The Times*, George Jones from the *Telegraph* and David Wastell from the *Sunday Telegraph* all made it down the Central Line, and simply because we all knew each other from my four years in Westminster, the atmosphere was relaxed and extremely enjoyable.

As far as the outcome of the by-election was concerned, the

smart money was always on a Tory win, albeit with a reduced majority. By then, the Liberal/SDP Alliance had fallen apart and the two parties were putting up candidates against each other. I thus had not only the usual rash of fringies, inevitably including David Sutch, but I also had a split Alliance vote. Nonetheless, the Liberal, Andrew Thompson, looked as if he was likely to be the only serious threat. Labour's Stephen Murray, son of Len Murray, the old TUC boss whose family home was in the constituency, tried hard. Walworth Road threw in a large, if not totally convinced team, including my old chum from Oxford East, Andrew Smith, who stood on the top deck of an open bus touring the constituency with a singular campaign line. 'I am living proof that you can beat Steve Norris' was the oft repeated theme. Virtually all the other main candidates were locals, so inevitably the carpet-bagger charge was thrown at me but thankfully to little effect.

The only real hiccup was induced by that patron saint of political tact herself, Edwina Currie, by now the Junior Health Minister and fond of lecturing the nation on its appalling disregard for its own health. She chose that moment to announce her infamous view that most eggs contained salmonella, and when the patent absurdity of this remark was pointed out to her, refused to back down. Two days after the story broke an agitated canvasser rushed up to me in Chigwell and told me I needed to follow him quickly. A voter wanted an urgent personal word. He took me to a large house with an XJS parked in the drive, and an equally large irate owner standing in the hallway. 'I've got a bone to pick with you,' he said. 'Do you know what I do for a living?' I gave up. 'I'm an egg merchant.' My heart sank. I could only mumble that I was terribly, terribly sorry. 'You bloody well should be. I normally take £500 a day at Romford market and do you know what I took today?' I hardly dared ask. '£27.50,' he said, 'and it is all that bloody Currie woman's fault.' I decided there was little to be lost. 'Look,' I said, 'I know she's a complete prat, but she's not standing here. I am.' 'I know that,' he said, 'but it's your bloody party and she's your bloody Minister.' There was a lot of blood around that evening. 'Look,' I said again, 'I promise that I will write her an extremely rude letter outlining all your concerns, put it in the post tomorrow morning and send you a copy.' He softened. 'Well, I'll want to see it before I make up my mind.' I sensed that this was as good as I was going to get and beat a hasty retreat past the XJS. £27.50 was hardly going to keep up the payments on that little number. I did as I had promised, knowing perfectly well that Edwina would neither see nor reply to the letter for weeks thereafter, but such was my virulence – not entirely contrived in any event – that he was hugely impressed and sent a message to campaign headquarters promising he would do his duty on the day.

Polling day arrived soon enough and the melee in Waltham Abbey Town Hall where the count was to take place was chaotic. The result was far from a foregone conclusion, and I was all too well aware that not only would apathy and Christmas shopping conspire against us, but that none of my own local canvassers had any real experience of fighting an election. They normally just weighed the Tory vote in Epping Forest, to save the formality of counting the huge Tory majority, and polling day was more of a social than a political occasion. Indeed, as I had done the rounds of our committee rooms earlier in the day, I had found a great many well-meaning ladies expending their efforts on delicious cups of tea and cucumber sandwiches without crusts whilst their friends crossed the names of those who had voted off our hard-won canvassing lists in the belief that it was simply a helpful exercise to find out how big our win was going to be.

I was mentally tearing my hair out by the time we gathered in the rather small and undistinguished Victorian building and Tricia Gurnett fed us news of our progress. Just before the result she told me that we had won, but that the majority was heavily down. As we walked on the platform, the Returning Officer, who inexplicably insisted in arriving in his full RAF dress uniform, proceeded to read out the result. I had indeed won by a margin of just over 4,000.

At that precise moment I can record that my overwhelming feeling was of depression rather than elation. Of course, it was wonderful to be back, but I was well aware that all of the next day's headlines would concentrate on the missing 16,000 from the Tory majority. Had I lost, I would have happily entered a monastery, but to have won by that small a margin was deeply depressing. Without a great deal of emotion I made the shortest by-election acceptance speech on record. I did remember to thank all those who had worked for me including Tricia, my mother and Vicky, the magnificent Central Office team and all my friends who, loyal as ever, had once more done their duty. I even managed to thank the Returning Officer, who, having made an unholy meal of reading out the admittedly lengthy result, had capped it by announcing 'I therefore declare Stephen Murray . . .' before hurriedly correcting himself. I was wheeled on to an interview with David Dimbleby in time-honoured fashion and we went through the motions and ritual which accompany every such occasion. His questions were as predictable as my answers, but the net result was that the Conservative majority had slumped from 41.6 per cent to 13.5 per cent on a poll of under half the total electorate. Central Office had produced the then Chief Secretary to the Treasury, John Major, to say nice things about the candidate and, earning my eternal gratitude, he duly did. It was not, however, the best of nights for me. I awoke the next day to the inevitable headlines which treated the victory as a failure. I consoled myself that whatever they said, I was in. A majority of one is, as every MP knows, enough to ensure the remainder of a parliamentary term. It was back to the old routine.

10

Second Maidenhood

During the by-election my father had been very ill. He had given up a heavy smoking habit after a serious angina attack fifteen years earlier, but his heart had been badly affected, so the morning after the result, I went to see him. An hour or so after I arrived, Margaret Thatcher rang, and having congratulated me, asked immediately after my dad. No doubt a Central Office hack had told her why I had had to take time out, but it was a kind thought nonetheless. A couple of days later I took my seat in the time-honoured fashion for by-election victors. Flanked by Marcus Fox, the Chairman of the 1922 Committee, and Bernard Braine, the Father of the House, I stood at the bar of the Commons Chamber nervously waiting for the end of Questions whilst colleagues swapped the odd ribald pleasantry. Eventually the Speaker called 'Members desirous of taking their seats' and we walked forward five paces, stopped, bowed, and walked on to stand in front of the Speaker's table. There we bowed again and I was allowed through to take the oath, sign the register, shake Jack's hand, and disappear behind the back of the Chair. The whole process only takes a couple of minutes, but of course in my case, most Members knew me and the Tories certainly put up a good cheer, if only because most of them were pleased that their by-election canvassing efforts had paid off.

Epping Forest is a great contrast to Oxford East. The Forest has a rather special place in the hearts of many Eastenders. If you do well in Bethnal Green, you move to Ilford, Romford or Wanstead. But if your children do well from there, they move to Chigwell, Loughton or Buckhurst Hill. The whole area is rich, rather ostentatious suburbia. Whilst Epping is a pretty market town and can still boast the high street building from which Churchill addressed his own election meetings, the rest of the patch is strung out along the eastern end of the Central Line. Massive detached houses sit cheek by jowl literally a few yards apart, regulation Mercedes convertible in the drive. Chigwell, of course, is famous as the home of *Birds of a Feather*, and I can only say that the social observation in that series is particularly accurate. Alan Sugar, the original barrow boy made good and now king of Tottenham Hotspur, is a constituent, as is David Sullivan, the soft-porn genius who created the smutty mag and *Sunday Sport* newspaper empire, bought himself Birmingham City Football Club for his Saturday afternoon diversions, and then set about building the largest private house in England since the war near the delightfully named Theydon Bois (Boyz for the uninitiated). It was recently rumoured that Marlon Brando had visited the Old Kings Head pub in Chigwell village, itself mentioned by Dickens in Martin Chuzzlewit, and certainly if Marlon is looking for a British home, Chigwell should suit his outsize personality down to the ground. I remember on one occasion describing myself as the ideal Member for Epping Forest – 'Lots of money and no taste.' It was painfully near the mark both for them and for me.

Despite all this ostentatious vulgarity, the philosophy most of my constituents adopted was close to my heart. They worked hard, they asked nothing from the State, and they expected the State to take as little as possible from them. 'I vote Tory for tax,' was David Sullivan's pithy summary, and most of my constituents would have echoed his sentiment. They were and are open and straight people who enjoy their wealth whilst putting on remarkably few pretentious airs and graces. If they do tend to buy a disproportionate number of nipple-pink XR3i convertibles, it is simply because they think they are the most beautiful cars in the world. They do not do things because other people do. They do exactly what they want to do themselves. They take holidays in the Caribbean, they were shellsuits of an unspeakable hue that cost hundreds of pounds, they are by *Dynasty* out of *EastEnders*, and most of all, they hugely enjoy themselves.

During my selection the association committee had made it clear that they expected the successful candidate to move into the constituency. John Biggs-Davison had been only a very occasional visitor during his thirty-three years, and right to the end, Tricia Gurnett, the agent, had to whisper the name of the constituency chairman in his ear. As far as I was concerned, it was clear that whilst the triangle of Hampstead Norris, Oxford and London was bearable, Wylye was nearly a hundred miles from Epping and was simply not a practical proposition. Much to Vicky's regret, we sold the house and looked for somewhere in the constituency. As it happens, we did not move directly. I sold Wylye for nearly twice what we had paid for it two years earlier – not an uncommon event in those days – and bought an elegant mews house in Holland Park which Anthony Ince, my Managing Director at Salisbury and I decided to do up with advice from Victor Owen, my old friend from Oxford Polytechnic, who had decided to be done with the appalling politics of the higher education world and is now an extremely successful interior designer. From this new vantage point, we looked at the constituency, but after Wylye it was hard to find anything that looked remotely attractive. I deeply resented the idea of paying half a million pounds for a piece of north-east London kitsch. In any event there were what ultimately proved to be fatal signs that the property market was stalling, and it seemed wiser to rent until the position stabilised. Fortunately, I met Nick Haggar, who owned a private school in Loughton and was just about to set up another at Coopersale Hall near Epping. This was a fine early nineteenth-century building which had been the home of Lord Lyle of sugar fame, and was reputed to be where Churchill had first dined on visiting his prospective new seat. Nick had acquired one of a pair of large semi-detached Tudor cottages, with the ultimate intention of using it for classroom space when the school expanded, but in the meantime, he offered me the chance to rent it and I enthusiastically agreed. Our neighbours, Jim and Ingrid Muscat, could not have been more delightful, and we found that in Ochard Cottage we were not only in possession of a very serviceable large house, but also of a squash court, tennis courts, lawns, lake and woodland, all courtesy of the extensive school grounds. Edward also had a school on his doorstep, but as the children were gone by three in the afternoon, and did not attend at weekends, it was an ideal spot. We virtually had the whole estate to ourselves.

At Westminster I found myself billeted in a tiny room above the Chamber with Tony Marlow, the Northampton MP who is one of the most colourful characters in the House. Tony is loved by some, including me, and hated by others (including most of the Whips' office). He is in fact a whip's nightmare – totally independent and quite prepared to speak, or indeed bellow, his mind. Tony is no wallflower. When he thought Thatcher should go, he told her so in no uncertain terms, heedless of the opprobrium which he must have known would promptly be heaped on him. When he took a similar view of John Major because of what he saw as John's vacillation on Europe, he said so again. In the 1995 leadership context he memorably and predictably backed John Redwood, and helped to wreck the latter's chances of success by appearing beside him in a bizarre blazer which he occasionally sported and which gave him the air of a superannuated gondolier, whilst poor John appeared to have his head sandwiched between Teresa Gorman's ample bosoms. If John Redwood's personal genie offered him two wishes, I suspect the first would be to destroy that spool of tape of him opening and closing his mouth like a hysterical goldfish during the singing of the Welsh National Anthem at the Welsh Party Conference, and the second would be to destroy all known copies of that fateful picture. Tony and I were sufficiently similar in temperament to click right from the start and despite the fact that we were cooped up in a space that would have sent an RSPCA man into orbit if we had been a couple of broilers, we have remained on good terms ever since.

As I started a new term as an Essex MP, I also decided that I needed to have my constituency work done from Parliament rather than Salisbury. Debbie had been an extremely competent secretary and a loyal friend, but I was visiting Salisbury less and less, and dragging her up to London was proving exhausting for her and not exactly convenient for me. I was very reluctant to change, but I can see, looking back, that I had become so wound up in my new life that Salisbury scarcely figured. As I have already mentioned, that was to prove fatal as far as the business was concerned. I had simply allowed myself to believe that it was an endless money machine that would go on churning out a fortune with or without me. As long as the boom continued, that was true, but the bubble would soon burst.

At this point, I was discovered by Caroline Edmondson. She had recently abruptly finished working for Hugo Somerson, a rather naïve young bachelor whom Caroline had just nominated as most romantic MP in a Mills and Boon competition. Unfortunately for her, the object of his affections was soon to be installed in Caroline's place, and she was told she was no longer wanted. It was not the most gentlemanly of reasons for disposing of a secretary, and the tabloids had a high old time with poor Hugo.

I should explain that Caroline is extremely good looking, was then twenty-five years old and in the habit of wearing wide belts which masqueraded as skirts. Mummy and daddy live in a magnificent Tudor manor house in Worcestershire where the gunpowder plotters met before travelling to London and meeting their grisly end. She is the quintessential Sloane Ranger, with a huge personality, and whose self-evident disinterest in shorthand and typing was more than compensated for by her kindness, brightness and huge sense of fun. She could handle constituents like a poacher tickling a trout, and most of them ended up loving her. I greatly enjoyed working for her and listening to her gripping tales about appalling scenes in Annabel's which had inevitably caused her to be late the next morning. 'Well, how on earth do you expect me to be in by nine if I did not get to bed until five?' It seemed a perfectly logical reason for not arriving until eleven, and Adrian's cocktail party at six obviously dictated that the rest of the correspondence would have to wait until the next morning. She was a delight, and I am enormously fond of her.

Unfortunately my reintroduction to the business of the House was not so enjoyable. As the Official Secrets Bill wound its way through the Commons after the Christmas recess, I became more and more convinced that it was fundamentally flawed. Maurice Frankel, Des Wilson and I once more joined forces and this time, in company with Richard Shepherd and several others, I found myself voting against the Government on a three line whip. Right or wrong, a large black mark was entered against my name in the Whips' register, and I knew my chances of promotion would be hindered. I was clear, too, that I wanted to be a Minister and I thought long and hard before I made my decision. It emphasises the great power that the whips enjoy when both parliamentary parties are frequented by young meritocrats for whom ministerial office is a prime ambition. Nonetheless, voting against his own party is something that any half-decent Member is likely to do at least once in his career.

A few months later I was enjoying a coffee in the tea-room when Nicholas Soames, Nick Ridley's PPS at the Department of Trade and Industry, asked me if I would put down what is known as a 'planted' question for DTI Oral Questions a couple of weeks later. This practice of planting friendly questions goes on all the time, despite being loudly deprecated by Ted Heath and others, and I, like virtually all of my younger backbench colleagues, had no qualms. The question Nicholas offered me was simple enough. 'To ask the Secretary of State for Trade and Industry what plans he has to expand his department'. My own private view was that there was no merit whatever in simply adding more bureaucrats at the DTI; what Britain's industry needed was less government rather than more, and I determined to say so. I duly planned my supplementary, but when Nick rose, his answer was typically direct, if not what I had expected: 'None, sir.' He sat down and I decided it was time to be equally unconventional. 'Mr Speaker, given that my right honourable friend has just delivered exactly the answer I was looking for, I see no reason for any further supplementary.' As I sat down amid laughter Nick turned and gave me a wide grin.

Nick Soames came into the Commons with me in 1983 although that was about all we had in common. He is huge, larger than life in every way, an appalling bully if he thinks he can get away with it, but the funniest man bar none in the Commons, and someone for whom I came to develop an enormous affection. He is now in his element at Defence. He looks and sounds the part, and is clearly enjoying himself enormously with the top brass. I have heard him confess to being the only man to have bounced a cheque on the Prince of Wales. He served him as Equerry, and remains the most loyal of friends. After Nick Ridley, he rather bizarrely teamed up as PPS to John Gummer. They were an odd couple. One was reminded of Noël Coward's quip when a fellow observer of the Coronation saw Queen Salote of Tonga riding in her carriage with a tiny man sitting beside her who, it transpired, was a Tongan diplomat. 'Who is that riding with Queen Salote?' Noël's friend enquired. 'That, dear boy, is her lunch.'

I had no way of knowing that Nicholas Soames was about to resign, but a few days later he did so and, I suspect, with our exchange fresh in his mind, Nick asked me to take on the job. I was delighted, because Nick was not only a full member of Cabinet, but also close to Margaret Thatcher. And frankly, I knew he desperately needed help. Although I had come to like him a lot during those few weeks we were together at the DoE,

Nick's own personal PR was appalling. Once again, I could see that another languid old Etonian needed a touch of the Institute.

Right from the start we seemed to click. What the public saw was a tall, austere man who cared little for his appearance and even less for the opinion of others. What was less evident was his enormous sense of fun, a total lack of pomposity and a consideration for his Junior Ministers and officials that was second to none in the whole Whitehall machine. In the rough world of politics, the invariable rule is that when there is bad news, it is the Junior Minister who delivers it. When success is to be trumpeted, the occasion will normally be reserved for the Secretary of State. Nick reversed the order. 'Here, give it to me. I'll do it,' was his invariable response to a Junior Minister's potential embarrassment, and when good news was around it was he who would offer the Parliamentary Under Secretary a moment of glory at the dispatch box. Predictably, they loved him for it. Officials, too, overcame his public reputation very quickly. Martin Stanley, Nick's principal private secretary, told me after his death that he had never enjoyed a posting more, and his verdict was shared by many. Nick's purported arrogance was a deliberate front. Privately, he was considerate, thoughtful, and often ahead even of the brightest minds in the department. He was a born deregulator and free marketeer, but above all an instinctive iconoclast. Nick revelled in challenging conventional wisdoms, cleverly, wittily and occasionally provocatively. It was of course the latter adverb which eventually led to his undoing. Nick was by then also enormously happy in his private life. His second marriage to Judy was a great source of comfort to him. He was much older than she, but neither saw the difference in age as important. Judy was vivacious, outgoing and warm. In a sense she was everything, at least in public, which Nick was not. Privately, she looked after him and – I can find no better words for it – cared for him.

Despite my best efforts, talking Nick's achievements up constantly to lobby correspondents and any other interested hacks, Nick was determined not to be popular. I remember on one occasion dining with Ian Stewart, and during conversation it emerged that Ian was extremely unhappy at what he felt had been Nick's rudeness to him in a recent exchange which I had not heard. 'I'm quite sure Nick intended no discourtesy,' I said.

'I shall certainly tell him about your unhappiness, and I know he will be very upset.' Nothing could have been further from the truth. When I retold the story to Nick, his response was brief and to the point. 'The man's a fool – and what's more, he's wrong.' I tried my best to remonstrate, but Nick was having none of it. 'Look,' I said, 'he may be everything you say, but I don't like people bad-mouthing you behind your back. It makes it look as though I am not doing my job properly. So be nice to him, can't you?' I was desperate. 'Just do it for me, for God's sake.' Nick, who had been writing at his desk, looked up. A very slight grin erupted at the corner of his mouth. 'All right, Steve,' he said, 'I'll talk to him. But only for you, mind. He's still a bloody fool.'

Two incidents dominated my time with Nicholas Ridley. The first proved to be a cloud no bigger than a man's hand which went on to cover the whole of John Major's sky. The Iraqi supergun affair had begun as a farce. Customs and Excise announced that they had detained a shipment of large heavy metal pipes bound for Iraq and that another consignment, already travelling by lorry on the continent, was being sought. Incredible as it seemed, customs officers alleged that the pipes were not, as the official order indicated, destined for a chemical plant, but rather part of a huge Heath Robinson contraption intended to propel lethal missiles miles inside Iran. Millions of words have since been written about the Arms to Iraq affair, but in the very early days, we were not even sure whether Customs and Excise had got it right. Nick and I also faced the wrath of Hal Miller, the MP for Bromsgrove in whose constituency some of the pipes had been manufactured. He believed that his constituents had been effectively set up by the MoD, and was determined to defend them. As one who had always believed in the cock-up rather than the conspiracy theory of politics, I poured scorn on Hal's suggestion. I did so in my customary direct way. Unfortunately, Anthony Bevins, the political editor of the *Independent* and a man blessed with a wicked sense of fun, reported me rather too literally. 'A source close to Mr Ridley described Sir Hal's assertions as "bollocks"', was the way he described it. No one in the entire House of Commons was in any doubt who the 'source close to Mr Ridley' was. Hal, typically generously, never held it against me, and of course subsequent events proved that whilst he was not right in every detail, there was a great deal more to the story than originally met the eye. Little did Nick know that over at Defence, Alan Clark had a very different view of the proceedings.

The second event proved too difficult for any of us to handle. Like most political explosions, the story originated from humble beginnings. Jean Caines, Nick's loyal and expert press officer at the DTI, was asked by Dominic Lawson, the editor of the *Spectator*, if she would forward his request for an interview with the Secretary of State. Jean was frankly wary of the whole idea. Young Lawson had earned a reputation for stitching colleagues up, and Jean's note to Nick, whilst faithfully passing on the message, noted this – pointing particularly to a recent printed interview with Chris Patten which had not portrayed Chris in a particularly flattering light. Nick, however, was intrigued. He had privately been irritated when, after the June 1983 general election, it had been Nigel Lawson whom Margaret chose as Chancellor, leaving Nick outside the Cabinet as Financial Secretary. Their rivalry was as personal as it was ideological, and Nick saw the opportunity to discuss Lawson *père* as too great a temptation to resist.

Dominic Lawson has his own account of their meeting, but Nick himself told me that it had been part on, and part off the record. I am sure, knowing Nick's indifference to the media generally, that his understanding of the conventions would have been less than crystal clear, and I know that the relevant sections of the long conversation, which continued over lunch, were not, as far as Nick was concerned, even part of the interview. But young Dominic had his own ideas and without bothering to ask Nick to verify any of the contents, which I would have thought an elementary courtesy, he produced a piece which portrayed Ridley as violently anti-German, complete with a number of intemperate quotations and topped with a lethal front page cartoon by Nicholas Garland in which Nick was seen running away from a poster of the German Chancellor, Helmut Kohl, on which he had apparently just daubed the hair and moustache of Adolf Hitler. Nick was, of course, not only an original pre-Thatcherite, but a Euro-sceptic before the term enjoyed wide currency. As in so many other areas, he saw the dangers long before his colleagues. I had myself heard Nick talk in precisely the way Lawson recorded so I knew that the words were likely to be accurate as far as they went. But I also knew that Nick was a man whose style of debate was deliberately provocative. To suggest that Kohl was achieving in peacetime what Hitler had never managed to achieve by war – namely, the effective domination of Europe – was, in Nick's eyes, chillingly accurate. It was certainly not to suggest that Kohl was Hitler either in thought or deed.

Anyone listening to the man would have known precisely what he intended, and, what is more, I suspect agreed with him. But the way Lawson printed the story left Nick in a desperately vulnerable situation. He was on a trade mission in Hungary when the story broke, and Martin Stanley frantically tried to contact him via our embassy in Budapest. Camera crews jetted out to find him, and Nick – thankfully, with Judy by his side – was hounded by the ratpack at every turn. Thankfully he managed to add nothing further to his problems, but at home, the story was making front page news. The Opposition predictably condemned him and called for his head. More to the point, a few of his Cabinet colleagues who had long regarded him as an unwelcome irritant saw their chance, and even Charles Powell, Margaret's Foreign Affairs advisor, and privately a friend of Nick's, told Margaret that Ridley was fast becoming a liability.

Our immediate problem was how to deal with his return to Britain. He was due to fly back on the Friday, and Martin and I decided that it might make sense to find somewhere private and away from prying eyes so Nick could relax a little, understand the position he was in, and try to find a way out. I agreed that I would handle the transport arrangements and the Heathrow authorities allowed me to bring my car onto the tarmac and have a route which would spirit me directly away. It all worked like a dream. As the plane taxied to a halt, passengers – including a large number of journalists who had travelled with him in the hope of a story – began to disembark through the forward door. A few moments later, the rear door opened and Judy and Nick swiftly descended. A few bright sparks from the media did follow, but Nick was able to jump into my large silver BMW and a few moments later, we were hastening down the M4 towards the west country at a quite indecent speed. The hacks were furious, including the occupants of a Ford Cortina which had tried to follow us. The irony of German technical excellence was not lost on my passenger who was finding the whole experience somewhat unnerving. So unnerving in fact that Nick did

142

something that no one had done in my car for the last fifteen years. He lit a cigarette. Smoking in a company car was about the only instant sacking offence in the Steve Norris Limited employee manual, but I had forgotten how hard it would be to impress this fact on the Secretary of State and before I knew it, he had lit up. I thought discretion the better part of valour and said nothing. Only days later did I discover a neat round hole in the leather as a permanent and deeply irritating reminder of his distinguished presence.

I had, however, managed to find somewhere secret for Nick and Judy to stay, and having made sure they were comfortable with friends, I set off for home. Nick was immediately in touch with Number 10, and friends and supporters like Michael Howard and Norman Lamont rang to offer support. Michael Forsyth had already issued a press statement supporting Nick and dismissing the idea of his resignation, and I thought, perhaps we could build on this; but canvassing the Cabinet, it was clear to me that the cards were stacked against Nick. Douglas Hurd, in particular, was furious with him and John Major was distinctly tight-lipped. There would be little if any support from that quarter. Other opinion in the party was equally hostile and it was clear Margaret felt under real pressure. On so many occasions, Nick had been her bulwark against the wets, both on economic matters generally and on Europe, and she was personally very fond of him. I know that she agonised for some time about his fate, not only because she liked him, but also because she realised that part of the attack on Nick was directed at her.

I spend most of the Saturday in Salisbury, constantly on the telephone to John Cole and others trying desperately to counter the stories running on the BBC during the morning that Nick's resignation was imminent. I was not yet prepared to see him fall – not least because I believed that Margaret would personally have wanted him to stay. I did successfully persuade John to change the lunchtime bulletins. Once again, 'sources close to Mr Ridley' were quoted as countering rumours of his resignation but by four o'clock in the afternoon it all came to nought. Margaret and Nick spoke, she told him that, much as she valued and trusted him, she simply could not keep him and he, a gentleman to the last, immediately resigned.

I was devastated by the injustice of it all. It was perfectly clear

143

to anyone who knew the man that Nick had been traduced. It was equally clear that Margaret had been forced to lose a valued ally. I was angry with Lawson and his fellow blood suckers, angry with those colleagues who had taken advantage of Nick's weakness, and angry with Margaret for not standing up to them in the way that I always assumed she would. My bitter, last ditch defence of Nick, which culminated in a few of us wearing large lapel badges with the slogan 'Ridley was right', clearly did me no good in the Whips' office. They dislike mavericks, and having a PPS rushing around like a bull in a china shop was not their idea of soundness. Several senior colleagues, including Christopher Patten, told me that it subsequently counted heavily against me when promotion was otherwise on the cards. All I can say is that I am utterly unrepentant, now as I was then. Nick may have been naïve, and Lawson *fils* clearly believed that he was justified, although his subsequent defence of his actions cut no ice with me whatsoever; but Nick was too substantial a figure to be brought down in this cruel and unnecessary way. If I were ever in the position of having to defend him again, I hope I would have the decency to do exactly as I did on that occasion.

Nick too was devastated by his peremptory execution. He and I, both now summarily returned to the backbenches, kept in close touch. During Mrs Thatcher's second leadership challenge in 1990, we talked almost every day. He was loyal to her to the end. In practice, he took no further part in active politics, although he produced an autobiography which crept in to the top-ten best seller list, but in typical Ridley style it lacked any great popular appeal. In 1992 he retired from the Commons and went to the Lords as Baron Ridley of Liddesdale. Although he made one or two splendid interventions in their Lordships' House, his health deteriorated rapidly. I suspect his enormous and painful rejection, and the sense of having let Margaret down which I know bore heavily on him, conspired with all those decades of heavy smoking and took their fatal toll. He died in March of 1993. His memorial service was hugely well attended in St Margaret's Westminster, and I was deeply touched when Judy asked me if I would be an usher. Both John Major and Margaret Thatcher were present, but my interest was in a fellow usher, Norman Lamont. John had just disposed of Norman as Chancellor, and the latter was not best pleased. Theoretically, we were both responsible for shepherding the new arrivals to their places but as any member of the Cabinet arrived, Norman, with a face like thunder, would whisper, 'You look after them, I'm damned if I will.' If Nick were looking down on our tribute to him, I have no doubt he would have been hugely amused.

11

That Bloody Woman

Nick Ridley had resigned on 14 July 1990, and by 28 November of that year, Margaret Thatcher had been forced out of office as Prime Minister. The story of her demise is the most fascinating story of contemporary politics, and it is one that I observed at first hand. I believe that the seeds of Margaret's eventual demise were sown on 30 July 1990, only a fortnight after Nick's resignation, when the IRA, in a typically cowardly act, placed a bomb in Ian Gow's Montego car. Ian was blown to smithereens the second he turned the ignition key.

Ian Gow was the complete politician, and certainly cleverer than most of his ministerial colleagues. As Margaret's PPS from 1979 to 1983, he was utterly loyal to her, whilst at the same time persuading his colleagues that they should share their deepest confidences with him without the slightest risk that they would be betrayed. Not for nothing was he known as Deep Throat. He was also one of the best speakers ever to have addressed the House of Commons. When he was serious, he made his points directly, firmly and with great clarity. He was formidably convincing. And when Ian intended to be light-hearted, as he was when he proposed the Loyal Address to Parliament in 1989, he made the funniest speech that any of us present had ever heard. His style was deadpan but devastating. He looked what he had originally been – a provincial solicitor. Of medium height, he had little hair, and large, round glasses. He invariably wore a three-piece suit and – one of his many affectations – he carried his handkerchief in his cuff rather than his pocket. To the casual observer he would have seemed stuffy and pompous, but he was not. As may be evident, I liked him enormously and was genuinely grateful to count him as a friend.

I was not alone, of course. Ian had that rare ability to make everyone around him seem special. He drank nothing but white ladies – a vile concoction of gin and other unmentionables that he quaffed like water. He smoked copious cigarettes, and, a naturally clubbable man, was frequently to be found in the Smoking Room as the day's business drew to a close. He would join in conversation, weighing every word, coaxing endless indiscretions out of his colleagues often by recounting outrageously funny stories about Margaret, but all in an affectionate way which never suggested indifference or dislike. Nor did he ever pretend that Margaret was anything other than she was. That struck a particular chord with me. I admired the lady greatly, but it was clear as the years rolled by that she was becoming a parody of herself, and Ian, too, was capable of seeing her in that light.

In recent years the role of the Parliamentary Private Secretary has altered tremendously. Originally, the idea had been that as an MP became a Secretary of State, the opportunity to spend time in the House of Commons diminished. Ministers were at risk of becoming remote from their colleagues, and insensitive to backbench feelings. The Parliamentary Private Secretary was always an honorary title, as distinct from the Minister's Principal Private Secretary, who is a civil servant. The PPS is ideally his master's eyes and ears, taking messages from the Minister to the backbenches and feeding back gossip and intelligence. The PPS would be a personal friend of the Minister and in earlier times when not every backbencher wanted to carry a ministerial baton in his knapsack, such relationships endured for many years. Christopher Soames, Nicholas' father, was not only Churchill's son-in-law, but his PPS too. Such was the emphasis on the role of conduit that by tradition a PPS would never speak publicly about his mentor's departmental interest. I remember Michael McNair-Wilson, when PPS to Peter Walker at Agriculture, specifically declining an invitation to talk about agriculture matters to his many farming voters on precisely these grounds.

No one changed this system more than Margaret Thatcher. She, or more likely those around her, recognized that as ministerial ambition became a more prominent feature of political motivation, appointment as a Parliamentary Private Secretary could be seen as the first step on the ladder of preferment, and as such, a PPS could be counted a member of the payroll vote. The 'payroll' in parliamentary terms refers to all Ministers on the government payroll. They can be relied

147

upon to vote at the Whips' bidding on what are technically free votes. It is an uncomfortable arrangement but an effective one. It forcefully underlines the notion of collective Cabinet responsibility. These days, the payroll vote now includes the unpaid PPSs, although this seems not to have worried the whips who can now include them in the private army on whom they can rely. So PPSs have become political eunuchs. They have honorary titles, they have no specific powers, they tailor their pronouncements to their individual Minister, and despite holding no government office, they are denied the opportunity for even mild dissent. A PPS is bound in silken chains, and the Government's tally of automatic loyalists is doubled overnight.

I have always believed that central to Margaret's predicament in her latter years was her decision to promote Ian to the Department of Environment as Housing Minister. Ian was the last of the great old school of PPSs. He was indeed a perfect conduit, and Margaret herself has frequently acknowledged his firm and yet always constructive advice which steered her away from so many potential pitfalls during their time together. Margaret was subsequently served by four PPSs, Michael Alison, Archie Hamilton, Mark Lennox-Boyd, and Peter Morrison, all of whom adored her, and carried her bag with distinction. She loved a toff, and was enormously susceptible to their flattery and foppery. The first three were genuinely popular with their colleagues, but none could match Ian's subtlety and political insight. As long as he was alive he was unofficially Margaret's eyes and ears and her most reliable guide to the mood of her colleagues.

Michael Alison is as admirable a Christian politician as it is possible to meet, but I recall occasions when Michael would put his head around the Smoking Room door and if he saw any colleagues there, immediately beat a hasty retreat. Admittedly, there are the odd Smoking Room bores like the late John Stradling-Thomas, who would ensnare the unsuspecting Member and recount endlessly the same tales of his days in the Whips' office, but the Smoking Room is nonetheless where members go to relax, and Ian Gow, who probably privately hated the whole idea, invariably made it his business to be there.

Archie Hamilton suffered from being so tall that when the weather was bad, it was difficult to pick out his face. A military man by training and inclination, he had a tendency to treat the

148

younger of our flock like privates on parade. He was infinitely happier in his subsequent incarnation as Minister of State for Defence, where he looked and sounded the part to perfection. Mark Lennox-Boyd carried on the great bag-carrier tradition with natural elegance and flair, but I doubt he knew the names of most of the young grammar-school novices whose mutterings he was supposed to distil for prime ministerial consumption.

Her fourth and final PPS was an unmitigated disaster. Peter Morrison was the younger brother of Charles, the MP for Devizes and both were sons of Lord Margadale, the enormously wealthy former Chairman of the 1922 Committee who amongst other baubles, owned the Isle of Islay. Peter had a fine political brain, but he also enjoyed every aspect of the good life. He was a toff's toff, and made it very clear from the outset that he did not intend to spend time talking to the plebs. Such friends as he had were snobs of the Alan Clark variety, all brandy goblets and country seats. Among the no doubt apocryphal tales of his grandeur, it is said that on one occasion Peter's ministerial car was irretrievably caught up in traffic whilst Peter was required for an urgent meeting in Whitehall. His private secretary diffidently suggested that they might have to swap their car for the Underground. Far from dismissing the notion, Peter thought this a capital idea and, large cigar in hand, they descended the steps of the nearest station. This was clearly a voyage of discovery for Peter, and as the train rushed into the station, he was heard to enquire at the top of his voice 'Which end is the restaurant car?'

All of this is significant only because if there is one feature of Margaret's tenure of office between 1987 and her demise in 1990, it was her growing isolation from her colleagues and a burgeoning unreality in many of her utterances. She had arrived in office as many things. The antidote to Heath, the first woman Prime Minister, a strong monetarist, a disciplinarian, and a powerful right-winger. She had become a war heroine along the way. But above all she had been portrayed as being in touch with ordinary people, with the aspirations of Middle England. And it was true. Not only did her kitchen economics resonate, but her views on law and order, on benefit scroungers and welfare, on home ownership, on the civil service, all chimed exactly with those of the Conservative Party's natural support- ers. But power corrupts, and as the years went by, she was given so few opportunities to mix with these same ordinary people – indeed, it was literally impossible to find a group who would not be cowed or otherwise affected by the presence of the Leaderine – that her sensitive touch became numbed. This was not Margaret's fault. Sycophancy naturally surrounds the powerful, particularly when they have such extensive powers of patronage through both the honours system and government appointments. Disengaging from it and finding a way to cut through to honest opinions is nigh impossible. At the same time, Margaret never saw a traffic jam. Here again, it was not her fault that she was such a high-profile target for terrorist attack that her passage needed to be smoothed at every turn. It was said that she hated the railways, but the truth is that a railway carriage is much more vulnerable than a fast armour-plated limousine flanked by motor cycle outriders. The Downing Street gates were long overdue and an elementary precaution, yet Labour portrayed them as evidence of her imperiousness.

In any event, Margaret encouraged more sycophancy than most, simply by her style. As is well known, she brooked no dissent, but what is perhaps less appreciated, though it features in many of the memoirs of her former Cabinet colleagues, is that her idea of a conversation was everyone else's idea of a monologue. I certainly had my own direct and painful experiences to bear witness. I remember on one occasion she invited the Conservative Members of the Electricity Bill Committee to meet her in her room behind the Chair in the House of Commons to discuss the bill's progress and our views on the ideas it contained. As we sat down for what promised to be a thirty-minute meeting, she launched into an exposition of the virtues of privatisation, the particular virtue of this bill, and the weakness of the opposition arguments. Her address lasted twenty-seven minutes. Three minutes of unadulterated brown-nosing later, we reeled into the corridor, bemused. 'I thought she was supposed to listen to us,' a querulous voice exclaimed. 'We didn't get a word in edgeways.' Business as usual at the Court of Queen Margaret.

But there was a serious side to this. Her refusal to listen was beginning to cost her dear. In particular, she never began to understand the pain the community charge caused to her backbench colleagues in the north. No doubt in Finchley, as in Epping Forest, the whole notion went down a storm, but in whole swathes of Lancashire, Yorkshire and the Midlands, Tories in marginals, and indeed those in quite comfortable middle-class areas, were being deluged with angry complaints from constituents which frightened them to death. They could see their seats disappearing from under them, and they demanded change. This was not the only issue which set her on a collision course with many in her party. Europe, as now, played a significant part, although not in the way that many commentators imagined. I had been part of the team of helpers, significantly still led by Ian Gow in 1989, who had seen off the challenge of the rabid pro-European Anthony Meyer, but like many of her loyal supporters, over the next twelve months I was more and more worried by her increasing unpredictability on a whole range of European issues. She talked tough on Europe and then in negotiation caved in at the last minute. She made her brilliant Bruges speech, and then allowed John Major, by then her Chancellor, to roll her into the ERM despite the fact that none of the three conditions precedent to membership, which she herself had set, had been fulfilled. Increasingly, Ministers listened to the Today programme to find out what government policy was, and it was clear that Margaret, like so many great political figures before her, was now infinitely more popular abroad than at home, and was beginning to act accordingly.

In many ways, she deserved the stories that circulated in the bars and tea-rooms of Westminster of her increasingly quixotic imperialism. Typical was the account of her dining with her Cabinet colleagues and being asked by the waiter what dish she had chosen. 'I'll have the steak,' she promptly dictated. 'And what about the vegetables?' 'Oh, they'll have steak too.' I had seen that at the Downing Street dinner on the eve of the Queen's Speech in 1986, and like all good stories, it was uncomfortably close to the truth.

In the event, the end came quickly. Michael Heseltine had managed to manoeuvre himself into a virtual commitment to stand against her by the time Geoffrey Howe delivered his devastating resignation speech on 13 November 1990, and gave Michael the chance he was looking for. My own view of Margaret had certainly changed significantly over the previous twelve months. In 1989 when Ian Gow had approached me, I had promptly agreed to help. He gave me a list of ten names and asked me to verify their intentions. His instructions were to the point. The conversation would need to be quiet and oblique, and any apparent commitments tested more than once for sincerity. I duly reported on my names, and was given some more to canvass. When it was all over I had a handwritten note from him, and then one from Margaret herself thanking me for my help. But twelve months on, I, like so many of my colleagues, had become deeply depressed. Margaret seemed to have run amok, was increasingly unpredictable, and all the polls told the same story. The chances of us winning the forthcoming general election with her as our leader were looking more and more remote. Although I had never liked him, I was also clear that the only person who could possibly dislodge her was Michael Heseltine. I was not particularly enamoured of swapping one blonde dictator for another, and I regarded neither as a particular friend, but not only was Michael a substantial figure in his own right, he was also untainted by the previous regime, and in particular by the community charge.

That summer, before the recess, I determined that I would talk to him privately on exactly these lines, and invited him to lunch at the Caprice. I did not mince my words. I told him that I thought we could no longer win with Margaret. I told him that I admired her for her achievements, but the reaction I had from so many people, including many Conservative voters, was that she was unelectable. I also told him directly that he was the man to bring about the change.

Michael was matter of fact. He did not seem the slightest bit surprised to hear what I had to say, and I suspected immediately that he had heard it many times before. He emphasised repeatedly that I had invited him, rather than the other way round. He pointed out that he had not at any time approached me, or promised me any inducement to gain my support. All that was absolutely true. He may have been rather more amenable than the disinterested patriarch I had first encountered during the 1983 election, but in exile, we all knew he had played his cards cleverly. He was equally direct. 'I think you know I will not do anything unless I believe I can succeed. To try and fail would be suicidal and pointless.' He confirmed that he was constantly being told he was the only person who could stop Margaret, and, making no promises, he left. My final words were of encouragement. 'You're the only man who can do it for the party, Michael. I don't want to see us in opposition just yet.'

On the day that Heseltine issued his formal challenge I spoke to Nick Ridley. He was naturally completely loyal to Margaret, and we had one of our most difficult conversations when I told him more in sorrow than in anger, that the view I held was shared by the majority of my younger colleagues. On both the left and right of the political divide, there was this sense of her having lost touch with reality. I know that Nick was deeply troubled because he genuinely respected my judgement, but he had seen me as a natural Thatcherite.

Given that I had not only worked for her the previous year but had been acknowledged as a member of her team, I was not looking forward to being invited to support her this time. I need not have worried, however, because the call never came. At first I assumed this was because Ian Gow's records had died with him, and that as we had operated on a one-to-one basis, he might be the only person to understand that full network. But I realised immediately that that could not be true. Margaret herself knew the names of her supporters and either John Whittingdale, her private secretary, or some other member of her team must surely have kept a list. It became clear, too, that many other much more obvious supporters were in exactly the same position as me. Fergus Montgomery had a room near mine and we exchanged a few words in the corridor. There was only one subject of conversation and simply by way of something to say, I remarked that no one had approached me from the Thatcher camp to help. Fergus had not only been Margaret's PPS during the early years in opposition, but she had been particularly loyal to him when he had had his own personal difficulties to contend with. Predictably, he utterly worshipped her, and was itching to help. It was quite clear that whilst my enthusiasm was manufactured, his was genuine and equally plain that the problem was Peter Morrison. Right from the outset Margaret's campaign team was shambolic. George Younger, John Moore and one or two others were dragooned into action and no doubt they did their best, but Peter, who had little feeling for the mood of colleagues at the best of times, clearly thought the whole affair could be disposed of as easily as she had been shot of Anthony Meyer. Because he believed that no colleague could be so disloyal as to vote against an incumbent Prime Minister, he scarcely thought it worth asking for the views of colleagues. And when he did, he was naïve enough, idle enough or both to take what he was told at face value. I met him just outside the library in the Commons. 'I trust we can count on you?' he barked. 'Absolutely no problem,' was my suitably delphic response. But that was enough for Peter. 'Jolly good' he said. 'That's another one.' 'How many do you think she'll win by?' I asked. 'Oh, I reckon we're home and dry by about 24 – if all the people who have pledged their support come good.' Whilst I was not proud of my own neat evasions, I simply point out in my defence that I saw no reason to blow my chances of preferment forever in the event that Margaret won by making my opposition obvious at this stage, particularly when the ballot was secret. More to the point, if I could mislead him, then so could another 24.

Margaret, too, seemed persuaded that she should remain aloof from the contest. That may well have been good advice against Meyer who was nothing more than a stalking horse; no one would have been more horrified than Anthony if he had been elected; but Heseltine was a different kettle of fish. Every single day of the campaign found him occupying the Members' Lobby, accompanied by Michael Mates or Keith Hampson, and like a demented Ancient Mariner, stopping every colleague who passed. The atmosphere during those days was quite extraordinary. The opposition parties were simply not in it as colleague argued with colleague on our benches, endlessly, furtively and passionately. And then, immediately before the first ballot, Margaret did something quite remarkably stupid. She left the country, and more to the point, the Palace of Westminster, for Paris. I assume the idea was for her to be portrayed as not only above the petty wrangling of the contest, but as a great European statesperson. If so, the strategy was profoundly misguided. It seemed to many of my friends to smack more of classic Thatcherite indifference to our opinions, coupled with her greater enthusiasm for foreign plaudits than domestic debate, and we were unimpressed. The miscalculation was fatal: 'Not quite so good as we had hoped' was Morrison's gloss on her 204 votes to Michael Heseltine's 152 with 16 abstentions. She had not won by enough to avoid a second ballot. Even more remarkably, she had failed by only two votes to secure the necessary margin.

I am quite clear, as are many others who were around at the time, that Peter Morrison cost her that election. I hesitate to speak ill of the dead because Peter died at a very early age a few years later, and it might seem cowardly to lay all the blame at his door. He was clearly not the only one responsible for the débâcle, but he failed Margaret on two counts. Firstly, he took no precautions to ensure, as Ian Gow had done, that pledges of support were real. Taking politicians at their word is naïve at the best of times, but from a fellow politician it was an act of almost criminal neglect. Secondly, Peter should never have allowed Margaret to leave the country. If she had spent the days of the campaign talking to as many of her colleagues as possible, she could have done it. She would have reminded some of past successes, of campaigns won and battle honours snatched from the enemy; promised others the longed-for knighthood, teased the young Turks with promises of recognition and preferment – in short, used all the massive power and authority that rests with a British Prime Minister. She might have turned thirty, possibly fifty if she had really tried. All this was thrown away, senselessly and gratuitously.

I offer only two observations. The first is that the very miscalculation which led Margaret to squander her massive powers during the campaign were precisely the reason why so many of us saw the need to remove her. She had simply lost touch with her colleagues, and more fatally, with the country. It was entirely predictable that our party members in the Conservative associations would be massively supportive of the leader. They had, after all, been equally loyal to Ted when Margaret had defeated him in 1975, but it is the responsibility of the members of the Parliamentary party to see the dangers lurking ahead and act accordingly. She showed by her indifference and incompetence that she deserved to be beaten. I am as convinced today as I was at that time that had she continued as Prime Minister, we would have been defeated in 1992.

My second observation is that had Margaret managed to canvass that extra thirty or forty, she might well have been tempted to fight on. Had she done so, there is every chance that she would have beaten Heseltine in the second round, but her victory could never have been other than pyrrhic. She would have been fatally wounded and discredited both in Parliament and the country. The Opposition would have made mischief endlessly. It would have hastened an even more ignominious end. At least this way Margaret could point to three out of three decisive general election victories.

My personal discomfort was not over on the first ballot. Although I had persuaded Heseltine to stand, my motives were more negative than positive. I voted for him on the first ballot as the lesser of two evils, and the result was an ideal one for me. Michael had achieved my fundamental objective of removing Thatcher, but not by a sufficient margin to ensure his own automatic election. In the second round contest, I switched allegiance to Douglas Hurd. My reasons for doing so were very clear. I knew that Michael would be hugely unpopular with the vast majority of constituency members. 'He who wields the dagger will never wear the crown.' I had also worked for Douglas and he seemed to me exactly the sort of man Britain needed. Decent, honourable, articulate, committed to public service and full of integrity, I regarded his Etonian background as irrelevant. I could well see that he was not immediately media-friendly, but I believed that his essential worth would shine through very quickly, and that we could rely on the quality of his judgement. I was in distinguished company. Both the Pattens, Tristan Garel-Jones and Tim Yeo, Douglas' PPS, were all involved in Douglas' campaign.

At the time, I hardly knew John Major. I had the impression that he had been extraordinarily fortunate to be selected by Margaret merely by having been in the right place at the right time. His meteoric elevation from Junior Social Security Minister to Chief Secretary, then Foreign Secretary and ultimately Chancellor seemed symptomatic of Margaret's erratic and self-indulgent management style rather than an indication of merit. That is not to say that John had not acquitted himself perfectly competently, for he had. But if John had succeeded because of her, Douglas had plainly succeeded despite her, and for me, that gave him the edge.

I never told my constituents that I voted against Margaret Thatcher in the first ballot. For me, at least, discretion was the better part of valour. I could see no useful purpose in generating a massive row with my own association when, in any event, the damage was done and the voting secret. While it gave me no pleasure to dissemble, I continue to believe that I, and the many colleagues who acted similarly, did the right thing. Enough blood had been shed in those November days. What was important was to get on with the task of rebuilding our electoral fortunes, healing the wounds, and uniting behind our new leader, John Major. In the event, John won for one overriding reason. Margaret in her grief could not bring herself to support the man who had assassinated her, even though she recognised him as a politician of genuine stature. Regarding Douglas as hopelessly wet, she allowed herself to be persuaded that John Major was a man in her own image. She duly touched him on the shoulder and her loyal supporters – devastated at her own demise – took her line without question. All of us in the Hurd camp at least were happy to see John succeed. Little did Margaret know however, that he would turn out to be anything but a classic Thatcherite.

12

Annus Horribilis

Politicians around the world simply refused to believe that Margaret had actually been removed from power. They knew she had been succeeded as Party Leader, but they simply could not comprehend that she was no longer Prime Minister. It was hard even for the Parliamentary party to take on board what was happening. She had been so much a part of our lives for so long that even those who had voted against her could scarcely understand what had happened, and the atmosphere was generally sombre. John immediately set about forming his first Government, installing Norman Lamont as Chancellor, and leaving Douglas as Foreign Secretary. He awarded the fourth great office of State, the Home Office, to Kenneth Baker.

Ken, as Margaret's Party Chairman, had had a bruising few weeks. As I have already observed, he is a man who, above all things, believes in loyalty. He had been a loyal PPS to Edward Heath, and he had transferred that loyalty totally to Margaret, rewarding her brilliantly for her confidence in him. She needed persuading at first, because he was a left of centre Conservative by instinct, but she could see his value, both in terms of technical skill, and his ability to handle the media. Having done such a good job at Environment and then Education, it was he who had lobbied her hard to appoint him Chairman of the Party. After piloting 'Gerbil' through Parliament, Ken felt his best work at Education was done. It might also be true that he would have been bored with the subsequent detailed implementation, but in any event he was looking for a fresh challenge and once again, he persuaded Margaret that he was the man for the job.

By all accounts he initially performed well at Central Office, not least by brilliantly defending a thoroughly lousy set of local government election results. Ken somehow managed to convince the entire world's press that the only two councils in

Britain that mattered were Westminster and Wandsworth. When we held those triumphantly, Ken trumpeted our success to the rooftops. The pundits fell for it hook, line and sinker, ignoring the massive swathes of red that were covering every other part of the UK map. But that was Ken at his best. In the latter weeks of the Thatcher premiership, he had had a less easy ride. I do not in all honesty believe he saw what was about to happen, and when the crisis did occur, his natural instinct was to stay loyal. Right to the end, he urged her to carry on and pledged his total support. I argue that had she heeded his words, the outcome would have been a disaster for the Conservatives, but it was typical of Ken that he was prepared to go down with his ship. It also meant that he had a good election, in the way that some brave soldiers are deemed to have had a good war. Colleagues from both wings of the party admired his loyalty to the lady, and by shrewdly not offering himself as a candidate, he was ideally placed to play the role of elder statesman. His translation to Home Secretary was regarded as well-deserved. Nontheless, I am not sure that Ken himself was at all well prepared, either politically or emotionally, for his new job.

I know that he was preoccupied by two thoughts. The first was that he now knew that his own chance of ever becoming Leader of the Conservative Party had gone. John Major was a significantly younger man, and whatever his life expectancy, the party was unlikely to turn back the clock to find a successor. For many years, Ken had been regarded as a viable contender and there were quite a few in the party who saw him as potential prime ministerial material, but his star had waned rapidly, if unfairly, with the unpopularity of the Community Charge, the dreaded Poll Tax with which Labour assiduously associated him. 'Summer heat on Labour', Ken's costly advertising brain-child at Central Office, had also been derided by the hacks as amateurish and expensive. In that sense, Kenneth did not see his new job as the climax of a great career. He must have been bitterly disappointed, too, not to have been offered either of the other two jobs, but Douglas was far too well entrenched at the Foreign Office, and Norman, John's campaign manager, demanded and received appropriate reward for services rendered. Ken must have known in his heart of hearts that this was as far as he was going to go. After a lifetime of meteoric ascent in politics, he had reached his final ministerial resting place.

Just as significant was Ken's lack of preparedness for the Home Office. He had enjoyed an almost unique career in the previous decade. He had deliberately sought and obtained each government job he had held. He had created his first post as Technology Minister from nothing, and succeeded in it brilliantly. He had deserved his move to Environment, and effectively seen off Patrick Jenkin. He had quite openly campaigned for Margaret to put him in Education, and cleaned up the mess left by the Mad Monk, Keith Joseph, and he had then lobbied just as hard to be released to take on the challenge of Central Office. In every one of these moves there had been an element of intention, of driving his career forward and upward, of positioning himself ever more crucially at the centre of the Tory hierarchy. This last move, however, clearly came as a complete surprise to him. It was obvious to those around him that he had not previously turned his mind to the challenges of the Home Office and that it caused him some difficulty to do so in those first few weeks and months. I am not sure he was ever totally focused on the portfolio in the same way that he was at Environment or Education. His essentially liberal instincts were constrained by what he saw as the political requirements of the job, and he was dogged by bad luck, as so many of his predecessors had been. He did in fact achieve a considerable amount in the short time he was there. He was one of the very few Home Secretaries to really care about the conditions of prisoners, recognising that brutalising young people and cooping them up three to a cell with no sanitation might satisfy the blood lust of the tabloids but would do little to prevent re-offending. Where Douglas Hurd had begun the campaign to eradicate slopping out, Ken accelerated it, and backed up his interest by insisting on visiting prisons regularly, something almost without exception no other Home Secretary had ever done.

A few days after the reshuffle Ken telephoned me to tell me that his PPS, Alistair Burt, had decided that after several years of loyal service he should concentrate on his marginal Bury constituency. Ken offered me the chance to replace him. I had been disappointed but not entirely surprised when my own telephone had not rung, so the opportunity to work with Ken, to be attached to a senior department and one that I knew a little about, was irresistible. It was certainly the next best thing to a ministerial post. I thoroughly enjoyed reading myself into the part of the department's work I had not previously encountered, and Ken was kind enough to let me attend as many of his meetings as I liked. He also allowed me to offer my own opinions which I fear I all too often did. Ken refers to me in his own autobiography as 'articulate and robust'. I interpret that as being a pain in the backside who insisted on putting his twopennorth in at every opportunity.

I did however work hard at trying to avoid the many elephant traps which surround the Home Office. The department has a hugely wide remit ranging from immigration and asylum through the police, prisons, crime prevention, race relations, security and the administration of the Official Secrets Act, to drugs. The list is virtually endless and the consequence is that every MP is involved with the Home Office in one way or another, generally in circumstances which are not easy to resolve. As well as having worked with the police and the crime prevention team, I had also had plenty of dealings with the immigration service and it was obvious that communications would take a great deal of handling. The huge and amorphous spread of responsibilities is one of the reasons why the Home Office has traditionally been regarded as a political bed of nails, and it was not long before Ken began to resemble a devout fakir.

He was lucky to have Tony Kerpel alongside him as his Special Advisor. Tony had been with him since DoE days and was his staunchest support. Special Advisors, like PPSs, are a unique breed. They are the only civil servants to be selected individually by the Secretary of State and, as such, when he goes, they go. Because of the nature of the appointment, the Special Advisor will tend to follow his or her boss from department to department because they are employed less for their specialist advice and more for their ability to put a political gloss on public announcements or policy development. Between us, Ken, Tony and I made a good team. Ken was at the Home Office from November 1990 to April 1992, a short seventeen months. In that time, he had to deal with the Guildford Four and the Birmingham Six, the retention of the mandatory life sentence, dogs biting children ad lib, and the Brixton breakout. All mixed with a dash of national lottery, to form a fairly typical Home Office cocktail.

The cases of the Guildford Four and the Birmingham Six had been referred back to the Courts by Ken's predecessors. When

161

the verdicts were declared unsound and the Irish prisoners acquitted, Ken came under a tremendous barrage from all sides. Editorials fulminated against the police, the Courts, various forensic scientists and, of course, Ministers. Yet as Ken persistently pointed out, there are few countries in the world where the sort of doubts which had been raised by the forensic evidence being re-examined would have led to such an outcome. There are many more countries where that evidence would simply have been lost, buried or tampered with. Here, however painful the political fallout, the process of law took its course and the Home Secretary duly authorised the men to be released. Ken, of course, received no credit at all for this. To read the press you would imagine that he had personally planted the evidence.

The mandatory life sentence debate is of course still current. The sentence was offered as a sop to the supporters of capital punishment during the abolition debate, and it was based on the idea that a mandatory life sentence was automatically handed down on conviction for murder. The trial judge then recommends an appropriate length of imprisonment to the Home Secretary who can, subject to safeguards, order release or continued detention. The whole idea of a recommendation process was to take account of the wide spectrum of capital offences that occur. On the one hand, crimes of passion might imply a need for leniency, whilst on the other, the gunning down of an innocent passer-by in a bank raid might give rise to a very heavy penalty indeed. Endless meetings took place to determine whether it was right to preserve the mandatory sentence, or whether it should not be abolished in favour of a system that would allow the trial judge to impose the appropriate penalty himself. I mention all this only to recall the occasion when Ken offered his own verse contribution to a bemused meeting of the great and good.

> *Lord Dawson of Penn*
> *Has killed many men.*
> *And so we sing,*
> *God save the King.*

As we all strained to appreciate the precise significance of this offering, Ken explained. Lord Dawson had been personal physician to King George V. As the King lay dying, Dawson was left in no doubt that the Empire demanded an orderly transition to his successor. Knowing that the King was mortally ill, he is said to have taken a card from the Sandringham breakfast table on which he wrote the immortal words 'The King's life is drawing peacefully to a close'. He ordered this bulletin to be pinned to the Palace gates, and it is alleged that he then administered a sufficient dose of morphine to ensure that events took their inevitable course. The King died shortly thereafter, precisely on cue. If true, it was a clear case of regicide, but no doubt after the mandatory life sentence had been passed, a strong plea in mitigation would have been entered on his behalf. Ken's abiding interest in British political history and his thirst for poetry and literature enlivened many an otherwise tedious meeting and make him the delightful and fascinating companion which he always is.

During the summer of 1991, a dog bit a child. Indeed, several dogs bit several children as they have done since man first domesticated the mutt. Unfortunately, one or two of these attacks really were quite horrific and provided the media with endless pictures of a poor tot lying bound and bruised in a hospital bed. In an otherwise slack news time, the 'dog bites child' bandwagon took off, and cub reporters up and down the country were told to go out and find further horrors. Within hours, and true to form, editorials were blaming the Government. We were impotent, indifferent and callous and Ken, as Home Secretary, was the Man Who Ought To Do Something. The problem was that it was not entirely clear what that Something was. Dogs are not generally terribly good readers, and nor is it easy to deal through legislation with a three-year-old who attempts to remove a canine eye with a bent stick. I told Ken that my strong advice was that we should simply let the whole affair blow over. Hard cases do invariably make bad law, and there seemed little to be gained from implying otherwise. Tony Kerpel felt as I did, although he was always concerned about how the issue was playing with our supporters. Officials were happy to offer advice on options, including the prospect of dealing with the worst offenders who emerged as a terrifying new breed of American pit bull terrier. This, at least, was a genuine new development. These incredibly unattractive specimens were apparently specifically bred for their single-minded willingness to dig their teeth in and hold on till the death. They were apparently cult ikons for a certain class of young bruiser who would parade his ugly charge complete with studded collar and thick metal chain as little short of an offensive weapon. Officials advised Ken that there were something like 10,000 of these animals in Britain, and once the press latched on to the fact, the calls for action became ever more strident. Even at this level, however, there were several difficulties with framing any legislation. Firstly, it was almost impossible to decide what a pit bull terrier actually was. To the untrained eye they looked like Staffordshire bull terriers which, although I personally cannot abide the look of them, are a much loved and ancient British breed, complete with Kennel Club certification. Secondly, although pit bulls might be a large part of the problem, any dog could turn violent under extreme provocation and there were enough reports of alsatians and rottweilers going haywire to indicate that the legislation would have to be widely drawn. Unfortunately, the more widely drawn it was, the less easy it would be to enforce. Ken clearly felt under enormous pressure, particularly when he appeared on the David Frost programme in the wake of the Conservative by-election defeat at Monmouth, and found the discussion turned toward dangerous dogs. Frostie was urging him to promise to slaughter all 10,000 pit bulls, whilst at the time, Ken stuck with the line that legislation would be difficult and complex. The next day he was predictably lambasted by most of the tabloids. Downing Street was becoming jittery, and asked for guidance, which is another way of saying that the Prime Minister is worried and wants to know how to explain this nonsense if he has to.

The constant accusations of impotence were getting under Ken's skin, and Central Office were telling him the party was uneasy. Under the combined weight of pressure from the press, Smith Square and Number 10, he buckled. Tony Kerpel and I were horrified to hear him announce on television that he Intended to Act. Ken allowed himself to be persuaded that he could legislate for all pit bull terriers to be muzzled at all times on pain of instant death, and that he could force them to be neutered, insured and registered. He could also ban any further imports. As officials hurriedly prepared a bill, he set about consulting interested parties like the Kennel Club, the RSPCA and the veterinary colleges. All of them seemed sympathetic in

164

private. The Kennel Club pointed out that they would not register pit bulls as a recognised breed because they felt fighting dogs had no place in a civilized society. The RSPCA also agreed that something (dangerously undefined) needed to be done, and the vets alarmed us all by stating that in their view, all pit bulls would manifest extreme violence at some point in their lives, and that it was not a question of if, but rather when. Once Ken published his proposals, however, believing that he had all these vested interests on his side, he was roughly disabused. The advice he had received in private was not repeated in public. The RSPCA in particular took the opportunity to flog their own hobby horse of a national dog registration system, although it is hard to see how registering a dog actually prevents it from biting a child. Once the bill began its passage through Parliament, the dog registration debate grew louder and louder as passions were inflamed on both sides. Eventually, the bill received Royal Assent, but from the day it hit the Statute Book it has been dogged (if I may be forgiven) by controversy. To this day, distraught owners tearfully argue for their dog's life as the magistrates order a canine execution. Buster the dog inspired more press coverage during his time on death row than Ruth Ellis, and the general verdict of most observers is that the Dangerous Dogs Act has been, to put it politely, less than satisfactory in its application. Ironically, the neutering of so many pit bull terriers does seem to have reduced the scale of the immediate problem, and probably by rather more than the media are prepared to admit, but as an object lesson in the dangers of knee-jerk legislation, the Dangerous Dogs Act will still take some beating.

One of Ken's lesser known but arguably most significant achievements was to advance the idea of a national lottery. He did not dream up the notion himself. He was introduced to it by Dennis Vaughan, a tall, elegant former orchestral conductor for whom the lottery had become a lifetime obsession. Dennis had seen lotteries operating overseas, and more to the point, had seen how significant were the funds that were generated. He believed that Britain, too, could benefit its arts, charities and heritage precisely as these other countries had done. He delighted in pointing out that only two European countries did not have a national lottery – Albania and Britain, and the

Albanians promptly added to our embarrassment by introducing their own lottery immediately the velvet revolution was over. If anyone is owed the credit for the British national lottery, it is Dennis Vaughan. But he had toiled away for years with no reward, lobbying successive Home Secretaries, and in Kenneth he met a man with the vision and imagination to take him seriously. The whole idea, of course, was anathema to certain churchmen. It had been this fear of a repetition of the Sunday Trading débâcle that had prevented Ken's predecessors from publicly supporting the idea, but Ken was impressed by the huge sums which Dennis suggested the lottery might raise. He could immediately see the political benefit of being able to invest literally hundreds of millions in sport, arts and culture. He had, as we all had, listened for decades to the moans of generations of luvvies about the imminent collapse of British art and drama. He knew from his days at Environment how strong was the call for extra investment in sporting facilities and he could instantly see the value of restoration projects which would never obtain funding by conventional means. He took the decision to face down the bishops and bring forward an enabling bill, with Tony Kerpel and myself in strong support. He also had to beat off the pools industry worried about the effect of the lottery on their revenues, and appease the small charities who feared that their income would dry up as potential donations were spent on the lottery instead. Ken stuck with his original bill, however, and not only negotiated it through the House, but persuaded Norman Lamont as Chancellor to take a sensible view of the tax implications. Peter Brooke, David Mellor, Stephen Dorrell and Virginia Bottomley have all subsequently enjoyed a thousand photo opportunities as a consequence of the lottery, whilst Ken himself did the difficult bit. Ken does have one consolation. His wife Mary is a director of Camelot.

In the final months of his tenure, Ken faced his most testing challenge. Two category A prisoners remanded on terrorist charges escaped from Brixton Prison by acquiring a gun which was smuggled in inside a shoe, shooting a warder, vaulting over the prison wall, and escaping in a hijacked car. It was an almost incredible catalogue of incompetence. The home-made gun had been secreted in the heel of a trainer shoe, which then managed to pass through all of the security checks at the prison without detection. The men had been allowed to associate with each

166

other. They had trained themselves to a high degree of physical fitness, and knew the layout of the prison well. In hindsight, it was astonishingly easy for them to escape, and Kenneth was justifiably very angry. The Prison Officers' Association, who always get their retaliation in first, huffed that in their opinion, the whole matter was a question of inadequate resources. It was an oft-played and scratchy record which sounded particularly unconvincing on this occasion. There were even calls for Ken himself to resign, but Tony Kerpel told him firmly that he should only do so if he felt himself responsible for the incident. It was quite clear that real responsibility lay further down the chain of command. At a press conference Ken let it be known that he believed that staff at the prison were clearly at fault. On any evidence he was entitled to draw that conclusion, but by making such a firm statement, he placed himself in great danger. The Prison Governors' Association closed ranks and inisted that the Home Secretary had no right to jump to conclusions before their man had a chance to defend himself. The prison officers reiterated their complaint about inadequate pay, conditions, training, indeed inadequate everything except their members' attention span.

Unfortunately, Ken was technically in the wrong. A formal inquiry would indeed need to take place, and although the conclusion was inevitable, prejudging the outcome was presented as inexcusable. The unions managed to turn the tables on Ken and within a few days, it was he who was in the dock. Stephen Tumin, the Chief Inspector of Prisons, conducted the original inquiry, and his conclusions did not make happy reading. There had been prior knowledge of the escape attempt, a prison officer had struck up a relationship with one of the men and knew that they were interested in obtaining a gun. The information was passed on, but although the officer was moved elsewhere the two prisoners were not separated. None of the staff at the prison from the top down appeared to come out of the report particularly happily. Tumin also recommended that, for self-evident security reasons, only part of his report should be published, and Ken agreed. The media, however, seized on this as evidence of a cover up. Had there been, for example, some covert operation to allow the men to escape so that they could be followed and their contacts identified? It was constantly suggested that Ken knew more than he was prepared to say, and once again the Home Secretary was under pressure. To my certain knowledge there was no foundation for the allegation of a cover up, but the affair did not end with Ken's strong denial. He had been on holiday when the Tumin Report was first published, came back to London to announce the conclusions, and then returned to his house in France. The press, without a shred of real evidence, decided that he had run for cover and for the next few days played Hunt the Home Secretary in the Dordogne. As dozens of hacks sharpened their expense account pencils and salivated at the prospect of some French cuisine, Ken initially lay low. No one knew the exact location of his small family holiday home, but within 24 hours there were sightings in the village, and Kenneth decided to return. He arrived back in Westminster before any of the hacks realised it, and Tony and I took great pleasure in advising their editors that further expense claims ought not to be entertained as the Home Secretary was available for interview in 50 Queen Anne's Gate.

Whilst Ken was having a tough time of it, life was not proving quite as pleasant for me either.

Two things happened in quick succession one of which was merely a taste of things to come; the other would quite simply change my life. I tell elsewhere the reality behind some of the lurid headlines about me in the tabloids in October 1993, but suffice to say that in 1991 I was to all intents and purposes living with Sheila Gunn, a lobby correspondent on *The Times*. Whilst I was not screaming the fact from the rooftops, neither was it any great secret. Given that our usual daily meeting place was the Press Gallery bar at the House of Commons, I invite readers to draw their own conclusions. Lobby correspondents are generally rather a good lot, and very different from the hacks who make their excuses and leave for the smuttier of the tabloids. The lobby generally could not have cared less about what was clearly private business and took no notice. There is, however, one bad apple in every barrel. One morning the phone rang at 6.00 a.m. in Sheila's farmhouse in Sussex. A local farmer had driven past and been suspicious of two men sitting in a car outside the house. Rapid investigation identified an obvious, large telephoto lens. It was clear what was happening. That Sunday the *People* produced a typical wink-and-nudge account of our affair, but buried inside the newspaper, and fortunately, not repeated elsewhere. I have my suspicions as to who decided to cash in. I understand he got £1,500 for his pains. When I knew the story was happening, apart from letting Vicky know, I told Ken Baker and the Chief Whip, Richard Ryder. They were both reassuring and supportive, but it was an unpleasant experience to say the least. I know I will never forget seeing that large prying lens poking from the rear window of the reporter's car. It may be harmless, but the whole experience is somehow deeply unnerving. I do believe that the least pleasant aspect of being in the public eye is the unwelcome paparazzo. In law, the definition of assault does not require physical contact. It is sufficient to put a person in reasonable fear of attack. Something like that surrounds an encounter with a snapper, particularly one who hides himself away either in order to spring out at the crucial moment, or as has happened to me on more than one occasion, to keep himself out of sight and subsequently produce photographs of mind-blowing banality which can still make the front page of the *Sun* on a quiet day. I understand the Princess of Wales who has suffered more than anyone describes the emotion as almost a feeling of being raped. I can understand that all too well.

Unpleasant as the experience with the *People* was, the serious bad news for me was happening on the business front. By this time as well as having two Volkswagen and Audi dealerships at Salisbury and Weston-Super-Mare, I had also made a large investment in a company called Glentronic. The company was based in Livingstone, just outside Edinburgh, and was formed to break into a new high-tech market for a special form of equipment which controlled the speed of electric motors. I was introduced to it by a business contact and was persuaded that the company was just about to achieve a technological break-through which would then offer limitless growth prospects. After carrying out as much due diligence as I could, I became chairman and a sizeable shareholder. Just to round off my business portfolio, Anthony Ince and I dabbled in the property market, having some spectacular success with a site in Salisbury which we bought and sold for a very large profit in a matter of weeks, and with some residential property where we had also been modestly successful. All of this, of course, was on a raging bull market in which, in retrospect, it would have been more difficult not to make money. The trouble is, raging bulls are impossible animals to ride forever, and this particular one threw me off in spades.

The first sign of trouble was when it became crushingly obvious that although Glentronic had a theoretically exciting future, it always seemed to be around the next corner. In a nutshell, the product never worked. I found myself staring down a large black hole, having committed the two most elementary business sins. I had invested in a high-tech company and a near-market product when only large companies with bottomless wells of cash should ever do so, and worse, I was starting to throw good money after bad. As several tens of thousands of pounds were swallowed up each month keeping the factory open and the team together, the acrid smell of burning of my own business funeral pyre was already hanging in the air. Just at this dreadful time, the market in new cars simply disappeared.

One of the terrifying aspects of a recession is how quickly it hits you. One minute, you are taking orders and the next minute they simply disappear like snow in midsummer. We had just undertaken an expensive refurbishment of the Salisbury show-rooms, borrowing yet more money against our theoretically golden future, and that debt weighed heavily on the balance sheet. The golden fruit machine was suddenly failing to show the three strawberries. As I looked around for ways to restabilise the business, a property which had been valued at £850,000 proved impossible to sell for half that price. And our latest property venture, the mews house in Holland Park valued at half a million pounds, was beginning to look distinctly vulnerable. Suddenly, I knew I had to work fast. I bit the bullet at Glentronic and put the company into voluntary liquidation. Every penny I had put in was instantly lost and that meant I was down about a third of a million pounds. I sold the Holland Park house and was about the last person in London to be able to gazump my way into a deal which just about got me out quits, and I then faced up to the biggest problem of the lot, the motor business.

Frankly I had few options open to me. One was to try to bring the company round under my own steam. I rapidly concluded that would simply not be practicable. The damage was getting worse, and I knew I would never have the time as long as I stayed in Parliament. What is more, I was not sure that I would be successful. It was clear the recession was going to get even worse before it got better. The second option was to go bankrupt – draw a line in the sand, and start again. But that would have involved taking the Chiltern Hundreds and I was determined, having managed to find Epping Forest, not to go down that path unless it was absolutely inevitable. The third was to cut my losses, and sell out to the highest bidder. To cut a long and extremely painful story short, I effectively gave the business to Anthony Ince, and not only did I pass it over for nothing, but I actually had to find quite a large dowry from my own personal reserves to have it taken off my hands. Once again, the entire investment was written off. I was forty-six, and everything I had built had disappeared. I had the clothes I stood up in (even though most of them were £1,400 Savile Row suits) and a tolerant bank manager who was about to learn the joys of managing my overdraft. I had my parliamentary salary, but although it is perfectly possible for anyone to live on £30,000 a year, it is a darned sight more difficult when you have been used to £150,000. This may sound pathetic, but it is true.

To add insult to injury, I had had only one outside interest in a company called Haven Management Services, a subsidiary of Anglia Secure Homes. Anglia, which was run by Peter Edmondson, had been a glory stock in the heady days, and indeed, I had sold some of my own holding at four or five times the issue price to buy Bargemon. But being so heavily centred on the property market, and as highly geared as most businesses were at that time, we saw the shares fall from a high of more than £5 to less than 10p. I was wiped out, at least as near as made no difference. Bargemon had to go, too. As I looked at my personal life at the end of 1991, there did not seem a great deal more which could go wrong. Time, however, would suggest otherwise.

13

Yes, Minister

I was distracted from my personal problems by the pressing and unwelcome prospect of the 1992 general election. Frankly, our prospects looked pretty terrible. We had seen the Lawson boom evaporate, interest rates were rocketing, the property market was in free fall and I was certainly not the only entrepreneur in deep trouble. I remember some of the most harrowing interviews I ever had in my advice surgery during that time. People would come in who had worked hard all their lives to build up a business, who had bought a respectable house in Loughton or Buckhurst Hill, had two cars, regular holidays abroad and two children in private school. They had been doing well and no doubt were as much seduced by the boom as I was, but their experience had been identical to mine. Generally husband and wife both came. They almost all looked tired, drawn and grey. Their stories were heartbreaking. They would talk of a bank which had been throwing money at them only weeks before suddenly turning nasty and demanding repayment, and when denied that possibility, having no compunction about putting the business into liquidation. They talked of the repossession of their home and the loss of their entire equity. Many of them were facing a future in Norway House, an ugly, airless, cramped former hospital building on the fringe of Epping Forest, which was the local council's hostel accommodation for the homeless. It was all they had to look forward to after a lifetime's work. I did the best I could for them, staving off banks and building societies wherever possible and helping them to find private accommodation where we could, but I often felt a huge lump in my throat as I listened to their stories. They were almost always apologetic, knowing perhaps that there was little I could do, but just grateful for a friendly face and a sympathetic ear. I would often tell them what had happened to me because somehow I

172

felt it might make it better for them to know that there were so many other people in the same boat. Perhaps it also helped them feel less hate and shame, that curious combination that over-takes you when you realise the sickening truth that you are totally and utterly on your own.

On any rational analysis, the Tories should have been swept from office, but politics is never a rational business and for all sorts of reasons, the outcome was to be quite counter-intuitive. From the Tory's side, John Major was not Margaret Thatcher. The party had a least lanced that boil, and Michael Heseltine, now restored to government in his old job at Environment, had taken on the task of ditching the disastrous community charge. He and Michael Portillo had brilliantly defused the powder keg, and effectively taken the issue of local taxes off the political agenda. John, too, came across as a sane and normal human being in stark contrast to his predecesor who had looked increasingly manic and unreal during the last days of her empire. John was obviously going to be a much harder opponent for Labour than she.

The change of leader however would probably not have saved the Tories from defeat had it not been for the effective campaign masterminded by Chris Patten to undermine Labour's credibil-ity on two major issues. The first was the Tory attack on Neil Kinnock as a potential Prime Minister. The Tories ceaselessly played on the Welsh windbag image of a man clearly unfit to govern. Neil himself, of course, unwittingly helped the Tory onslaught by playing to type and crowning his election cam-paign with the appalling misjudgement at the Sheffield rally. The second attack proved even more effective. When I first saw the pair of boxing gloves and the corny 'double whammy' slogan I could not bring myself to take it seriously. It seemed so puerile as to not be worth bothering with. I could not have been more wrong. Chris Patten had quite rightly decided that Labour's Achilles heel was the economy. Apart from all their wild spending pledges, John Smith had been induced to produce his fatal shadow budget just immediately prior to the election which quite clearly spelled out that anyone earning more than £25,000 a year would be significantly worse off. That might have been a line which would have played well in Monklands East, but in my constituency, where a small three bedroomed semi-detached house cost upwards of £130,000, it was an insult. Nothing so comprehensively defeated Labour in Basildon as John Smith's tax proposals. John's early death shocked his colleagues and their genuine sorrow was shared on all sides. We were all saddened. Yet on several significant issues it has to be said that John Smith was fundamentally wrong. He was wrong ever to have fallen for the trap of a shadow budget. He totally misjudged the aspirations of middle-class people at least in the south east of England if not elsewhere. He urged Nigel Lawson to take interest rates even lower during the latter part of 1987 when the great boom in cheap money and inexhaustible credit was raging, when in retrospect that was a disastrous misjudgement, and when it was clear that we had stayed too long in the Exchange Rate Mechanism and at totally the wrong rate, John Smith was standing shoulder to shoulder with Norman Lamont urging resolution. On all three counts he misjudged badly. It will hardly disturb his reputation for me to enter this quiet caveat, but I do not personally believe he would have been anything like as formidable an adversary for John Major as Tony Blair. Nor, incidentally, would he have had either the heart or the mind to bring about the changes in the Labour Party which Tony Blair has already accomplished.

For me, this reluctant recognition by the electorate that they simply could not afford Labour became much more apparent in the second and third weeks of the campaign. In the first few days I was genuinely worried. The punters would look rather embarrassedly over my shoulder when I asked for their support. 'Well, I haven't quite made up my mind' was the invariable response. What they meant, of course, was that they were not happy with us, but not yet clear where else to go. 'What do you mean, you haven't made up your mind. It's either Major or Kinnock isn't it?' Was my usual reply. 'Oh, I don't want Labour' was the invariable quick response. 'Well then, there's only one choice, isn't there?' And that message got home. Within ten days of the campaign starting, I met several voters who told me they were Liberals, that there was no point in my calling for the local government elections because they would still be Liberals, but that they were going to vote for me in 1992 'because the alternative doesn't bear thinking about'. It was a flat, negative and generally unedifying campaign ranging from John Major's Val Doonican-like bar stool performance with an improbable Jeffrey Archer prominent in the front row of every audience, to Kinnock's own sub-Nuremberg effort in the People's Republic of South Yorkshire, yet the contrast between the simple integrity of the soapbox underlining Major's obvious gritty determination, and the flag-waving triumphalism and ersatz glitz from the brothers, proved telling.

Having won my by-election nearly four years earlier by a majority of just over 4,000, I had made a quick calculation of my own prospects. John Biggs-Davison had handed me a majority of over 20,000, but I could hardly see the 1987 performance being repeated. I reckoned 10,000 would be a good margin and it was in that frame of mind that I arrived at St John's School in Epping where the count was taking place. Tricia was there, having masterminded a first-class campaign for the previous three weeks in which, as ever, Vicky and my mother figured prominently. She was as confident of success as in all honesty was I, but her estimate of the majority was higher. 'I would be disappointed if we weren't around 15,000 at least,' she said.

As the count took place in the school hall, a television had been set up in one of the adjacent classrooms. Early on in that memorable night the beaming smile of David Amess announced our success in Basildon. At the time, whilst we were all delighted because he is genuinely popular, the true significance of the result did not sink in. By one o'clock in the morning my own count was complete. I had polled 32, 407, the highest Conservative vote ever recorded in the Epping Forest constituency. Our majority was well over 20,000. It was far beyond my wildest dreams and the whole team were delighted and rightly pleased with themselves. As we went back to Orchard Cottage for an impromptu celebration, the television showed the results pouring in and by the time we eventually got to bed around six in the morning it was clear that we had won a quite astonishing victory.

Afterwards, acres of newsprint were devoted to analysing how badly the pollsters got it wrong. I am not sure they ever did. From my experience, voters probably got as far as the polling booth itself before their hands hovered over the ballot paper and, faced with the moment of truth, came down against the Conservative name. Nobody loved us in that election, but we were distinctly the lesser of two evils.

It has been suggested that for the Conservatives at least, this would have been a good election to lose. Given that the economy was far deeper in recession than anyone imagined, the Tories certainly paid the price of having to raise taxes to bridge the public spending gap when their whole strategy and stated objective was to do precisely the opposite. Had, however, Neil Kinnock become Prime Minister, then he and his Cabinet, faced with precisely the same deep recession, would have endured a torrid time at the hands of the market and their own left wing. I have no doubt that had Labour won in 1992, they would never have lasted a single full term. As Francis Pym had discovered, however, there is no justification for believing in a good time to lose. I was clear the country could not afford Labour, and I believed the voters had made the right decision. A vote is not an opportunity to deliver a verdict on the outgoing government. It shapes the character of the next.

As the 1991 Government re-shuffle was taking place, I took a call from a voice that enquired 'Mr Norris?' 'Yes.' 'Number 10 here. Can you hold a second, I have the Prime Minister for you.' A long pause, and then my old friend Brian Deacon from Radio Oxford: 'It's all right Steve, it's only me.' He hooted with mirth. He had certainly had the reaction he was looking for. In those few seconds I had mentally come to attention, momentarily exultant that the prize I had coveted was within my grasp. I could happily have throttled him. The following year I was in the bath when Vicky told me Number 10 were on the phone. This time I was determinedly casual. 'Tell them I'll ring back' was my languid response. Even so, I could feel the adrenalin pumping again. This was surely not someone else winding me up. The number they left was one I certainly recognised, and the operator dispelled my last doubts. A harassed private secretary asked me if I could make myself available to see the Prime Minister later on in the day, and I was fairly confident I could squeeze the engagement in. I arranged to be at Number 10 around lunchtime. I parked my car in the Commons and walked over. I was shown to an upstairs room and asked to wait but after only a minute I was ushered into a small study.

John was there with one private secretary, and after a brief exchange of congratulations, he got down to business. 'I'd like you to go to join the Government, Steve.' I was suitably grateful. 'I want you to go to . . . Transport.' I noticed the momentary hesitation as the Prime Minister's right forefinger traced a complex diagram which presumably held the details of all the new appointments until he came across my name. 'Thank you very much, Prime Minister' was my enormously imaginative response, and after no more than thirty seconds of further pleasantry, I found myself back out in Downing Street. As I walked through the gates, I saw Caroline with John Whitting-dale, Margaret Thatcher's old political secretary who had just been elected for one of the Colchester seats and was an old friend of hers. 'Well?' she asked. 'What have you got?' 'Transport.' 'Sort of trains and boats and planes?' 'Sort of.' As we went off to a Whitehall wine bar to celebrate our two successes – my elevation and John's election – I have to say I was not massively enthusiastic about my new brief. Over my nine years since first being elected I had served as a PPS at the Department of the Environment, founded a crime prevention charity for the Home Office, set up an educational trust for the Department for Education and Science, been a Cabinet Minister's PPS at the Department of Trade and Industry and in the latter days before the general election, been a PPS to the Home Secretary and founded a charity with a friend of mine, Brian Arbery, which provided residential treatment facilities for drug and alcohol abusers. And I got Transport. If there was a vast eternal plan around, I couldn't see it.

Lunch over, I started to wonder what I should do next. The trouble with Westminster is that there is no rule book. None when you first arrive as Member of Parliament, no plan of the building, and certainly no induction course for would-be Ministers. The sensible course seemed to be to ring Malcolm Rifkind's office at the Department. I knew that Malcolm had been replaced by John MacGregor, but his was the name in the Commons telephone directory. 'John MacGregor's office,' answered Stephen Allen, the assistant private secretary. The King is dead, Long Live the King. 'You won't know me,' I answered by way of introduction, 'but my name's Steve Norris and I've got a job in your department.' 'Yes, Minister' was Stephen's immortal reply.

From our conversation I learned that John MacGregor wanted to see me and the rest of his new team the next morning, but that I was very welcome at the Department where my new office awaited me. At that time, DoT occupied the southern end of London's least attractive building, the triple-towered mon-strosity known formally as 2 Marsham Street and as the

177

Lubianka to anyone who has worked there. Transport shares the building with Environment, so I was no stranger to its unreliable lifts and endless Kafkaesque corridors. Immediately I arrived I was shepherded to the twelfth floor, and greeted by Paul Hogg, who introduced himself as my assistant private secretary. He apologised for the absence of my principal private secretary, Paul Downie, who had sensibly chosen that moment to be on his honeymoon. These two were the cornerstone of my private office, and our team was completed by Magdalene Nestor, a bubbly girl who kept the diary in good order, and the rest of us smiling. My room had previously been home to Patrick McGloughlin, the young miner who had inherited Matthew Parris's Derbyshire seat and who had been Minister for Shipping. There were several rather dull Victorian paintings of tea clippers in full sail around the walls, an obvious reproduction desk with a large leather chair, and a table around which a dozen people could meet. The only relieving features of this charmless collection were a comfortable chintz-covered armchair and sofa which would not have been out of place in a suburban drawing room, and a large standard lamp. The one asset that 2 Marsham Street possesses is unrivalled views of London, and mine was superb. Big Ben was my office clock, and I looked out over Westminster Abbey, and the City of London beyond. Paul did tell me I could change the furniture if I wished, but the extravagance of that gesture was not one I was prepared to indulge in. I settled for changing the pictures and arranged a visit to the Government art collection, housed in an anonymous colourless sixties concrete block on the south bank of the Thames in Southwark. Here the Government's large store of paintings are racked according to rank. Major works for Secretaries of State, good quality oils and a few famous prints for Ministers of State, and a large number of desperately tedious architectural drawings and ancient cartoons for Parliamentary Under-Secretaries. Fortunately, I was able to ferret out three ideal colourful prints by Julian Trevelyan and the assistant curator dug around for a 1930s woodcut by Cyril Powers of a London tube station.

When I went to see John MacGregor the next morning, he told me that he wanted me to take on the new post of Minister for Transport in London. This was apparently one of our manifesto commitments but as I have never troubled to read a manifesto in my life, preferring the bliss of ignorance, I actually had no idea what he was talking about. A quick glance at the London section of the usual turgid 1992 effort revealed three commitments. First, an organization to bring the voice of business more prominently into decision-making in the capital, second, a Cabinet subcommittee with particular responsibility for London, and third, the appointment of a Transport Minister who would be responsible for all modes of travel across the city. This was in fact a fairly revolutionary suggestion. Previously, under both complexions of government, transport had been organised on a straightforward modal split. There was a Minister for shipping, one for aviation, one for roads, and a fourth for railways. There were obvious advantages to this arrangement; officials could determine at a glance which division and Minister was responsible for which issue. But it had become increasingly obvious, even in 1992, that this sort of division ignored the reality that producing a sensible transport strategy, particularly in urban areas, can only make sense when the inter-relationship between the road network, the buses, trains, even airports and ferries are all taken into account. Although men were taken out and shot for less during the Thatcher years, we were going to have to relearn the words 'integrated transport strategy'.

Within a few days, I was hooked. The Ministry worked on the tried and tested basis of 'predict and provide'. Half the department attempted to predict the growth in traffic, while the other endeavoured to build the roads and railways that were needed to satisfy that demand. If there were any politics involved, they were simply the Opposition calling for more, and the government of the day mouthing the usual platitudes about the inadequacy of resources. By the late eighties, however, every country in the world was facing a frightening new paradox. On the one hand, the growth in demand for traffic, and particularly for motorcars, showed no signs of abating. On the other, concern about the consequences of unrestricted traffic growth, particularly the problems posed by vehicle emissions and congestion were beginning to be recognised as challenges on a global scale. The task of reconciling the two is one of the most important we will all face in the twenty-first century.

The other instant attraction for me in my new job was London. The first time I had visited our capital city was when I went to watch Widnes play St Helen's in the Rugby League Cup Final one year in the late sixties. 'Sew your pockets up when you go down there, lad', was the general tenor of the advice. We went in a friend's car, parked at Wembley, saw the match, and left. I repeated the experience the following year when Everton beat Sheffield Wednesday in the Cup Final, but inexperience and lack of resources meant that yet again the visit never got beyond the North Circular Road. Come Oxford, and I had found the delights of a few fleshpots at the instigation of Dorian St George Bond, Christopher 'Party' Bird and others, and then after Oxford, and the last vacation driving John Relph's red beer wagon, London became my home. When I had been with Burroughs, I had literally walked every yard of the square mile, and knew it intimately. During that time I never bothered to own a car, simply because it never struck me that I had any need of one. The tubes, buses and occasional taxies served me perfectly well. Later, when we lived in Notting Hill, I got to know the West End and some of the more interesting suburbs. I have always been a voracious learner, and by the time I went into Parliament could have made a passable living as a mini-cab driver.

In the intervening nine years I had come not just to know, but to love London. It is not as grand a city as Paris, its infrastructure may be more antiquated than Tokyo and life marginally less frenetic than New York, but the glories of London are timeless and all the more remarkable for being often so unexpected. That first view of St Paul's from Fleet Street as one approaches Ludgate Hill, the Mansion House tucked into the corner of the old city, Somerset House, almost invisible from the Strand but majestic from the river, are all gems to lay alongside the view of Buckingham Palace through Admiralty Arch, Westminster Abbey, the Palace of Westminster itself, and the green lungs of St James' Park, Hyde Park, Green Park, Regents Park: the list is endless. But nor is London simply a collection of magnificent buildings and historic palaces. The city houses some of the finest art galleries, the best theatres and, these days, the most varied cuisine in the world. The River Thames is probably London's most under-utilised asset but the views from a tripper boat still more than repay the investment. Londoners of course scarcely bother with the river boats, which is a shame because London from the river from Putney to

Greenwich is arguably the best day out money can buy in the whole United Kingdom. And where in the world can you enjoy the clubs of St James's, each with its own unique character, the excitement of Covent Garden or Soho, the extraordinary range of concerts and exhibitions along the South Bank, not to mention the West End shops, the Park Lane hotels, the city churches, livery halls and Lord Mayor, the pomp and ceremony of the State Opening, the colour of the Notting Hill Carnival, the community spirit of the Lord Mayor's show, black taxis, red buses, beefeaters at the Tower, punks in the Kings Road, eurotrash in Bond Street. The elegance of Belgravia, Kensington or Holland Park, the quieter charm of Clapham, Putney or St John's Wood, the bustle of Campden Lock, Portobello Road or Upper Street, Islington, are all my London and then only a tiny part of it. The opportunity to play a small role in making it a better city was one I was determined to make full use of.

Every Jim Hacker needs a Sir Humphrey, and on my first day, I met the Permanent Secretary at the Department of Transport, Patrick Brown. Patrick is no archetypal mandarin. There was a time not long ago when every single permanent secretary arrived via Oxbridge and in nearly every case, a classics degree. Both Anthony Sampson and later Jeremy Paxman exposed the narrow outlook which this produced, the worst effect of which was the undervaluation of engineering, industry and commerce, architecture and all the other practical skills associated with trade rather than the professions. It is arguably our most debilitating national inheritance. Patrick was five years older than me. He had attended the Royal Grammar School in Newcastle and then went on to the school of Slavonic and Eastern Studies at London. He worked abroad for Carreras, did a spell as a management consultant and then joined the civil service as a high-flyer late entrant. He had been given the unenviable task of sorting out the Property Services Agency, and having successfully accomplished that, moved to Transport as Permanent Secretary the previous year. He is a true professional. Inevitably his political antennae are finely tuned and over the years I have watched him deal with three widely different Secretaries of State, John MacGregor, Brian Mawhinney and George Young, and saw how quickly he had the measure of every one, adapting his style to theirs, giving them exactly what they wanted but always on the basis of understanding where the lines were to be drawn that the politicians must never cross. Patrick of course had responsibility for the whole department and his main contact was with the Secretary of State. My own senior official was one of the four deputy secretaries in the department, Nick Montagu. Superficially, he was more in the mandarin mould than Patrick. Oxford educated, where he was a leading light in the Union, he had entered the service as a graduate, and been assigned to the old Department of Health and Social Security. He was head and shoulders above his contemporaries and had risen swiftly to the top, along the way finding himself dealing with a young Junior Social Security Minister called John Major. He had only recently transferred to Transport, but had effortlessly mastered the brief, and his command of all the issues was impressive. Much more to the point, he had a wicked sense of humour, very little time for pomposity, and an encyclopaedic knowledge of the names and qualities of practically every person in the department from the tea lady to the Secretary of State. He was much liked, and he and I got on like a house on fire. We shared the belief that you get the best out of people by encouraging them rather than kicking them, that the carrot is more of an incentive than the stick, and most important of all, as Brian Walden once remarked, that most things in life don't matter very much, and the rest don't matter at all. Nick never takes himself seriously, is never pompous and always on the ball. Like me, he takes the job itself enormously seriously. Between them, he, Patrick and Phillip Wood, who was then in charge of the railways division, put together the framework of the whole of rail privatisation.

Whilst Nick and his staff provided the technical input to my job, I soon realised that the key to success for any minister lies in the quality of his private office. A Minister's day is long and tiring. I would wake before seven, arrive at the office around eight, and spend the next twelve hours on meetings scheduled roughly every 45 minutes on perhaps a dozen different subjects. I would then go over to the House of Commons when it was in session, vote where necessary, and then go home with at least one, but often three or four red dispatch boxes full of letters to be signed and submissions to be cleared before the next day. In four and a half years I can count on the fingers of one hand the working days that ended on the same day they began. Under that sort of pressure, you never survive unless the people around you support you to the hilt. No account of my ministerial career, however brief, would be complete without recording my enormous debt to my Principal Private Secretaries; the two Pauls, John Nicholls, who was there when the balloon went up in October 1993, Bruce Bendell and for the last eighteen months, the excellent Stephen Heard. They were supported by Karen Dee, who replaced Paul Hogg, by Carole Hulks, who replaced Magdalene, and finally by the two girls who were not only excellent workers but delightful friends, Heather Pilley, who joined us from the department's Dockland's office when Karen moved on, and Rachel England who arrived in 1994 when I took on a wider portfolio and acquired a second assistant private secretary. Heather has a wicked sense of humour, whilst Rachel treated me like an errant ten-year old, rather in the manner of a tolerant and fond nanny. When Angela Marlow took over from Carole as diary secretary on Stephen's recommendation, our team was as good as any in Whitehall. Certainly, no Minister at any rank was better served, and I rate our output comparable with any in the private sector. We worked well together, we never had a cross word or a dull day, and our work rate was prodigious. I owe them and all their predecessors enormous thanks.

Ministers enjoy one other relationship which is just as important as any they may enjoy with their officials. The other person to whom I was introduced on my first day was my driver, John Underwood. Cars are allocated on a strict hierarchical basis in government. The Prime Minister has an armour-plated Daimler, Secretaries of State have Rover Sterlings and Junior Ministers are allocated a variety of small family saloons. The phrase 'ministerial limo' would cause a hollow laugh in my tiny Rover 400, particularly with three officials cramped into the rear. No wonder Alan Clark and Michael Heseltine, who could both afford to do so, declined the official car and chose to keep their own.

John is a quiet, tall, former merchant seaman from Plumstead who says little, enjoys his pipe and his own company and the occasional swift one in the social club at weekends. He also happens to be extremely loyal and discreet. The drivers see all, hear all, and invariably know all. On re-shuffle days when Parliament is caught up in a paroxysm of excitement, the first to know who has gone where are always the drivers. John was with me for more than three years until he eventually had the chance to add a large amount to his earnings by going to work on a longer range job elsewhere, and John Hougham, whom I already knew, took his place. The two Johns were terrific; never late, always there when I wanted them and hardly ever complaining when I was later leaving the House of Commons or a nearby restaurant than I had originally predicted.

The Minister's car is frequently targeted by the tabloids as a great luxury, but the truth is the job could simply not be done without it. The timetable is so tight, and the amount of paperwork each Minister has to take home every night so great that, however much I would have enjoyed coming in on my bicycle, the whole notion was simply impractical. A tight programme of meetings, speeches, conferences, seminars and more meetings in the department, the Cabinet office, Parliament, and every major venue in the city, not to mention frequent trips out of London by rail and air, all require precision timing, and a minimum of delay. I was actually unusual in being the first and probably only Minister to decide to use the tube to avoid delay and sample the product at first hand. On occasions it made real sense, but normally there simply wasn't the time to indulge in politically correct tokenism. And at the end of a seventeen-hour day, a lift home was more of a necessity than a luxury. In any event, in typically British fashion the car disappeared on Thursday evening, because Friday is traditionally a constituency day for Ministers as it is for backbenchers. As it is only available for government business, I would bid John a good weekend on Thursday evening and meet him again on Monday morning. I have always thought it a silly notion that somehow Transport Ministers might be unaware of the delights of London Underground or the pleasures of the Routemaster. As far as I was concerned, not only had they been my staple diet for the previous twenty years, they continued to be throughout my time in the department.

14

Mind the Gap

The largest part of my London portfolio was dealing with London Transport. It was not my first experience of the organisation. On 18 November 1987, thirty-one people had died in a horrific fire at King's Cross Underground station. A day or so later Des Wilson rang. He knew I was free of my parliamentary responsibilities, and he put a proposition to me. He and his friend Godfrey Bradman, the property developer, wanted to do something for the victims of the disaster, but Godfrey had sensibly decided that the best way was not simply to make a donation, but to use his own money to fund a team who could then campaign throughout the capital for funds. Des was looking for someone to head up the appeal, and preferably to be able to open the necessary doors in a hurry. Never being able to resist Des, I agreed and a day or so later found myself quartered in a portakabin on the forecourt of King's Cross station. We set about organising a three day street collection in London, a carol concert in Leicester Square which Des's wife, Jane, co-ordinated with as many personalities as we could gently pressgang into turning up, and various other activities. The portakabin was not intended to be more than co-ordinating centre but I was enormously moved by the number of people who put their heads round the door and proffered a blue or a brown note. 'Take it,' they said. 'I can't bear to think what happened to them.' In the end, we simply left a large white plastic bucket at the door, and by the end of the day it was always full. We needed publicity fast and staff at J. Walter Thompson gave us their time for nothing and produced a brilliant poster showing the blackened burned out escalator and underneath in large black lettering, 'There but for the grace of God . . .' I thought it was brilliant but when I went to see the Chairman of London Underground, Dr Tony Ridley, he

185

refused point blank to allow it to be displayed on the Underground. He argued that it would frighten passengers and not be helpful as they began the task of reconstruction.

We argued but to no avail. We certainly used the poster outside, but produced a watered down version for the railway which nonetheless produced a flood of donations. The report which Desmond Fennell subsequently produced blamed the disaster on simple mismanagement. The Underground had become complacent about safety, and management was sloppy and disinterested. Reading the report I was struck by how King's Cross was almost inevitable and it was a miracle that the disaster had not happened sooner.

The team at the head of London Transport had replaced Tony Ridley and his managing director, Keith Bright, both of whom resigned in the aftermath of King's Cross. Wilfrid Newton was an inspired choice as chairman. A native South African, he had spent the majority of his business life as an accountant in the oil industry, moving into transportation systems and then to the chairmanship of the Hong Kong Mass Transit System which was renowned throughout the world as one of the finest metro systems ever built. Tall and imposing, he had suffered badly in a car accident, losing a leg and the sight of one eye. He had lost none of his sharpness however, and remained a director of Hong Kong and Shanghai Bank where he was Chairman of the audit committee. He had a wicked sense of humour and his favourite trick on his frequent air trips to Hong Kong was to retreat to the toilet once the plane had taken off, unscrew his leg and hand it to a horrified stewardess for safe keeping. He was tough, competent and experienced and he brought a much-needed discipline to the whole organisation.

Denis Tunnicliffe had been appointed managing director of London Underground. He had begun his career as a pilot, shot up the ladder of promotion at British Airways but managed to fall out with its then boss, John King. He later joined Harry Goodman and ran Airtours until he fell out with Harry, and then joined the Underground. He never disguised his Labour sympathies, but he was a brilliant change agent who was an ideal choice to transform the culture of the old Underground and produce a more efficient, slimmer, safer and more reliable railway. Denis has a devilish iconoclastic streak which makes him quite difficult for some ministers to handle, but I could tell that here was a rare talent that ought to be nurtured as much as it needed to be protected, and Wilfrid too recognized Denis's value and talked to him like a Dutch uncle when necessary.

King's Cross had left an indelible mark on London Transport. The silver lining on that tragic cloud was that the event at least proved a catalyst for major change. Smoking was banned almost overnight, with scarcely a murmur of objection from the public. Denis instituted a complete overhaul of the system, developing a company plan to improve management and produce a safety regime comparable with the best in the world. Wilfrid kept a tight hold on the finances and a watchful eye on every aspect of the business. Government too had begun to respond to the obvious need for investment in a system that had been crumbling for decades. Under governments of both complexions the Underground had been starved whilst successive Chancellors of the Exchequer found more pressing demands elsewhere. It is a tragedy that the great mistake made by the Labour Government immediately after the war was that nationalised industries would be given the funding they would need because they were owned by the State. The reality was precisely the reverse. Rather like our originally magnificent Victorian sewerage system, out of sight was out of mind. Trains had become old and unreliable, signalling was equally antiquated whilst some of the wiring was so ancient that when it failed, it simply had to be bypassed for fear that if it was touched, it might crumble. Embankments which were jerry-built from tunnel spoil by the Victorians were now in danger of slipping, and even the track bed resembled a roller coaster in places. As water ingressed at various locations, and wooden escalators frequently broke down, the once greatest system in the world was far from healthy.

By the time I arrived in 1992 the recovery was well underway. Denis's company plan had reduced the staffing by a quarter, whilst output and efficiency had rocketed. Malcolm Rifkind had supervised a record investment of more than £700 million in 1991, and morale was massively improved. There was much still to be done and battling for resources with the Treasury would be one of my main tasks in office. I became convinced early on that if we were to persuade people to use our public transport system, providing one that was decent, reliable, clean and frequent was the most important priority. Price, unfortunately, had to be a secondary consideration. During my time I took a lot of flak for pushing fares up beyond the rate of inflation but I was always conscious that the Underground got its money either from the taxpayer or the fare box. There is no other source of revenue as far as I am aware.

I also knew of Ken Livingstone's experience when the GLC ran London Transport. Ken believed that lower fares would lead to more people using the system, less cars, less polution and less congestion. His 'Fare's Fair' scheme, which slashed prices across the board, was ostensibly a perfectly sensible proposition and although Nicholas Ridley, then Transport Secretary, took Ken to Court to force him to abandon it, it was a valuable, if expensive experiment in a capital city. Sadly, the outcome was not quite as predicted. After fares were slashed, more people did indeed use the system, but not in sufficient numbers to bring revenue back to its previous levels. As a result, several hundred million pounds which could have been invested in improvements was needed simply to cover operating costs. More importantly, not enough of the new passengers were people transferring out of cars. They were mostly Londoners who suddenly discovered all sorts of journeys they could make which they had not previously been able to do. There might be a sizeable social benefit in encouraging people to be more mobile, but Fares' Fair proved an extremely expensive way of bringing that about, and it was not, unfortunately, what I needed it to be, namely a way of seducing people out of their cars and onto public transport.

I remember trying to explain this to the Environment Select Committee in 1994. I pointed out that the private car is an extraordinarily attractive way to travel. It is very difficult to mirror all its advantages in public transport. Have you noticed how when you are late leaving, it waits for you, and allows you to access it right outside your front door? Have you noticed how, if you want to stop for a newspaper, or have forgotten your sandwiches, it obeys your command? And then you can dial your own temperature, your own radio station, and indeed not have to sit next to all those dreadful human beings on public transport.

That is of course the reality, and quite serious research shows that making public transport absolutely free will reduce car use by only around 6 per cent in cities, compared to, for example, abolishing private non-residential parking which will reduce it by 48 per cent. My feeble attempt at irony was not lost on the Select Committee, who understood perfectly well what I was trying to convey. As a public transport user myself, I was pointing out that simply providing better trains and buses, even when they were more reliable and cheaper, would not of itself solve our problem. I had, of course, forgotten the golden rule that irony does not travel. Some mischievous hack picked up the quote and took it completely out of context, suggesting that I was personally being sniffy about commuters. It was a daft idea that any examination of the Hansard text would have shown, but on a quiet news day it was manna from heaven for the hacks and they worked it hard. Wonderful cartoons, screaming headlines, even a querulous intervention on *Any Questions* for Brian Mawhinney to field ensued. Fortunately, after the first day or so, the cavalry rode in. As ever with journalists, the intelligent variety doesn't follow the herd, and to my astonishment, several defended me robustly, including Jonathon Porritt, the environmental guru and no particular friend of the Conservatives. He headlined his piece in the *Weekend Telegraph* 'What's truly dreadful is that Steven Norris is right' and having outlined precisely my arguments, concluded, 'meanwhile, we have a serving Minister who is not just in danger of understanding the real issue (the ravening monster that Modern Man has become) but of doing something about it. So let's hear it for Steven Norris.' That will do for me.

Meanwhile the battle for more resources to improve the system never let up. On the Underground we faced two tasks, the renewal of existing infrastructure and providing the vital new pieces that would relieve some of the strains on the existing system, and open up new opportunities for the city. Just before I took over, London Underground had started the complete renewal of the Central Line for around £830 million, which was good news for my constituents in Epping Forest. What was less clear was how we could afford to upgrade the rest of the system on anything like a creditable timetable. As far as new schemes were concerned, we were just about to embark on the largest project in London since the Victoria Line, the extension of the Jubilee Line from Green Park through Westminster, then on to

Southwark, Surrey Quays, Canary Wharf, North Greenwich and up to Stratford, when the Reichmanns went bust.

Paul Reichmann had sold the vision of Canary Wharf to Margaret Thatcher and convinced her to be an enthusiastic supporter of the project. Part of the plan was to give Canary Wharf access to the main tube system, and a vital link to the West End. A deal had been hammered out under which Canary Wharf would contribute £400 million in cash toward the £2 billion project, and it now looked as if all that might be at risk.

Two things were immediately clear to me. One was that the Treasury quietly regarded this as a blessing in disguise. The Treasury hates spending in all forms, and for them, the opportunity to cancel the project on the basis that the private sector contribution was not forthcoming was attractive. The second was that although the scheme was expensive, it clearly had the capacity to transform a whole swathe of London which would otherwise always be cut off from access to jobs by lack of adequate public transport. The Jubilee Line would bring West End jobs to Southwark, Bermondsey and the new Docklands development south of the river. It would kick-start the reclamation of the massive British Gas site on the Greenwich peninsula which, although tantalisingly close to the city, was a derelict wasteland. And by linking in to Stratford station, the new system would relieve overcrowding for Central Line passengers which was otherwise still a problem even after the line was upgraded. It was also obvious that whether or not Canary Wharf was now owned by the Reichmanns, the building was still standing. Without access to the rest of London, it was likely to be the ultimate gargantuan white elephant and for all the high quality of its accommodation, destined to be nothing more than back office space let at a massive loss. With transport access, however, the Reichmann vision could still be realised.

The Treasury line was predictably simple but brutal. If we wanted the extension, then the £400 million contribution had to be forthcoming, and not a penny less would be acceptable. It was a tall order, not made easier by my knowing that Michael Portillo, the then Chief Secretary but a predecessor of mine at Transport, would not have been entirely displeased had we failed.

We set about talking to the group of banks who now found themselves the reluctant owners of Canary Wharf. There were more than a dozen from every corner of the globe involved and co-ordinating them would not be easy. Nonetheless, we began the task and Nick Montagu and one of our senior officials, Geoff Skinner, determined that we would pull it off. The press picked up on this three-way battle between ourselves, Treasury and the banks. We were given little chance, particularly with unattributable Treasury briefings hinting that all was lost. At the 1992 Party Conference in Brighton Philip Stephens of the *Financial Times* was quite blunt. 'It's all over isn't it, Steve?' he said. 'You've lost.' 'The hell I have!' was my John Wayne rejoinder. 'Well, Treasury have told me it's dead,' persisted Phil. Then we still did not have the private sector contribution in the bag and time was certainly running out. But I was not giving up just yet. 'Look, Phil,' I said, 'the opera's not over until the fat lady sings, and this particular diva hasn't even got her music out yet. I bet you a large bottle of champagne we'll do the deal.' Phil agreed. He was sufficiently sure of his sources to have no doubt who would buy the bubbly. He had, however, reckoned without Nick, Geoff and our team. They worked night and day, answering every single objection thrown at them by a disparate group of bankers who all needed to be satisfied on every individual point about the deal. (When I was discussing our difficulties at a press conference on one occasion a journalist who was hard of hearing reported my reference to a 'desperate group of bankers'. It practically sent the City into free fall for a morning, but fortunately no lasting damage was done.)

Even within the department there were those who worried whether the Jubilee Line extension was the right way to spend the department's money. John MacGregor as a former Chief Secretary to the Treasury was no easy touch where spending was concerned, and not the least of my jobs was to make sure that he too remained fully signed up to the project. My key argument to him was that if the project was cancelled, the money would simply not be available elsewhere. The Jubilee Line budget was, in Treasury jargon, ring-fenced, in other words the funds were available only for that project and in the event that they were unused, they returned back to Treasury. I argued hard with John that to abandon the Line would be to secure nothing in return whereas if we pressed on, his negotiating position on other parts of the budget would be no worse off.

Fortunately, John accepted the argument and the scheme was preserved.

Over at London Transport, Wilfrid and Denis were also keen to see the project happen. For them, as for me, it was a litmus test of our seriousness about regenerating London as well as a project on which they had expended literally years of time, effort and money. Fortunately, and entirely because of the superhuman effort of everyone concerned, we eventually lined up every single ball in a row, and left the Treasury no alternative but to agree grudgingly that the project could go forward. One of my proudest moments was the day that John MacGregor and Wilfrid Newton signed off the project which I believe will be the greatest achievement of my time in office. The Prime Minister set the first pile driver off at Canary Wharf, and at the time of writing the project is well underway. The great tunnel has been dug from east to west, the new stations are beginning to be visible and the trains are rolling off the production line. '*Si monumentum requiris, circumspice*' wrote Christopher Wren on the Rotunda of St Paul's. Whilst not suggesting the achievement is comparable, if you seek mine, look for the Jubilee Line extension a hundred years from now. I guarantee it will still be serving London.

The railways are certainly important in London but they are by no means the whole of the picture. The tube carries 2.5 million people every day but the buses carry 3.5 million, and I could see from the outset that we needed to make bus use more attractive. The most obvious way was to inject private sector management and resources by transferring the London bus companies owned by LT to the private sector. We then needed to concentrate on other ways of making buses more attractive such as better information systems, more advanced ticketing, and, in particular, bus priority lanes so that buses can enjoy a genuine advantage over private cars on the road.

In London, the main method of delivering these was the red route programme which I had inherited from Cecil Parkinson. By 1992 red routes were about the hottest political issue in the capital and although none had actually been installed, they were still seen as extremely unpopular. Unfortunately, Cecil's announcement had given the impression that red routes were the equivalent of urban motorways and unsurprisingly they had found few friends. Even if they were likely to appeal to my outer

London voters in Epping Forest, their enthusiasm would be far outweighed by the thousands of people who lived alongside these roads and saw their communities threatened. It was clear we were going to have to correct a very damaging misapprehension. Derek Turner had been appointed as the first Traffic Director for London, and he and I set about doing so.

We spoke to innumerable conferences and talked to endless local authorities and pressure groups, all of whom were initially extremely sceptical, but we persuaded them that red routes were about better bus priority, special measures to avoid rat-running down small adjacent side roads to make them safer, better cycle crossings, more pedestrian crossings and so on. All of this had always been part of the package but the message had been buried. Fortunately, the pilot scheme Derek developed in North London worked well, but it still took us four years to persuade Londoners that red routes were actually welcome. By the time I left, the only political argument was that many of the boroughs were asking for faster implementation than I had the budget to deliver.

As far as the sale of the London buses was concerned, I had inherited a rather strange proposition that we should deregulate buses and then privatise them. Unfortunately, in many people's minds the two concepts were interchangeable, but the steer that Norman Fowler, then Party Chairman, had had from the Tory constituency associations in London was that whilst they were relaxed about privatisation, they were worried about what they had been told would be a deregulated free for all in London. I argued strongly that the original idea was bad business, and we should reverse the order of play. Some of the young ideologues in the Treasury actually suggested that this would depress proceeds because the great deregulated market opportunities would not be available in London.

I knew perfectly well that the opposite would be true. Only those who have never worked in business imagine that businesses like competition. On the contrary, what businesses like are cosy monopolies that generate vast amounts of cash. I knew that although one or two potential bidders might be disappointed not to have the advantage of a completely free market, many more would be encouraged by the relative stability that the regulated market after sale would produce and in the event, I was right. The Treasury estimated we would raise £100 million. Wilfrid Newton was not even sure we would reach that figure, and being a cautious accountant, argued that we should reserve nothing in the accounts until the sales had actually been achieved. I told him that not only would we make £100 million, we would actually more than double it and I solemnly bet him a crate of champagne that I was right. Wilfrid, clearly thinking that I had lost my marbles, accepted. In the event, we raised £233 million and I still have a few bottles left to savour. Each of the companies was sold individually during August and September of 1994. I actually approved several of them from Sydney's holiday flat in Gran Canaria where the steam-driven fax machine was whirring within an hour of our arrival.

When I arrived I also inherited a big road programme, some of which clearly had to go ahead, particularly finishing the upgrading of the North Circular which was already half complete, and offered the chance of relieving a lot of the local road network of rat-running through traffic. On any analysis, too, the A13 needed upgrading if we were to attract the new jobs which were so badly needed in Docklands. The Docklands Highway linking Canary Wharf to Tower Hill was already underway and, together with the Jubilee Line extension and the improvement of the Docklands Light Railway would transform the attractiveness of the whole Docklands area. But I also inherited two extremely controversial schemes. The first linked the north and south banks of the Thames and continued on through Oxleas Wood to the A2. There was no doubt the road would be valuable, but Oxleas Wood is one of the oldest identified woodlands in Britain, and a vocal protest movement had grown to save it. They had actually managed to turn up at the Rio Summit, and it was claimed that the European Environment Commissioner, Carlo Ripa di Meana (the grim Ripa, as he was known in the department), actually kept an acorn from Oxleas Wood on his desk. When I visited the site early on, I could see that not only would the road do a great deal of damage to the woodland, but any of the alternatives, such as cut and cover or even a bored tunnel were, for all sorts of technical reasons, no better.

At the same time that we were taking flak from environmentalists, I knew we had no money in the budget to build the scheme. It was likely to cost £350 million and I could think of a dozen better ways to spend that sort of money improving

London's transport before building that road. I argued hard to John MacGregor that we should take it out of the programme, freeing up the resources for better purposes, and at the same time ridding ourselves of an unpopular irritant. John agreed, and I announced that the scheme had been withdrawn. The greens claimed it as a great success, and having spent so long opposing it, that was natural, but in reality the sight and sound of the protesters had never figured particularly strongly with me. I doubt there are many more effective recruiting sergeants for the Conservative Party than the great unwashed appearing on television, clambering over the tops of cherry pickers, screaming abuse at policemen. I would not go so far as to say that I welcomed trouble, but as I showed on our other controversial scheme in London, I was perfectly prepared to countenance it if we had to.

Whilst I was sure that we could neither afford Oxleas Wood nor would it serve a sufficiently valuable purpose, I was equally convinced that we ought to go ahead with the scheme to join the bottom of the M11 to the Blackwall Tunnel approaches. Anyone who uses that part of east London knows how the Leytonstone Road was impossible, and the whole area dogged by noise, fumes and endless streams of cars. The Hackney-M11 scheme, as it became known, is designed to alleviate that pressure by funnelling traffic in one major road. Once it is complete, the community will have a chance to breathe again. Here too, there was an active anti-roads protest movement. Some people did not like the idea of giving up their homes which I well understood, although most of them had been bought by the time I arrived and were in a dreadful state. Far more vocal was the roving band of anti-roadies who, having failed at Twyford Down, were determined to halt the project. They promised house-to-house fighting, literally guerilla war, if we went ahead. They made elaborate arrangements to booby-trap houses, and barricade themselves in, but the DoT staff and police were more than a match, and the road is now well on its way to completion.

During my time at Transport I realised we needed to rethink our old 'predict and provide' mentality. Cities are not prepared to contemplate the bulldozer and the concrete mixer to solve their congestion problems and there is a growing recognition that new roads will often simply generate new traffic and move the problem from one place to another. That does not mean that there is no place for new roads. As long as there are communities which currently have large arterials ploughing through their centre, there will be strong demands for bypasses. The most vociferous supporters of the Batheaston or Newbury schemes are the local people themselves. And there will also be a role for roads as economic generators. There are many parts of Britain which will only be able to fulfil their potential to create new jobs if they have the road infrastructure which will bring people and goods to and from their premises. These are roads for which rail, sadly, cannot provide a viable alternative. Railways can certainly carry more passengers between large settlements and ferry more freight, particularly now that the Channel Tunnel is open, but just to put the freight issue in context, more than half of truck journeys are under sixty miles in length and rail in that context makes no economic or even environmental sense.

After two years in the department I walked round to the Institution of Civil Engineers just off Parliament Square to attend the launch of the national cycleway project known as SUSTRANS. John Grimshaw, its founder, used some slides to introduce his subject, and there and then I realised that there was something very straightforward missing from our transport strategy, and it was under my nose. John pointed out that 60 per cent of journeys are under two miles, and yet only $2\frac{1}{2}$ per cent of them in Britain are done by cycle. In Holland, predictably, cycling accounts for well over 20 per cent of journeys, but more tellingly, the German figure is 12 per cent, with similar performances by the Scandinavians, French and even the Swiss. So Britain seemed to be cycling a lot less than elsewhere in Europe.

My immediate reaction to comparisons with Holland was, I suspect, fairly typical. We all know why they cycle in Holland: it is dead flat. Unfortunately, you can say what you like about Switzerland, but it is not flat! At the same time, we complained that the French enjoy better weather, yet the Scandinavians spend half the year in snow and darkness. No, there was clearly some other explanation for the difference. John produced one which was frighteningly convincing. Cycling was seven or eight times less safe in Britain even allowing for us having the best overall road safety record in the western world. People did not cycle in Britain because they rightly believed it was dangerous. As the presentation went on, I heard Graham Webb, an old friend of mine whom I knew to be a cycle nut, complain that in his local borough the highway authority had managed to spend £300,000 on a road scheme and produce a result which was worse for cyclists.

I went back to the office and thought hard about what I had heard. When I asked a senior engineer why we did so little for cycling on our new roads, his answer was direct. 'We don't build cycling provision because not many people cycle.' QED. The more I saw, the more I was convinced that it was precisely that attitude which was the problem. It was not about finding massive resources, it was simply about thinking more intelligently, and if the needs of cyclists were taken into account sufficiently early on, then there was often no extra cost for the scheme.

Britain is the only country in Europe where a transport minister, George Young, is known as the Bicycling Baronet. Sir Robin Butler is better known for cycling to work than for anything he has achieved in government, and Sir Richard Scott is more famous for cycling to his inquiry than for the report he eventually produced. I want Britain to be like other countries in Europe, where people cycle regardless of income, simply for the pleasure and the convenience. Here, I suspect most people think that cyclists are either mad or poor. One of my greatest thrills was to launch a national cycle strategy just before I left the department. It was an all-party affair, enthusiastically received up and down the country by transport professionals. I don't claim to have delivered much as yet, but the seeds are sown. I also made the nation a solemn promise: Lycra will never touch my body. It is a promise I have had no difficulty in keeping. I don't want cyclists to feel they have to dress up like the Tour de France before they set off. When I cycle, which I have even been known to do without a camera in attendance, I invariably do so in my jacket and tie. Cynics only have to visit York where the local council have gone out of their way to bring in an imaginative cycle strategy that has induced a great many more people onto two wheels than elsewhere in Britain. It can be done.

Cycling was not the only form of transport we had ignored.

Like most modern cities, traffic planners had too often over-looked making walking easy. This sounds an odd proposition on first hearing, redolent of a famous John Cleese sketch, but all of those barriers ostensibly designed for our protection, those complex road junctions and urban clearways – even those dank underpasses which are so prevalent in our cities – all show how planners have seen the pedestrian as a second-class citizen. Yet we are all pedestrians. If we can plan our city centres to make walking not only easier but more attractive, there again, there are tremendous gains to be made. It saddens me that in central London, apart from Covent Garden, Leicester Square and a small area around Carnaby Street, there is virtually no pedes-trianisation. We should be much more imaginative about ridding whole areas of London of the car. Richard Rogers has long suggested taking cars out of Trafalgar Square. Norman Foster has a scheme to remove them from Horseguards Parade (although he spoiled it by proposing underground car parks). I would add the idea of taking all cars out of Soho. There would be squeals of complaint at first, but once the scheme was in place, Soho would be massively improved, and every cafe, bar, restaurant, strip joint and bookshop would be the better for it. Again, there are plenty of precedents, and in nearly every case, the proposals were resisted through fear of the unknown.

Making London a more liveable city is, and to some extent has to be, a never-ending task. Certainly, a city without bustle, noise, and yes, some fumes and congestion, would be a dull place indeed. But several billions still need to be spent to improve the Underground and produce what Denis Tunnicliffe has described as a 'Decently Modern Metro'. We need to build not just the Jubilee Line, but ThamesLink 2000, the Channel Tunnel Rail Link, Crossrail and the new Chelsea-Hackney Line at least. We do need to complete some vital road schemes. We do need to put much more into improving the buses and using better traffic management systems. All of that remains undone, and it is deeply frustrating that a small-minded Treasury seem determined to undermine our best efforts. As Allen Sheppard, the Chairman of London First, remarked to the Cabinet Sub-Committee, 'It is just that we don't think you're taking us seriously.' I fear that is an all too valid criticism from business. We must invest in our capital city, not just for the sake of Londoners, but for the country as a whole. Very few business executives arriving at a potential factory location in Middles-brough, Mansfield or Merioneth arrive without first staying a night or two in London. Get London right, and the rest of the country benefits. Allow London to decline, and we will all feel the loss.

I have often been asked whether I believe that London should replace the old GLC. The stock answer from Conservative Ministers has always been that there was no value in an extra layer of bureaucracy and that argument is still valid. But I suspect that those who argue for a more powerful voice for London simply want the message about the need to invest in the capital to be heard more widely, and acted upon. I am convinced that London does need such a voice. Certainly not a GLC mark two, not even the Labour Party would countenance that. I favour instead the idea of a Chief Executive elected for a five year term on a non-party-political basis working in conjunction with a supervisory board of no more than a dozen chosen from all the present thirty-three boroughs, with tightly defined functions and a relatively small budget but with a clear mandate to take strategic decisions across the city, and above all, to articulate the case for London. I have said on more than one occasion that if any government in the future is prepared to contemplate such a body, I would most certainly be a candidate for the job.

15

Too Much Too Soon

Life as a Minister was certainly fun. It is enormously hard work but my private office were brilliantly supportive, the officials I worked with were interesting and entertaining, and the issues were ones that people actually cared about. You can't ask much more from a job than that. Unfortunately, as I learned to my cost, life in what is euphemistically known as the 'public eye' can have its less agreeable moments too. Just about the worst in my life started innocuously enough. On Thursday, 30 September 1993, Nigel Dempster led his *Daily Mail* column with a typical Dempster piece.

'Government Transport Minister, Steven Norris, 48, I can reveal, is living apart from his wife of 24 years, Admiral's daughter, Vicky Cecil-Gibson, and has found companionship with Jennifer Sharp, the Promotions Director of Harpers and Queen magazine. Oxford graduate Jennifer, 40, has known the MP for Epping Forest for nearly 20 years, but has become close to him in the past five months – after his wife moved out of his constituency to the west country with their sons, Anthony, 19, and eight-year-old Edward. Last night Norris, who lost his Oxford East seat in the 1987 general election and was then returned to Parliament in a December 1988 by-election, said 'Poor old Jennifer. She is a friend, but I do not know how she got embroiled in it all. I shall be going about my normal business.' Blue-stocking Jennifer, whose marriage to artist David Sharp was dissolved eleven years ago, ended a ten-year-old relationship with *Vogue* travel writer Andrew Powell earlier this year. Before joining H & Q in 1982 she helped Tina Brown launch *Tatler* magazine in 1979, and formerly worked as the membership secretary of Mortons, the exclusive Berkeley Square Club. She has told friends 'We are not living together. I have my flat in Kensington and Steven, who is an honourable, decent, and hardworking man, has a home near the House of Commons. What happened to his marriage has absolutely nothing to do with me.' A self-made millionaire who prospered in the car business, Norris married the daughter of Rear-Admiral Peter Cecil-Gibson in 1969. He was educated at the same Liverpool School as Paul McCartney and George Harrison, and graduated from Worcester College, Oxford. In 1991, before he was promoted to the Government, he was reported to be involved with Sheila Gunn, a political reporter for *The Times*. He had been spotted at Miss Gunn's farmhouse in Sussex, and she was also seen visiting Norris' London mews house. Vicky is said to be considering her options, and divorce has not been ruled out.'

By the standards of Fleet Street, the piece was a model. In just over three hundred words, the hacks managed one Government Minister, a Rear-Admiral, two Oxford graduates, three glossy magazines, four journalists, an artist, two pop mega-stars, and a rival national newspaper, not to mention a Sussex farmhouse, a London mews, a Berkeley Square night-club, a flat in Kensington and a vague reference to a west country home. As an object lesson in how to write a gossip column, it rated straight A's. For the next ten days, the subsequent story filled many a tabloid page. I shall tell the story of the events of that week later but it is first necessary to sketch the background that had led to the piece appearing in the first place. It is not a particularly lurid story. Indeed, in many respects it is depressingly familiar; I have been astonished at how many people have told me their own, very similar tale. It is not a story I am particularly proud of, nor one for which I have ever felt the need to apologise. There may be those who would criticise me for that. So be it. It is, I suppose, most of all the story of one man's human frailty and mistakes, and the impact they had on those closest and dearest to him. It is a sad story in some ways, but not tragic. It has moments of exquisite pleasure and happiness too. It is not a shocking tale other than to those of an extraordinarily nervous disposition, and the reader may conclude that it would not even be newsworthy were the central character not a Government Minister. I make no complaint about that. Politicians can hardly spend half their time courting the attentions of the press only to spend the other half complaining when those attentions are occasionally inconvenient.

It is platitudinous to say I married young. I was twenty-four, and Vicky was twenty-one. I married for love. No one in their right mind does anything else. Like most young men, I was emotionally immature and, in my case I suspect, insecure too. The late sixties may have been 'swinging', but in the days before the pill was routinely available, and in what was then a markedly different climate, people did not tend to live together before they were married. Everything began well enough for us, with a grand wedding, a comfortable flat in Notting Hill, and an easy lifestyle. Unfortunately within a year or so I was in Bournemouth with Ronnie Hoare, living from Monday to Friday in a hotel and later in a small flat, whilst Vicky was studying at Goldsmith's College in east London for her post-graduate teachers certificate. By the time she moved to Bournemouth, I was on my way to Liverpool where I lived with my mother. When Vicky arrived in Liverpool, we had some time together, but it was not long before I was off to Berkshire. That sort of absence would have put a strain on any relationship, but in my case it was combined with my finding all of my horizons opening wider and wider by the day. I was changing. In some ways I was achieving more than I had ever imagined possible and as that happened and my horizons broadened so I suppose I was impatient in other ways too. Marriage became a prison, and the more I shook the bars of the cell, the stronger they became. When I met Clare Marx in 1978, I was quite able to convince myself that I wanted something more from a marriage. It matters not what that something was, and I have long since given up trying to rationalise beyond Oscar Wilde's own confession that 'I can resist everything except temptation'.

Shortly after meeting Clare, I effectively began to lead two lives. It was certainly no fault of Vicky's. She was constant in her love, and deserved better from me. I lived in outward respectability with Vicky at weekends, and tried as far as I could to be a good father to Tony, who had been born in 1974. During the week, however, I lived with Clare as much as I could. She had qualified as a doctor a couple of years earlier and was specialising in orthopaedics. She was brilliantly good at her job and destined for great things. I kidded myself and her that Vicky and I would part, but however long our relationship continued, and even though Vicky was aware of Clare's existence, I was never able to bring myself to do the deed.

I have never been able to take tough decisions about those to whom I am closest, although I am sure that I have managed to hurt most of them more than I ought as a result. I always look to others to make those decisions for me. They eventually do, of course, but only after the most awful and unnecessary heartache. When Clare eventually became convinced that I was never going to leave, she took matters into her own hands. It is a tribute to her unfailing generosity of spirit that we parted amicably.

At that point in my life I really ought to have had the good sense to put all the complications behind me and concentrate on my family, but a dreadful restlessness, a constant obsession with wanting more, drove me on to repeat all my mistakes again. In 1986 I met Lynn Taylor in Salisbury. She was divorced and living in her own small house in a village not far away. I was rich by any standards and Lynn certainly enjoyed the good life. We ate well, travelled frequently and had a great time. Again, Vicky was aware if not approving of the arrangement, which I never went to any great lengths to conceal. In my defence I can only say that in a strange way this odd menage worked for me. I had my cake and ate it. I avoided the mess of divorce yet enjoyed the advantage of a new life. It is easy with hindsight to see how wrong I was, and how inevitable it was that the whole business would end in tears, but at the time none of that seemed important. Sufficient unto the day is the evil thereof.

Much later Lynn made a great deal of the idea that I had proposed marriage to her and given her a ring. I did indeed buy her a ring at one point, but only in response to a constant stream of badgering and certainly without ever having imagined that it would be interpreted in the way that it was. No doubt that was my naïvety, but I found it a bit hard to take when she alone of all the people in my life decided to pay off her mortgage by selling her story to that fearless investigator and fine upholder of morality, the *News of the World*. What was true, however, and I ought to be straight about it if there is any purpose in this account of my life, is that I did indeed talk to her about marriage after I had been divorced from Vicky. I believed what I said at the time, and to the extent that I had some years previously said the same thing to Clare, neither can I deny that I made the same mistake twice. In reality, however, this story had a slightly different ending. When I was back in the Commons in 1989, Lynn and I tended to see much less of each other and I had also come to doubt whether she was actually the person I wanted to spend the rest of my life with. Sometimes relationships which start well enough and are intensely enjoyable for a time simply don't work in the long term and as far as I was concerned, this was one of them. When I finished with Lynn it was because I, rather than she, wanted to. Perhaps that is why she has since seen me as fair game. I make no complaint about that.

At Westminster I had met Sheila Gunn, who was a lobby journalist for *The Times*. I had known her since Oxford East days and she had been a visitor to my by-election, but we became much more seriously involved from 1989 onwards, and as I have already told, were done over by the *People* for our pains. Sheila was the one person who convinced me that I simply could not go on living two lives and that I had to choose. Edward had been born in 1985 and he was as dear to me as Tony. I was worried and frightened by the idea of leaving them as much as Vicky, whom I could never bring myself to dislike for an instant. But I could see that not least, I had simply let too much water flow under the bridge, I had caused too much damage to that relationship for me to contemplate restoring it, and reluctantly or otherwise, I knew Sheila was right. Even then, I constantly prevaricated. There was always a good reason why today was not the right time, and it drove Sheila to distraction.

By April of 1992, she and I had reluctantly concluded that we were simply going to cause each other too much pain as long as there was no more tangible evidence of my actually having taken a decisive step. We drifted apart from each other in that we no longer lived together, although we saw each other often enough. I confess to feeling relief at having the pressure of a deadline removed, but Sheila's mark was indelible. I knew that she was right about my relationship with Vicky, however much I might have wished otherwise.

I met Emma Courtney in June of 1992, in the Commons where she worked as a secretary for my colleague, Henry Bellingham. She is very beautiful and much younger than I, but it was not that which attracted me. More important was that she was kind, gentle and understanding just at the time when those qualities were right at the top of my list of emotional demands.

She was a haven in what was then an entirely private storm, but just as painful for all that. I became to rely on her more and more, especially after Sheila had written to me in August of 1993, finally breaking off our relationship in no uncertain terms. She had learned that I had been to see Vicky and the boys during their summer holiday in Northumberland and was convinced that was the final evidence that I was not serious about ever leaving the marriage. Ironically she was wrong, because I had told Vicky some months earlier of my firm intention and we had agreed that when Edward started at his prep school in Berkshire she would move with him and find a house of her own. She was lucky to find a beautiful house in our old village of Hampstead Norris and that, at least, perhaps took some of the pain away.

I don't mind admitting that during that time I was even more emotionally unstable than usual. So many pressures seemed to be crowding in on me and nothing ever seemed to be easy. Every way I turned complications loomed, and all of them my fault and of my own making. I have never quite understood why I have so easily been able to dispose of business or political arguments, earning a reputation along the way as a pugnacious, blunt negotiator, yet been incapable of even the most straightforward decisions in my own life when they involve painful consequences. I know it all revolves around an obsession with being liked, and a consequent inability ever to say no. I cannot bear to see people in distress and I constantly internalise my own worries and fears. The people who have worked with me over thirty years will tell you that they have never seen me have a bad day. I am pathologically incapable of being rude, and I have a smile for everyone. It is often portrayed as a great asset. Perhaps it is, but I ought to admit that it is actually the more pleasant manifestation of a deep personal insecurity.

Finally into this minefield and quite unsuspecting came the person of my old friend Jennifer Sharp. Jenny and I had known each other for decades and I had always been utterly captivated by her enormously attractive personality and good looks. We had been out together a few times when the article appeared. On one occasion as we walked near Westminster a single photographer suddenly emerged, took a single flash photograph and then disappeared as quickly. I thought nothing of it at the time, except to wonder what on earth was of interest in a perfectly

205

normal photograph of two people walking openly down a London street, but I suppose as it accompanied the *Mail* article it might just have been taken by someone who was aware of our friendship, and had decided to take the usual tip-off fee of £50 from a diary. In any event, our scene is finally set: Vicky, by now living in Hampstead Norris, Clare somewhere in Suffolk, Lynn in Wiltshire, Sheila in the press gallery, Emma at the House of Commons and Jennifer, all about to find themselves embroiled in ten days of unpleasant, and in most cases wholly unwelcome intrusion into what they might well have been justified as regarding as their own private lives. In the next chapter I tell the story of the ten days which followed in more detail, from which it is perhaps fair to conclude that Lynn might not have been entirely averse to participating, but none of the others concerned either consented to, or enjoyed any of the press attention.

People like me can not only handle ourselves, but court publicity as part of our job. We should take whatever is thrown at us without complaint, and if stories are factually wrong, we have generous libel laws of which to avail ourselves. If a privacy law is justified, then it should not be for the protection of the super-rich or the famous. Those who are the most vulnerable to unwelcome harassment are those who make no claim on public attention, yet find themselves the helpless object of a cynical, ruthless and unpleasant aspect of journalism which cannot, in my opinion, ever be justified.

16

Never Complain, Never Explain

The story of how this mundane domestic drama with its pathetic anti-hero unfolded in the press is a tale in itself. Much of what was written was true – certainly enough to dissuade any sane individual from legal action – and some of it was not. There were lacings of pure invention, a dash of hyperbole and conjecture, all seasoned with a heavy dollop of prurience – the kind of dish we are told the British so much enjoy. I actually doubt that prurience is a uniquely British characteristic. All over the world people love to peer into the intimate details of others' lives, and the more tangled and complex those lives are, the better. The objects of their attention do not have to be famous, although celebrity undoubtedly helps. They do not have to be glamorous, although that too is useful. Lashings of intrigue, duplicity, passion, revenge or distress are what make a tasty dish to serve the waiting punters. Here, at least, good news is no news. The only good news for a newspaper editor is bad news.

As I explained in the Prologue, the day before the *Daily Mail* story I was meeting with Paul Condon, the Commissioner of the Metropolitan Police, at his office in Scotland Yard, and heard from John Nicholls, my private secretary, that the *Mail* had been on to our press office and were going to run a piece about my friendship with Jennifer. In traditional Fleet Street style they were inviting me to comment. I put the phone down calmly enough. The story was hardly shocking, nor indeed was there much to say. I could not, in all honesty, see what was remotely newsworthy. Even so, I thought it might just be worth trying to kill off the story and rang the proffered number. I kept my comments brief, and as they faithfully recorded, gave a very good impression of not being greatly concerned. And that is where the whole matter might have begun and ended were it not for what happened that Thursday, when Sheila Gunn read the diary piece. Although Sheila had ended our relationship in uncompromising terms, she clearly felt that I had been wrong to have had a relationship with Jennifer so soon after. Even now, I think it was she who had the wrong end of the stick, but logic is never centre-stage in affairs of the heart. Although a journalist herself, she took it all at face value and was upset. She was in the Press Gallery at the House, when she encountered Simon Walters of the *Sun* and Peter Hooley of the *Daily Express*, who both knew of our affair and, listening to her, immediately smelled the chance of a good story. Next day both papers ran with the revelation of a second mistress. When Sheila added for good measure, 'He has not behaved in an honourable or honest way', they knew they had struck gold. There was more of the same on Saturday, together with the first mention of a link with a House of Commons secretary, as yet unnamed.

Right from the outset, I had rung Emma, who was wonderfully understanding and supportive, and then Vicky to let her know what was going on. I also rang Tricia, my constituency secretary, and my constituency chairman, Peter Ashton. Vicky was predictably unhappy, but none of the story was particularly new to her. She simply blamed me for having given the press the chance to write the story in the first place, and also for the unwelcome attention she was already beginning to suffer. Peter was extremely good about it all. He is about my age, and as I was later to discover, he took the same view as the overwhelming majority of people both in and outside Epping Forest. He believed that my private life was my own affair, and that what mattered was whether I was doing my job properly as a Member of Parliament. Over the whole of the ten day period he was a great support and of course he killed any talk of censure from my local party stone dead. I also alerted John MacGregor, who could not have been kinder or more loyal, and Richard Ryder who was also encouragingly robust. Meanwhile, however, Adrian Lithgow, a political reporter on the *Mail on Sunday*, knew of my link to Emma. He did not have to stretch himself to discover the details, because he had been with a group of us including Caroline Edmondson, Emma and several other friends on many occasions. Here again, I had never seen the need to be furtive when as far as I was concerned, it was not only my own business, but unlikely to be of any interest to anyone but those directly involved. On that at least I proved spectacularly misguided. On Sunday, 3 October the *Mail on Sunday* duly revealed Mistress Number Three, and the following day some of the dailies carried her picture. By now some of the brighter hacks had started to realise there was nothing serious likely to emerge from the story beyond a good breakfast letch. Richard Littlejohn headed a brilliantly funny piece in the *Sun* ' 'Ello, Steve, got a new mistress?' Even I could see the funny side of that.

Since Lynn and I had parted we had kept in touch by telephone on odd occasions. Indeed, not long previously she had rung to ask if I would show her and a friend around Westminster, and I had happily agreed. We had a perfectly pleasant meeting at the end of which we parted as amicably as ever. By now I was sure that the tabloids would be searching hard for any other name they could get, so I thought it might be worth ringing her just to ask her to be discreet. Unfortunately, I was several hours too late. The *Sun* and the *News of the World* had beaten me to it and both had opened their cheque books. Lynn was not rich in her own right, and was not having an easy time on the job front. The prospect of many thousands of pounds for her version of these events, which I am sure she rationalised were now rapidly coming into the public domain anyway, was obviously irresistibly tempting. On Tuesday the *Sun* duly delivered Mistress Number Four.

By a stroke of fate that first week of October was also the week of the Party Conference which that year was due to feature the Transport debate just before lunch on Tuesday. Some weeks previously I had agreed to have dinner with Simon Walters, Trevor Kavanagh, the political editor, and one or two lads from the *Sun* at a hotel at Blackpool on the Monday evening and I was in any event due to be on the platform for the debate. There was no question in my mind of ducking either the debate or, for that matter, the dinner. As dozens of colleagues rang with their support I felt I owed it to them to press on. The whips in particular were still smarting over the demise of David Mellor, whom they saw as a victim of a newspaper vendetta, and the Tory hierarchy was in no mood to allow the press to dispose of another victim. I was also hugely reassured by Downing Street's only comment during the whole business. A two-line statement merely noted, 'It is well known that Steven Norris is separated, and his private life is his own affair.' No. 10 made no further public comment. I said a silent prayer of thanks to John Major for that, as I have done on many occasions since. His instinctive unwillingness to be censorious about colleagues is one of his most attractive characteristics.

So I was clear, as I contemplated my dinner engagement, that I was going to hold my ground as long as I could, not only because I believed that I had done nothing to justify resignation, but also because I too was not willing to let the tabloids select the Government rather than the Prime Minister. That may sound pompous, but if so, I spelled it out to both John MacGregor and the Chief Whip that my resignation was available at any point, present or future, if it were thought necessary, without fuss, complaint or bitterness. Had I been obliged to walk the plank, I would not have blamed either them or the party, but then as now, I regarded it as wholly unnecessary. I resolved to go to the dinner, attend the debate and then, in order to save the party and more importantly myself any further embarrassment, immediately return to London. I packed my overnight bag and went off to Blackpool by car where at least I could enjoy the privacy which I was so infamously later to extol.

During the long journey my phone never stopped. Elizabeth Buchanan, Cecil Parkinson's former special advisor and now with Tim Bell, rang to offer a helping hand. I knew she meant it, even though she was formidably busy as one of Margaret Thatcher's closest aides, and I was enormously grateful. She assured me that Tim, too, had offered to pitch in where necessary. We talked through how I felt, and how best to play the conference. I had taken a decision early on that there was no merit in talking to the press, and had rigidly adhered to that self-imposed rule even to the extent of occasionally simply replacing the receiver soundlessly when a freelance hack managed to get through. It seemed to me that anything I said would simply pour petrol on the flames. Any attempt at explanation would only provoke more questions. As Dennis Healey once remarked, when in a hole, stop digging. We agreed that it was the only sane policy and it was one I followed to the end. Other colleagues rang to cheer me up, stiffen my backbone and generally rail against the unpleasantness of it all. Every single one who did earned my undying gratitude. At times like that you are as alone as you will ever be in your whole life, and it is then that you need your real friends and learn very rapidly who those real friends are. Tricia Gurnett, for example, was absolutely magnificent in holding off the press at the constituency end. Since my business collapsed she had offered help with my workload when I could no longer afford Caroline and she was quite superb in stonewalling, offering helpful comments to the local media and generally guarding my back. She too earned a brownie point and a place in my personal Valhalla that week.

The meal with the *Sun* boys began by their firing all sorts of personal questions at me to which I was as noncommittal as I could be. I reminded them of what I considered to be my own business and none of theirs without losing my patience. The only point when my guard dropped was when Trevor Kavanagh put to me this odd notion which Lynn had apparently been peddling that I had proposed marriage to her accompanied by the much-fabled ring. The whole notion had an almost bigamous flavour to it and for once I saw red. I told him in no uncertain terms that I just did not accept her account of what had gone on between us and told him why. Despite the dinner being officially 'off the record', it gave him the headline he was looking for to fill the next day's paper. But I was determined to enjoy my dinner regardless. I had known Simon and Trevor for many years and I could understand that they were simply doing their job. They might even have been more embarrassed than I at having to ask their mildly salacious and obviously intrusive questions – they at least had the good grace to look embarrassed.

After an hour or so their line of inquiry was exhausted and the conversation turned to something I was genuinely interested in: how to deal with crime in the inner-cities. *Sun* journalists have a predictably right-wing punishment-centred view of these things and it was one that I passionately disagreed with. For the next hour or so I harangued them about Crime Concern's work and how strongly I felt about the need for prevention rather than conviction. They joined in what proved to be a vigorous debate and we went on late into the night. We parted as amicably as usual if not entirely sober, and as I walked back to my seaside digs, I knew I was right to have gone. Whether or not I survived politically, I had shown them I would not be beaten personally.

The next morning I walked along the dull, windy promenade at Blackpool feeling desperately self-conscious. At moments like those you imagine that the eyes of the world are upon you when in fact, of course, most people have no idea who you are, and even fewer care. Just at that moment, fate lent a friendly hand. As I was trying hard to appear nonchalant, I came across Sir Geoffrey Leigh and his wife Sylvia who were also on their way to the conference hall. I had known them both since we met at a weekend house party of Ken Baker's at Dorney Wood when Ken had the use of that beautiful Buckinghamshire government house during his time as Home Secretary. Geoffrey and I had proved a lethal combination at snooker, and I had enjoyed their company on several occasions since. It was an acid test. Would they cut me dead, or greet me as before?

I need not have worried; they could not have been more friendly. With an arm round my shoulder, they told me that I was walking the rest of the way with them. I cannot possibly convey how important that simple gesture was to me. I was obviously not looking forward to the rest of the morning, although thankfully, I had no speaking part. Nonetheless, even looking relaxed can be difficult when you know that the cameras are only there for the one second that you allow your guard to drop, and I needed to screw up every ounce of resolve before braving the Winter Gardens. With Geoffrey and Sylvia's support I made it inside and, thank goodness, everyone who met me was just as warm and sympathetic. When I went backstage towards the end of the previous debate John MacGregor, and my fellow Junior Ministers Roger Freeman, Malcolm Caithness and Robert Key knew I was under pressure and in a few words they, and John's special advisor, Eleanor Laing, put me at ease. There was no effusion, no grand gestures; that would not have been their style, but there was constant reassurance by gesture, body language, call it what you will.

As the sound of applause indicated the end of the previous debate, we went onto the platform and into the glare of the television lights. Immediately, the cameras started popping – mainly in my direction. Remembering Alan Durband's advice from my Institute days about acting, I determined to make myself relax and chatted as amiably as I could to Malcolm. The speeches from the floor were as dreadful as they always are at a Tory conference, and then John began his wind up. Every platform speech begins with the Secretary of State thanking his ministers, and John made a point of including me as warmly as the others in his own praise. He wisely included us all in a single sentence, so that when the audience applauded, we could each assume that at least part of the approbation was directed at us. I cannot remember a word of what John said. My mind was on one thing and one thing only. I had to look relaxed. I knew I must never frown. My appearance is fairly unprepossessing at the best of times, and I can often look less happy than I feel when my crumpled, rather jowley face is in repose, so I determined to look bright, cheerful and interested. I gazed, Nancy Reagan-like, directly at John trying desperately not to glance at the photographers or anywhere else in the audience. Mercifully, it was soon all over and, having applauded John warmly, we left the platform.

One or two journalists tried to buttonhole me as I came down the narrow platform steps but I refused to say a word. My only thought now was to get out of the building and away from the Conference as quickly as possible. Friends ushered me to the back of the hall where I hoped to make my way out unseen. Unfortunately, a couple of hacks followed me and started firing off questions whilst I looked around desperately for a promised taxi that had failed to materialise. 'How do you feel about these revelations, Mr Norris?' 'Why are you not resigning, Mr Norris?' 'Mr Norris, what have you got to say about the allegation that you promised marriage to several women?' And so on. It was all desperately predictable, and I was having none of it. I literally stood silent without uttering a word until thankfully, one of my pals hailed a passing cab and I clambered in. As we drove away, I can remember distinctly the feeling that at least now the worst had passed. Whatever else I had to do, or the newspapers chose to print, at least I now had my privacy. And by an extraordinary stroke of luck, I was due to leave Britain on Saturday for Hong Kong and Singapore, where Nick Montagu and I had long ago planned to see the bus and Metro systems, and talk generally about public transport to the two Governments.

On the way back from Blackpool I called in at my parents' home. They had known of my unhappiness, although I had never exposed them to the gory details. I felt I owed it to them to show them that I was holding up, that there was nothing to worry about, and that the wilder elements of some of the stories were untrue. They were as loving and supportive as only parents can be, and I felt much better for the visit. Any person who manages to reach their half-century with both of their parents around to enjoy the occasion should count themselves fortunate. I know I do. Returning to London I was determined to carry on with business as usual.

That week, as it turned out, was the high water mark of the press hysteria. The *Sun* triumphantly flourished poor Clare as Mistress Number Five. The *Daily Mail* produced a double page spread with pictures of the girls including Vicky, and the usual utter hypocrisy from hacks told to produce two hundred craven words on ministerial infidelity. The *Sun* cartoon, 'Do you want the small size condoms, the medium size or the Steve Norris?' was par for the course. Tony Banks couldn't resist a line either. 'That's the trouble with mistresses. None for years and then five turn up together.'

Even so, Martin Helm, the Department's chief press officer, told me he believed the worst was over. 'Stay quiet, out of sight as much as possible, but when you are seen, for God's sake, look normal and smile.' It was, as always, good advice. 'Never complain, never explain' was alleged to be Margaret's watchword. It stood me in good stead. Martin and his team in our press office kept stray journalists at bay and allowed me time to breathe. All of them, particularly my own press officer, David Stewart, turned in star performances. At home, I discovered the value of an answering machine, and simply ignored any calls I didn't recognize.

The only headline that truly annoyed me throughout the whole week was on the front page of the deservedly defunct and, as far as I am concerned, totally unlamented *Today*. Their political editor had apparently been talking to my old friend Mrs Currie. 'Political editor of *Today*' is as much oxymoron as 'humble backbencher', but even by their standards this was outrageous stuff. 'Minister tried to seduce me' was their screamer of a front-page headline. I simply could not believe it. Edwina had chosen that moment to retell our distant history as if I had pushed her up against the wall of the division lobby only the week before. It was as close as I ever came to anger. Whatever else Edwina is, she is not stupid, and she must have known the damage that her contribution was likely to cause. I could not help thinking that all this might have something to do with her forthcoming and much-heralded smutty novel for which she was desperately trying to drum up publicity. As far as I am concerned, she can produce as much soft porn as she likes. It rather suits her. But dragging a colleague in by way of publicity was a cheap shot. For the record, and rather uncharacteristically in my case, I have never spoken to her since. I simply cannot bring myself to be pleasant to someone who caused such unnecessary damage to a colleague. No doubt this earth-shattering revelation will cause her no distress. She has a hide like a rhinoceros and may even now see the opportunity for a nice spin-off piece in *Cosmopolitan* or *Marie Claire*. I would not put it past her.

Once the frenzy of Wednesday was over, tabloid attention, bereft of new leads, began to flag. On Thursday there were no photographers around when I left home in the morning, nor when I arrived at Marsham Street. Fortunately, Margaret Thatcher was helping to keep me off the front page with the revelations of her own memoirs, widely interpreted as being sceptical of John Major, and which were occupying most of the broadsheets. Incidentally, one of the features of the coverage of my story was that it was almost all confined to the tabloids with the exception of a short piece by the delectable Julie Kirkbride, later revealed as a 'close friend' of MP Stephen Milligan, in the *Daily Telegraph*, recording my leaving Blackpool, and an even sillier inside page item in *The Sunday Times*. No BBC or ITN news bulletin throughout the whole week covered the story either, although there was one short item on the Sky News channel which meant that friends of mine in South Africa knew more of the story than BBC-watching *Times* readers from Loughton. On that Thursday several papers did run the inevitable follow-up pieces. The *Daily Mail* speculated on 'Why Vicky will not divorce'. As neither I nor Vicky had ever spoken to them, they naturally made the whole thing up. It was obviously easier that way. The *Express* commented on my abrupt departure from Blackpool under the headline 'Minister disappears'. Nonetheless, the dailies had clearly begun to lose interest. Despite their best efforts they had not been able to unearth any other useful liaison. The *Mail* had tried rather unconvincingly with Tricia Gurnett, and Caroline Edmondson told me that one or two hacks had sniffed around her too, but even those intrepid sleuths scouring the country for Number Six failed to turn up the glimmer of a story. On Saturday, I breathed a huge sigh of relief and took off from Heathrow with Nick. He brought his usual good nature, and multitudinous greetings from friends in the department, some of whom I scarcely knew, all keen to offer support. We arrived in Singapore where the High Commissioner met us in his magnificent silver Daimler limousine, and whisked us off to his official residence. On Monday, John Nicholls faxed through a *News of the World* double-page spread which Lynn had generously provided. Thankfully, it was fairly innocuous and contained nothing new. A small piece in the *Sunday Mirror* and a couple of paragraphs in *The Sunday Times* were the only other remnants of the story. No one approached me in Singapore, nor when we arrived a few days later in Hong Kong, and for the first time, thanks to Nick's good company, I was able to relax. By the time I got back to Britain at the end of the week, my re-entry at Heathrow did not rate even a solitary freelance. The nightmare was over, and for the moment at least, I had survived.

Although selfishly, survival was my prime concern, others around me were not so fortunate. Vicky suffered the most. Photographers camped at the entrance to her drive for several days. When once I had tried to visit, we left the arrangements until fairly late, and then I spoke to her from my car. Within half an hour reporters miraculously appeared from nowhere. She happened to be using a cordless telephone, and it was obvious that one of the hacks was monitoring her calls. She immediately rang me with the news, and we agreed that it was not sensible for me to plough on. I turned back to London and within twenty minutes, the reporters were gone as quickly as they had arrived. She was rung up at all hours of the day, frequently by the same newspaper, and asked for a statement. She was offered thirty, forty, even fifty thousand pounds for an exclusive by more than one. Despite her refusal they persisted. Apparently the logic of this is that on day one, the aggrieved wife is likely to decline interviews. On day two, she may have second thoughts, and by day three might be open to a tempting offer. On day four she might accept, and bingo! Vicky heroically saw them all off. What was truly unforgivable was that reporters also tracked down her elderly parents who lived locally and pestered them unmercifully. They had nothing to say and were only indirectly involved but one journalist, allegedly from the *Daily Mail*, rang at four o'clock in the morning. My poor mother-in-law was unable to sleep for the rest of the night.

Jennifer too, found a crowd of photographers outside her office. Her solution was simple. She had recently had a rather attractive and much shorter haircut which, combined with a cloche hat, enabled her to enter and leave in front of the noses of the paparazzi without them once realising who she was. Thankfully, they soon lost interest, although they ring her to this day whenever my name is in the news and she is equally unfailingly polite and impenetrably noncommittal.

Emma had retreated to her parents' home in Norfolk, but the local paper and one or two nationals soon had teams outside her door. She too was offered money for her story but refused. Again they refused to take no for an answer. Finally, she agreed to be photographed if they in turn would leave her alone, and sensing that they were unlikely to be offered a better break, her pursuers agreed. Even so, she and her parents were besieged and pestered for several days when they had all made it quite plain from the outset they had nothing to say. Sheila, herself a political journalist and forced to be at Blackpool for the whole of the conference kept a low profile. Most of her colleagues were, in any event, sympathetic and the general feeling was that dog should not eat dog. Lynn I feel less sympathy for. She, at least, had a fat cheque to compensate. She has consistently made herself available for weddings, bar mitzvahs and late night television. As far as I am concerned, she is the one who must look at herself in the mirror each day.

For myself, I was always conscious that I was never in any physical danger, my property and friends were intact, and my job was secure. When I considered for a brief second all the dreadful fates that befall ordinary people and families each day, I know I have nothing to be resentful of, and a great deal to be thankful for. Whatever happened to me, I at least have only myself to blame. I may or may not have deserved the treatment I received. It may or may not have been in what is loosely called the 'public interest' to reveal the sad secrets of a rather solitary life. Turning the actual story into a six-in-a-bed sex-romp was second nature for the hacks and a godsend for the columnists. Like Nick Ridley, albeit in infinitely sillier circumstances, the cartoons probably did as much to implant the whole daft notion in people's minds as yards of tabloid text. All of that is academic now. Once Pandora's box is open, the damage, such as it is, is done. I could be thankful that at the end of it all, whatever other qualities I possessed, I knew that being lucky was far and away the most important.

17

Taking the Tabloids

Of itself, my story was simply not important enough to merit other than the tiniest footnote in British political history. As it transpired, however, it did become a part of those travails of the Major Government generally known as the Back to Basics scandals. I was not the first to be caught up in that net. Indeed, the famous speech itself was only delivered on the Friday after my conference appearance, and when the Norris story had all but subsided. Ironically, at the time it never struck the press to portray John's message as a call for a return to Victorian standards of prim public morality. The speech was a straightforward appeal to put aside those peripheral policy issues which so obsess the media on every issue, and return to the basic arguments beneath. On education, for example, John made the point that whilst the education press was full of fashionable contemporary education jargon, sneering at what was seen as blinkered and unimaginative learning by rote, what parents actually wanted was a return to quality teaching and high output. Whilst much of the debate on the health service raged around management and fundholdings, what patients wanted was a high quality service available where required, and provided on the basis of need rather than means. The subsequent revisionism which sought to distort John's words was only part of a continuous campaign of denigration which has dogged him almost from the first days of his premiership. For the Simon Heffers and Charles Moores of this world, Major has committed the ultimate crime of not being Margaret Thatcher, and will never be forgiven for it. The sneering tone of their and their colleagues comments are beneath contempt, although I believe they say more about the journalists than they do about John Major.

History is littered with scandalous stories of Members of

219

Parliament. From Palmerston and his innumerable mistresses through Gladstone whose nocturnal visits to Trafalgar Square to offer moral guidance to fallen women, right up to Profumo, Lambton, and all the others, they would all have given the *Sun* enough to gorge itself on for months in the nineties. What has changed, of course, is the attitude of the press toward publication. These days there are few taboos in Britain about revealing the intimate secrets of the Royal Family, let alone unimportant Junior Ministers. In any event, earlier in 1993 the Heritage Secretary, David Mellor, was revealed as having an affair with an actress, albeit not one that anyone had ever heard of. He had been the victim of hidden microphones picking up private conversations, but that did not seem to worry the newspapers who loved every prurient detail. At the time, and undoubtedly because he was much senior to me, he came in for significantly worse treatment than I ever endured. Part of that might have been because he was, ostensibly at least, happily married, whereas my circumstances were at least privately well known to the press. Even so, thanks to John Major's support, he looked as if he was about to survive when the press landed a fatal counterpunch. He had apparently enjoyed the hospitality of an Arab couple who had invited him and his family for a lavish foreign holiday. Despite the fact that the two families were already friends, the feeling was that David had committed at least the fatal sin of omitting to declare the hospitality at the time. He had also been a Foreign Office Minister, although the idea that his own views on the relationship between the Arabs and Israel were influenced by his holiday is faintly preposterous. Nonetheless, he was fatally weakened and obliged to resign.

If he felt sore, then others were just as angry. In particular, the whips felt that the press had bounced them into the resignation and were determined not to allow the press another sacrifice. When my own story broke, they were all determined that I was not going to be thrown to the wolves. They saw me as the sort of personality that could see them off, and to that extent at least, they were right. When the story faded from the headlines and normality resumed with the new parliamentary session, the party generally could see my survival as a collective success.

Unfortunately, that optimism was not to last. Hardly a month after I had faded from the news pages, Tim Yeo's was there in large type. His crime was to have fathered a child by a Tory councillor. Despite his wife standing loyally by him, he did not have, as I did, a helpful constituency association. One of his branch chairwomen, who was Mayor of a local town, clearly enjoying her fifteen minutes of fame, insisted on appearing on television wearing her Mayoral chain to condemn him. In the days that followed, his association decided that whilst, paradoxically, they would not seek to deselect him, they thought the Prime Minister should think again about his position as a Minister of State at Environment.

Tim was a competent and popular Minister and there was no suggestion that his personal arrangements made him unfit to perform his duties, especially since it was clear that he had come to an amicable arrangement with the mother of his child and indeed his wife, Diane. This, however, was a wonderfully juicy bone for the press to chew on and they were intent on making a meal of it. Andrew Mackay, the pairing whip who was a good mutual friend, rang me to suggest that I might give Tim the dubious benefit of my own experience. In all honesty, there was not a great deal to say except to advise Tim in the strongest terms I could think of never to explain and never to complain. I also told him to talk to as many people in his local association as he could, and to stay on as friendly terms as possible with the journalists. I have always liked Tim, and I desperately wanted him to survive. He listened to me politely enough, but even as I spoke, I was not sure he was actually listening all that attentively. I suspect he had called me because Andrew had asked him to, rather than on his own initiative, and that he was heavily distracted. I still do not know what possessed him to give any fodder to the journalists, never mind making formal statements, but he did. He also took Diane with him to his constituency meeting and there were several occasions when they were photographed together. She looked understandably tired and strained. I am sure she earned a huge amount of respect and sympathy for the dignity with which she carried herself but unfortunately, it rebounded badly on Tim, accentuating her misery with the underlying message that it was he who was at fault. Within a few days, the hacks had won their second scalp when Tim agreed with the Prime Minister that he should resign.

Thereafter, the stories seemed to tumble out endlessly. My good friend, Malcolm Caithness, resigned after his wife shot herself in a state of depression attributed to the relationship he was said to be having with Jan Fitzalan-Howard. Stephen Milligan died in the most bizarre circumstances involving plastic bags, oranges laced with amyl nitrate and ladies tights. By now the press were in full spate and baying for blood at every turn. In a Frankensteinian orgy, they supped on Robert Hughes, Michael Brown and Richard Spring in turn. Even poor old Hartley Booth was caught up. Even though a lowly PPS, he must be the only Member forced to resign for *not* bonking the girl.

Were all these resignations actually inevitable, or could others have acted as I had done and survive? I accept that those in public life cannot say one thing and do another with impunity. It is perfectly legitimate for the public to learn about any alleged discrepancy between what those who seek to represent them are alleged to do in private when that is significantly at variance with what they say or do in public. Nonetheless, there is a dividing line and I am very clear where it lies. If the business is essentially private, if those affected are all consenting adults and if no crime is committed, then I believe that politicians are entitled to be judged and treated like anyone else.

If I ever have a criticism of John Major it is that he takes too much notice of the newspapers. His predecessor never bothered with most of them, and was fed a carefully selected diet by Bernard Ingham. John appears to devour them all and worse, to react accordingly. As one who survived by luck rather than good judgement or merit, I can only comment that when Rod Richards, a Junior Welsh Office Minister, was forced to quit in 1996, the papers, as they always do, ran a list of Those Tory Scandals Again. Significantly, every one of those lists omitted me. This is not because I exercise some particular charm. It was very simply because I did not resign whilst the others did. These days, resignation is not seen as an honourable act by a politican keen to save his party from embarrassment regardless of the truth of allegations made against him. Resignation is now seen as a straightforward admission of guilt.

It is surely sad that that is so. There must be a place in public life for the honourable resignation of a Peter Carrington to whom no personal blame was attached, but just as no one expected Willie Whitelaw to resign when Michael Fagin broke into the Queen's bedroom, and nor were the press serious in suggesting that Ken Baker should go following the Brixton break-out, so we can conclude that the public is not stupid. It can see the difference between what is culpable and what is not. It can also smell a hypocrite a mile away and woe betide the politician who prattles on about family values in his election address if his private life might test those values to breaking point. I am not in favour of a privacy law, but I am in favour of politicians being accorded the same treatment as journalists. If the private lives of their accusers were trumpeted as widely as those of politicians, several Fleet Street papers would be heavily into the recruitment business. Ah yes, they cry, but we do not put ourselves up for election. I believe that argument to be bogus. I was elected to represent my constituents' interests. I have always tried hard to do so with as much success as most of my colleagues. I never moralise, and the only two Biblical quotations I care to quote are 'Judge not that ye be not judged' and 'Let him who is without sin cast the first stone.'

One enterprising national newspaper ran a poll of my constituents during that fateful week in October 1993. 20 per cent of those interviewed thought I was a shit. 20 per cent thought I was a hero. 60 per cent simply couldn't care less. They told their interlocutor that it was none of their business. For me, that says it all.

I survived because I was lucky, and because those around me wanted me to. Officials like Patrick Brown, Nick Montagu, Martin Helm and Simon Whiteley, not to mention John, Karen and Magdalene in my private office, all worked hard for me. John MacGregor, Roger, Malcolm and Robert, my fellow Ministers, the Whips from the Chief down, even the Prime Minister who had no need to do so, all made it possible. All I had to do was shut up. Unaccustomed as I was to such advice, I am eternally grateful that I took it. There was one amusing postscript. Each year the *Spectator* announces its annual parliamentary awards – best speaker, best campaigner, newcomer and so on. In 1993 The *Sun* political team decided to run their own award. I have it on a shelf somewhere. The inscription reads '*Sun* Parliamentary Awards – 1993. For Balls in Adversity – Steve Norris'.

18

Transport of Delight

As anyone who has experienced it will tell you, suffering the unwelcome attentions of the tabloids is rather like having an accident in your car. One minute you are bowling along without a care in the world and the next, disaster strikes and there is glass all over the road. There is no point in trying to replay the tape. The impact has happened, and the damage, such as it is, has been done. All you can do is to extricate yourself, thank your lucky stars for being alive, and get on with the rest of your life.

Once there were no more shock horror revelations, the story died as quickly as it had risen. In a sense, Andy Warhol's dictum about being famous for fifteen minutes is a reassurance. A butterfly has a massive attention span compared to a tabloid newspaper, and a small earthquake in Chile, or in my case, a small earthquake called Thatcher at Blackpool, will soon provide a distraction. In the weeks that followed, when I was determined to put the whole nonsense behind me and get on with my job, I would very occasionally be asked by a young inexperienced reporter for a comment on what they would always delicately refer to as my 'private life'. I simply never played ball, and even that small trickle soon dried.

Now, more than three years after the event, I am amused to find how many people have either forgotten, or never knew about the story in the first place. Popular indifference about Junior Government Ministers can be a blessing in disguise. In any event, that poll in Epping Forest did indeed turn out to be more accurate than I had dared believe. There were a few vocal complainants in Epping Forest, but they were hugely outnumbered – literally eight to one – by the people, many of whom I had never met, who wrote to offer their support: to tell me they thought I had done a good job for them, and to reassure me that they believed my private life was my own affair. All of that is enormously welcome when you are feeling low, and it did a great deal to restore my faith in human nature. Newspapers go bust unless they give their readers what they want, so I have to assume that some readers enjoy a bonk before breakfast. No doubt they do, but it is nice to know that they are quite capable of recognising fact from fiction.

Back at the Marsham Street ranch, I was pressing on with developing a coherent strategy for transport in London. It was helpful that most of what I was planning was not politically contentious. There may be a Marxist-Leninist view of traffic management, but I have yet to hear of it. Nor am I greatly impressed with the Adam Smith view, which I assume would mean switching off all traffic lights and letting market forces rule. As far as I was concerned, allowing people to move around efficiently and quickly in a way that also improved the quality of the environment and reduced the effect of traffic on the rest of the population was a practical and strategic challenge rather than a philosophical one. That is not to say that everyone shared the same priorities, but I worked hard to draw together as many of the politicians, environmentalists, planners and transport professionals as I could in a consensus about what needed to be done. I constantly stressed that of the £2 billion which the department spent in London, three quarters was spent on public transport and only a quarter on roads. I had no difficulty with the notion that improving public transport options was my biggest single priority, and that given that most Londoners rejected massive road-building wherever it was proposed, our work there should concentrate on managing the network more efficiently, as our red route programme was doing, and developing technical solutions based on computerised management techniques to make the city flow more efficiently. Not many people know this, as a well-known Eastender who did a bit in films once remarked, but the London traffic light management system, imaginatively known as SCOOT, is actually the best of its kind in the world. The governors of Sao Paulo and Bangkok both came to see it, and following a visit I made to Tokyo, the authorities there are now actively interested in transplanting our techniques.

I knew from the outset that the two qualities most needed in a Minister for Transport in London were broad shoulders and a sense of humour. Londoners grumble about delays on the tube or congestion on the roads, just as do New Yorkers, Parisiens or Berliners. It took the Foreign Press Association to remind me just how good the system actually is. I spoke to them at their elegant home in Carlton Gardens where I had laid out my plans for the capital. When the time came for questions, I expected the usual diatribe which generally held me responsible for every late train and every leaf on the line. 'I don't know what you're complaining about,' was the first response: 'it's brilliant here. The buses run everywhere, the tubes feel safe, your taxi drivers are the best in the world, and there is more room for parking in this city than in practically any outside the United States.' I was gently reminded that it was Tokyo, not London, where people are employed to push commuters on to trains during the morning rush. It was Paris, not London, where although the central area is brilliant, some of the outlying Metro lines experience horrendous levels of crime. Londoners are prone to believe that they are the only people in the world who suffer on the way to work. Anyone who reads the annual report of the RATP Passengers' Committee, the Paris equivalent, will be highly amused at the reference to unintelligible announcements, constant service disruptions and slow or dirty trains that fail to meet buses which in any event arrive three at a time.

The truth is that London is well served by its public transport system, particularly the massive bus network which is the most comprehensive of any major city anywhere in the world. But it is also a system that continues to need vast resources if it is to serve the needs of the population.

When the 1994 reshuffle came around, it was clear to his colleagues that John MacGregor would take the opportunity to stand down. Being John, he played his cards close to his chest. Not for nothing was he a member of the Magic Circle. But I talked to Eleanor Laing, his special advisor who was closer to him than anyone else in the department and whilst she, in true diplomatic fashion, refused to confirm or deny the rumours, I was clear from the body language that we were about to undergo a change at the top. That would hardly be unusual. By staying two whole years, John had already become one of the longest-lasting Transport Secretaries in recent times. Transport has so often been a stepping stone for those on the way up, as in the case of Malcolm Rifkind and Brian Mawhinney, who was John's successor, or the last stop before the terminus as it was for Paul Channon, Cecil Parkinson and John himself.

I was as sure as I could be that I would stay. The Prime Minister was very unlikely to have been so supportive of me in October only to remove me the following July, but more to the point I calculated that he would sooner simply leave me out of any reshuffle discussion on the grounds that it would be an additional distraction he did not need. I had no problem with that. Not only was I grateful to have survived, particularly because one or two colleagues had since bitten the dust, but I also loved the job I was doing and would not have wanted any other at my level. I knew that the chances of my being promoted were frankly nil, so I was able to regard the whole process with more than usual detached equanimity.

In the event the outcome was much more positive for me than it might have been. John MacGregor's legacy to the department was to have agreed with Patrick Brown, the Permanent Secretary, to reduce the department's administration budget by 20 per cent, and this involved shedding a Minister. We had been used to five, one of whom by tradition would be a peer, and that was now to be reduced to four. John MacKay had replaced the luckless Malcolm Caithness as our Lord's Minister and had been enormously impressive in his command of the aviation and shipping brief in the short time he had been with us. It was no great surprise when he, too, left us to be promoted to Minister of State at Social Security. Roger Freeman moved sideways to Defence, from which he had come to Transport three years earlier. He too had been tipped for the Cabinet but was destined to wait one more year. Most surprising of all was the demise of Robert Key. Robert had not had a happy time in the year he had been with us despite having, by all accounts, done well at Environment and National Heritage where he had the unenviable job of deputising for David Mellor when he was in his particular vale of tears. It would have been no surprise to anyone had Robert been promoted to Minister of State then. Indeed, there were several who suggested he would be an ideal replacement for his boss. Unfortunately, however, John MacGregor and Robert simply did not get on.

The relationship between a Secretary of State and his Ministers is an unusual one. At one level, they are all equal members of the House of Commons. They rely on their constituents rather than the Prime Minister for their continued presence, and the votes of the most junior backbencher count for the same weight as John Major's in any division. At the same time, the ministerial team work in a clear hierarchy. Indeed, in some departments, Parliamentary Under Secretaries report to Ministers of State rather than as I did, directly to the Secretary of State. Perhaps because the structure was commonplace in business I had no difficulty treating the Secretary of State of the day as my boss, albeit one who would be prepared to listen to my opinions. Robert, however, made it clear he had little respect for John and was not happy to have his decisions second-guessed. It was in John's nature to want to dot every i and cross every t, and a collision was inevitable. They fell out in particular when Robert, against John's better judgement, visited the scene of a coach crash on a Kent motorway. Robert was inevitably besieged by reporters demanding action from the Government on seatbelts in coaches, and was drawn into a protracted row over whether the British Government or Brussels had the power to act. John had been worried that precisely this sort of consequence might follow, and had recommended against the visit.

The whole issue of when a Transport Secretary or Minister attends a disaster scene had been particularly highlighted when Paul Cannon, after the Lockerbie disaster, had set off for his summer holidays in Mustique on what he thought the perfectly sensible basis that he would be more likely to be in the way than anything else. He was almost certainly right, but he reckoned without the hysterical press reaction which followed, portraying him as an indifferent toff more interested in sunshine than a major air disaster. Nonetheless, with the two Scots Johns, MacGregor and MacKay, Roger and Robert all gone, the supreme irony was that I was the only survivor of the entire Transport ministerial team.

The day's surprises were not over either, because John Major took the unusual step of appointing John Watts as a Minister of State at Transport, effectively number two, straight from the Chair of the Treasury Select Committee and with no previous experience as a Junior Minister. Giles Goschen was our new Lords Minister. Immensely tall, his only handicap was that he looked about thirteen. He thankfully has an old head on young shoulders and a wicked sense of humour. He has earned the respect of both the aviation and shipping industries, and I am sure it will not be long before Tom Strathclyde, the Chief Whip in the House of Lords, moves him on to higher things.

As soon as Brian Mawhinney arrived as Secretary of State, we agreed that I would keep my old job, and add local transport and road safety issues to the portfolio. It gave me arguably the longest title in government: Parliamentary Under Secretary of State, Minister for Transport in London and Minister for Local Transport and Road Safety. What an impossible mouthful. Unfortunately there is an invariable rule in politics that the length of titles are in inverse proportion to their importance!

On the first day Brian was appointed, I was working quietly in my office when the door was opened without ceremony, and in he came in his rolled up shirt sleeves. I quickly learned that this was a typical Brian gesture. In the two years I had worked for him, John MacGregor had never set foot in my office. On the rare ocasions he removed his jacket, his sleeves would have been neatly buttoned at the wrist. And had he wanted to see me, our respective private secretaries would have arranged an appointment. In one simple act, Brian swept all that aside and I knew we were in for a very different ride.

Brian Mawhinney is one of the most interesting men in British politics. He has a gritty, uncompromising manner, not given to easy banter, his accent instantly identifies him as an Ulsterman through and through, proud to be the first from the province to have made the Cabinet for goodness knows how many generations. Having been PPS to Tom King, the then Northern Ireland Secretary, Margaret had promoted him to Junior Minister in the province where he had remained for several years. One of the characteristics of Northern Ireland Ministers is that they are very rarely seen in the Commons. The whips arrange as many pairings as they can so as to avoid unnecessary travel and as the whole point of a territorial department is to provide a responsive government locally – nowhere more than in Northern Ireland – Ministers spend a great deal of time there. As a result, Brian was an unknown quantity when he moved to the Department of Health as number two to Virginia Bottomley, charged with implementing Virginia's plans for reforming London's hospitals.

Having been involved in the health service in Berkshire, I was well aware that the constant complaint from those outside the capital was over how much resource was sucked in by the large number of teaching hospitals in the centre of London. Nonetheless, Virginia's plans to close St Barts, merge St Thomas's and Guy's, close Westminster Hospital and build a replacement for St Stephen's in Fulham were, to say the least, brave. An elementary student of *Yes, Minister* will know that to a civil servant, the word 'brave' means deeply stupid, as in 'That is a very brave suggestion, Minister'; and certainly, there was a feeling that Mrs Bottomley had bitten off rather more than she could chew. Brian Mawhinney found himself having to negotiate the day-to-day details of implementing the reforms, and by all accounts, did so with considerable skill. Indeed, there had been many who had speculated that Brian would replace Virginia who was widely, if unfairly, thought to have lost the plot.

It is said that Brian is close to the Prime Minister and enjoys his confidence. They are certainly constituency neighbours and folklore has them frequently closeted in a Peterborough curry house, plotting their respective futures. I doubt, however, whether there was any nepotism involved in his promotion. Major would have recognised before most of us that Brian Mawhinney is an enormously shrewd operator and in a single year at the Department of Transport he certainly left his mark.

Ulstermen are a dour breed, no doubt honed by generations of conflict and aggression. Brian could certainly be blunt to a fault, and he could not suffer fools gladly. He is certainly bright, having lectured in medical physics before embarking on his political career, but I sensed that he was wary and resentful of what he clearly saw as patronising complacency among the upper echelons of the civil service. It is certainly useful advice to civil servants never to assume too much of their Ministers, and on occasions, as in all organisations, there is a temptation to explain that we do things this way because we have always done them this way. Even so, I had personally seen remarkably little evidence of this approach at Transport; neither Patrick Brown nor Nick Montagu fitted the conventional civil service mould. 'You just tell me what the facts are, and I'll decide what we do about them,' was a favourite Mawhinney rejoinder. It was intended to remind civil servants that however much they might believe otherwise, he was in charge. He has a combative debating style which could occasionally strike fear and loathing in the hearts of officials.

He was not loved, though I suspect this would not have disturbed him one iota. Nonetheless, he was an enormously shrewd judge of politics. He approached his portfolio with a genuinely open mind, and was keen to listen to my contribution and to weigh it with others before ever coming to a conclusion. An open mind is not an empty one. He had his agenda, the first item on which was to avoid shooting ourselves in the foot wherever possible, but he never made important decisions before listening to the arguments.

For all that I had enjoyed an excellent relationship with John MacGregor, John had been preoccupied with rail privatisation and, bluntly, there are not many tube lines in Norfolk. As a result, he allowed me to get on with the job in London but without any real debate. Even decisions like the cancellation of Oxleas Wood, which had won plaudits from environmentalists, had been taken for financial rather than green reasons. Brian Mawhinney inherited a department which, to borrow a transport metaphor, was at a crossroads. The great rail privatisation bandwagon was beginning to roll, but at the same time the Treasury were bearing down on a department which they saw as full of easy pickings.

Transport is virtually the only department where the majority of spending is not on running costs but on projects. Unlike, say, Health, where the scope for large-scale budget reductions is virtually nil, it was easy for the Treasury to tell Transport not to start as many new road improvements or bypasses in order to save money. What is not already there will not be missed, seems to be the rough logic. Whilst that pressure was particularly severe, Brian also inherited a growing concern about the department's perceived 'predict and provide' approach to transport planning. He also sensed that we were losing out quite unnecessarily by appearing indifferent to these concerns when in reality we had no option but to take them seriously. In his first few months he made a point of seeing not just the British Road Federation and the road hauliers, but Transport 2000, Greenpeace, Friends of the Earth, and even Alarm UK, home to many of the more radical road protesters who were delighted and frankly astonished to be invited to meet the Secretary of State in person.

I sat in on most of those meetings and Brian's approach was fascinating. He would listen to them talk, eyes often closed, and on occasions, seeming almost indifferent. When the spokesmen had delivered their peroration, his eyes would remain shut for a moment or two longer. It was wonderfully disconcerting. He would then seem to spring into life. His eyes wide, his face unsmiling, he would immediately come back with three or four shrewd questions which certainly indicated he had not misunderstood what he had heard. I suspect most of those who met him during those meetings would have found the experience vaguely uncomfortable, but then that too was very much Brian's style. Having spent time exploring the full range of opinion, Brian concluded, as I had, that there was really nothing of substance that divided intelligent opinion across the board. The hauliers were quite prepared to see the importance of protecting the environment, whilst even the most virulent anti-roads campaigner would eventually concede what all of the political parties plainly knew, which is that some road-building at least would continue to be needed for some years to come.

There was almost unanimous agreement on the problem. Too many road-based vehicles were seeking to access confined urban spaces, resulting in unacceptable pollution and congestion. The problem was that there was much less agreement as to the solution. Brian's response was to inaugurate a Great Debate on Transport with the aim of drawing together as much collective agreement as possible, and also identifying realistic and deliverable options for change. It was a bold and clever move, which immediately established his own green credentials and quietened much of the criticism of government policy by the pressure groups. The Opposition predictably portrayed it as an admission of having run out of ideas, but their grumbles fell on deaf ears. When the conclusions of the Great Debate were announced by George Young, Brian's successor, there were some who expressed disappointment that the document did not present any dynamic new and previously unforeseen solutions. That, however, was never likely to be the outcome; what did emerge, exactly as predicted, was a much stronger consensus around the direction to take, policy and a real reduction in the temperature of the political debate.

One of Brian's most significant attributes is that he never forgets that he is first and foremost a politician. Had he not pursued medical science and politics, he might well have made an excellent rugby player. He can kick a ball into touch from any position on the field. He looks at every issue on the basis of how it will play politically, and is cynical about 'brave' solutions that may command academic approbation but will sink like a stone in The Dog and Duck. He was, for example, much less keen on road pricing than his predecessor. John MacGregor saw it as a means of raising money. Transport nuts like me saw it as a way of reducing congestion using market mechanisms. Brian saw nothing but trouble. As far as he was concerned, voters would happily nod through the idea of road pricing until confronted with a toll booth. He told me the day he was appointed that his yardstick for approval of any new ideas would be their political saleability, and he never varied from that.

I was certainly not surprised when John Major moved him after only a year to be the Party Chairman in the run-up to the general election. Not only had Brian been one of John's campaign managers in his own leadership battle against John Redwood, but he saw his view of Brian as a political fixer as having already been vindicated by his performance at Transport. I cannot see a better Chairman in the Tory ranks. He has already honed a much sharper edge to our policy presentation. And he has begun to build a lean and mean fighting machine at Smith Square that looks at last as if it means business.

There are those who complain that Brian's abrupt, no-nonsense and frequently aggressive style is not sufficiently media-friendly. In normal circumstances, I would agree, but these are not normal times for the Tories. Although we were re-elected in 1992 with our highest share of the popular vote since 1979, that was a greater reflection on the failings of our opponents than it was natural enthusiasm for the Conservatives. There is no doubt that the biggest single enemy the Conservatives will face is anno domini. After seventeen years, a whole generation of voters has no practical experience of an alternative, and many old enough to have lived through a Labour government appear to have selective memories. The only chance for Conservative success is to spell out in uncompromising terms the consequences of a Labour government, which Britain simply cannot afford. Our message will be simple. You may not love us, you may not even like us anymore, you may long for a new set of faces, but those new faces, however prettily packaged, are neither affordable nor electable. It is a negative message, it is not even a particularly attractive one, but it is unarguable common sense and demonstrably accurate. Brian Mawhinney has exactly the personality and delivery to cut through the sentiment and short-term woolly-mindedness to remind voters of where their best interests actually lie. There is going to be blood on the floor at the next election. It will be useful to have someone leading our campaign who knows what the inside of an operating theatre looks like.

19

First Among Equals?

If the best intelligence system in Whitehall is the driving pool, Members' secretaries are a close second. When Emma rang me one fine June day in 1995 to tell me she had heard that the Prime Minister was about to make a personal statement, I simply didn't believe her. As usual, I was wrong. Within the hour, the rumour was confirmed. Something very big was obviously about to happen.

My first thought was that John Major had decided to call it a day. Right from the outset he had told the world he would leave in his own time and when it was least expected. I could quite imagine Norma, in her quiet way, pointing him in the direction of their Huntingdonshire home, and the guarantee of an infinitely quieter and more lucrative retirement. I would not have blamed him. No Prime Minister has surely had to undergo the sniping, sneering and outright hostility which he had endured, much of it from those whom he might have been tempted to think of as friends. I have already pointed out that to many Conservatives, his greatest crime was not being Margaret Thatcher. This was certainly true of the right, who also felt betrayed when it became clear that far from being a Thatcher clone, Major was his own man. It was, of course, she, not he, who had misrepresented what Major stood for. Always useless at selection, she had fluffed the most important selection of all, the choice of her successor.

There is no doubt that if Margaret had conceded in favour of Michael Heseltine, he would have won. She herself has acknowledged that possibility. She too, of course, had later become part of Major's problem, sniping from the sidelines in a way which she had so deprecated when Edward Heath had turned the same trick on her. Ironically, the issue was the same. It was on Europe that the differences between Major and

Thatcher were perceived to be greatest and there, too, where the party seemed intent on tearing itself apart.

Divisions on Europe are not confined to the Conservatives; Labour knows the seeds of dissent are sown within its ranks. I seldom heard more vitriolic criticism of the Commission than that levelled by Gwyneth Dunwoody, Nigel Spearing and Peter Shore not to mention Dennis Skinner, who is proud of never having obtained a passport, and his colleagues on the far left. Even the Liberals boast an anti-EU MP in the form of Nick Harvey. Given the paucity of Liberal MPs, that probably represents the greatest proportion of dissidents of the lot. Unfortunately for John Major, divisions among opposition parties are unimportant, whilst divisions within government are crucial. In his defence, it should not be forgotten that he has enjoyed a tiny Commons majority throughout most of his premiership. Any fool can push legislation through with a hundred or more majority to spare. Sadly, it often means ill-considered and rushed legislation reaching the Statute Book; the elective dictatorship is a double-edged sword.

On many issues, the Community Charge included, Margaret would happily burn off several dozen dissidents in her own ranks without being seriously troubled. John never enjoyed such luxury. When nine rebels decided to indulge themselves at the government's expense, they exercised an influence out of all proportion to their number. The most ludicrous example of the tail wagging the dog of course had nothing to do with Europe, other than the involvement of Hugh Dykes, the passionate Europhile who sits for Harrow. He and John Gorst allegedly held the entire government to ransom by threatening to vote against it if their local hospital was not protected. Whilst the air was thick with accusation and denial, many of us reflected on how convenient it would be to threaten to bring down the government if we did not get our own way on every single issue. No doubt our constituents would think us brave and principled. 'Doing a good job for us,' they would all cry, but they would be wrong. What all of us who were elected as Conservatives have never to forget is that our constituents put us there to support a Conservative government.

It must have been particularly galling for John Major to be described as weak in the face of this sort of threat. Weakness and strength do not come into it. A government with no majority is forced to find compromises, and by their very nature they are unlikely to satisfy everyone. It is one of the more ludicrous attacks on him, and entirely unwarranted. Where I do believe Major must bear some part of the blame is by having disconcerted and unsettled some of his backbenchers by being seen to blow alternatively hot and cold over Europe as individual issues arise. At times he has seemed more comfortable in Brussels or Strasbourg than in Westminster – understandably so, given that arguably his greatest success was the negotiation of the Maastricht agreement. At other times he has articulated the language of the Eurosceptics and whilst they have taken him at his word, it is clear that they have never entirely trusted him not to revert to type.

A classic example of this dilemma is the issue of a single currency. When opponents demanded a referendum it was precisely because they believed they knew what the outcome would be. The British people, they reasoned, would not wish to sell the Pound Sterling in exchange for a Euro, and they were probably right. Major's reluctance to deliver such a commitment was understandable from his perspective. He reasoned that he needed to maintain maximum flexibility in negotiations with his European partners, and that if he were seen to come down heavily against a single currency in advance of the negotiations, Britain's position at the table would not be credible. From the standpoint of a European negotiation he was right. Politically, he allowed his own natural scepticism about a single currency to be undervalued. Unfortunately, the perception even amongst sceptical Tory MPs was that he was equivocating because, to some degree at least, he shared the views of his Chancellor. These suspicions only redoubled the sceptics' efforts, and raised the temperature of the argument yet again. What makes matters worse is that 95 per cent of the parliamentary party and, I believe, the British people, would be prepared to agree a common position on Europe based on two equally valid principles.

The first is that Britain's immediate trade interests lie in being part of a community in which a third of all its inward investment comes to these shores. There are those who argue that Britain could not be ignored even if we were to leave. 'They need us more than we need them,' runs the logic. I wish I could believe that. The reality, I am sure, is that were we to quit, the other countries of Europe would tend increasingly to look inward, and we, forever lodged on the periphery of the continent, would run a serious risk of being marginalised.

The second and equally valid position, which unites virtually every Conservative, including those strongly committed to the European ideal, is that we ought to be enormously sceptical about the European Commission and all its works. I am clear that Euroscepticism in this sense is not Europhobia. Simple hostility to foreigners has no place in any civilised society and is in any event absurd; most of us have happily sought foreign shores for our holidays and enjoyed the experience. Eurosceptics, however, of which I am most certainly one, are deeply troubled by the way in which an unelected, bureaucratic and essentially imperialistic institution like the Commission exploits its sole right to initiate legislation. Having worked closely with the EU during my time as a Minister, seeing more and more policy areas falling within the scope of European directives, I have no doubt that this is not a case of reds under the duvet. It is true that in the past, over-enthusiatic British officials have been the culprits when seemingly insensitive legislation has been alleged to emanate from Brussels, but it is patently obvious that the Commission from M. Santer down, start from the perspective of looking for ways to take more and more areas of policy under the wing of the European Commission. One day, perhaps, generations to come will feel comfortable with a federal union in Europe, with or without a single currency. The federal system has, after all, delivered substantial benefits to the United States, as has the mighty dollar. But however internationalist the British or even the Germans become, I cannot conceive of them ever accepting such a fundamentally undemocratic apparatus as exists at the present time.

Against this background of personal criticism and bloody in-fighting, the conversation between John and Norma had evidently not been quite as I had predicted. I do believe he was close to resignation in June of 1995 and for two pins would have thrown in the towel. I suspect that when he issued his ultimatum 'Back me or sack me', he found a strength which came from not minding whichever way the result went.

At first it seemed that John would be returned unopposed. His gamble, for gamble it certainly was, looked to be more like a free throw. Rumours abounded that other candidates were about to declare, but when the challenge came, it was from an unexpected source.

Formidably bright, no doubt, John Redwood is the least clubbable member of the House of Commons, with no capacity for small talk or gladhanding whatever. His appointment to the Welsh Office, succeeding the enormously successful Peter Walker and David Hunt, had been greeted with a combination of terror and disbelief. He was known to be fiercely right-wing in an area which had come to rely heavily on regional aid. It was a classic case of putting Herod in charge of the crèche, and few could see the logic of the appointment. Once installed, Redwood had taken advantage of the breadth of his portfolio to produce an alternative health strategy much to Virginia's annoyance, and a number of other free market initiatives which had not endeared him to the indigenous population. He now resigned from the Cabinet and announced that he was standing on a Eurosceptic, free-market, right-wing agenda, which also managed to incorporate a strategy for saving the Royal Yacht. He soon attracted the majority of the outright Europhobes, including, famously, Teresa Gorman and Tony Marlow. More to the point, several ostensibly Tory newspapers talked him up hard. 'Redwood or Deadwood' was the *Sun*'s headline on the day voting took place. The *Daily Mail* opined that it was time to change the captain, and they were not alone. Both took it for granted Major was finished, and once the initial shock of the announcement was over, many commentators wondered if his actions had been wise.

I had been hugely disconcerted by Major's move. It would, after all, change the fundamental arithmetic. Our majority would remain the same, and nor could I believe that even if they were roundly defeated the Eurosceptics would go away. The result was unlikely to do more ther than crystallise opposition to the Prime Minister from within his own ranks, which up to that point, at least, had generally been muted and indirect. It was clear, too, from the many conversations I had with my constituents, that they were hopelessly divided. Many, probably the majority, wanted to see John Major win. Some were for Redwood, although they would have been hard pushed to pick his face out of an identity parade. Others were for Heseltine, or Portillo. One or two even supported Ken Clarke.

All of this seemed infinitely depressing. As I looked around at the options that were available, I could not see any candidate who could possibly improve on John Major. Michael Heseltine, no doubt prepared for the highest office as long as he was capable of drawing breath, was showing signs of ageing and, more importantly, was regarded as dangerously pro-European. On the same basis, Kenneth Clarke was a non-starter despite my personal admiration for the man. On the right, Michael Portillo was the only serious contender and was certainly the only other candidate to whom I would have considered lending my support. He, however, had made it plain that he would not be drawn into the contest, despite bizarre stories of extra telephone lines being installed at his home. When I talked to my colleagues, I discovered that many of them were treating the contest as being between right and left, wet and dry, whether on Europe, the economy or social policy. I was appalled. It was precisely the mistake which Labour had self-indulgently made during the seventies and which had culminated in the election of Michael Foot and their being out of power for a generation. If ever there was an example of how to commit political suicide it surely was there for us all to see; we were, after all, still enjoying the fruits of it.

I could also see that there was a risk that Redwood would attract those who simply wanted to exact their revenge. It is not given to man to tax and to please, nor is it given to Prime Ministers to re-shuffle their governments without upsetting as many as they delight. The longer any premier is in office, the greater that number of disgruntled and dispossessed living dead becomes, as Margaret had already found to her cost. That, at least, was not a problem for me. On the contrary, I was personally very grateful to Major for having stood by me when I needed him, and when John Redwood approached me personally I told him immediately that I would be voting for John Major.

More than anything else, I believe in one simple proposition. A bad Tory is better than a good Socialist. I could see no point whatever in bloodletting, nor in electing a candidate who would divide the party down the middle whether in Parliament or in the country, as John Redwood, right or wrong, inevitably would have done. I could see only one enemy – the increasingly likely prospect of a Labour government – unless the Conservative party buried its differences and started to turn its attention to the real enemy. I am not by nature a factionalist. I am not practised enough at hating, but more to the point, I remember the tale of the new Member sitting on the green leather benches of the Commons for the first time looking at the massed ranks of the party opposite and whispering to his older companion. 'It's like a battle, isn't it, seeing the enemy all lined up against you?' 'Remember, sonny,' said the veteran, 'over there is the Opposition, your enemies are all on this side!'

The Major camp set up its headquarters in Neil Thorne's house in Cowley Street and, frustrated by the lack of action, I rang to offer my help. James Arbuthnot, my parliamentary neighbour, answered. Given that television crews were frequently stationed outside the door filming all the comings and goings, it seemed to me that one useful gesture would simply be to be seen arriving. At least that would be an outward and visible sign to one's colleagues. In all honesty, the amount of campaigning that is ever possible with such a small and sophisticated – not to say cynical – electorate is minimal, and as Mrs Thatcher had discovered, most of the media involvement is irrelevant.

James was not exactly overwhelmed by my offer: 'Well, let me see . . .' I hung on. He appeared to be consulting others. Presumably they were discussing whether my arrival would be an advantage or an embarrassment. I cannot say I was greatly flattered – or impressed. After an interminable debate, James, polite as ever, advised me that everything seemed under control and my presence was 'probably not necessary'. Shades of Peter Morrison. 'Bugger them, then,' I thought. 'God knows why I bother.' The next day the Major camp rang to ask if they could count on my support. They clearly couldn't run a bunk-up in a brothel. But all the brown-noses did well. James is now a Minister of State.

When the day dawned, I voted early, and made sure that the press knew which way. There were one or two waverers in the Tea Room, and privately, I urged them to damn their principles and vote for their party, which in this case meant Major. It could not be clearer to me that whatever their view of Europe, indeed whatever view they took of Major personally, the only possible outcome that could be good for the party was a resounding victory for the Prime Minister and one in the eye for Tony Blair. Scraping home would be no more use than it would have been to his predecessor. It would leave him fatally crippled. Passing through the Lobby on my way back to the department I ran into Jon Sopel from the BBC. 'How did you vote, Steve?' he enquired. 'Oh, Major,' I said, 'I can't see that any of this is doing us any good, but as far as I'm concerned, if we do have to go through with this damned election, he's far and away the least worst option for any Tory.'

'Mind saying that to us outside?' he asked. 'Why not?' I retorted. 'Still a chance to get one or two of the waverers on side.'

There is nothing unusual about this type of interview. It happens literally all the time, and indeed College Green is now more television studio than open space; but I knew what message I wanted to put across. I knew that there were dozens of Tories who for one reason or another were going to vote for Redwood or abstain, and an abstention would be as bad as a vote against. The media had speculated that out of 327 votes available, anything less than 200 would be a disaster for Major, even though he could win on that basis under the rules. I agreed. I also knew that a paean of praise would simply be ignored by the only audience who mattered. That kind of wallpaper would never impress a colleague; they had to be reminded of the real bottom line – having in place a Prime Minister for the next general election who could show that he or she commanded the support of a clear majority of colleagues on a secret ballot.

So I repeated what I had said to John in front of the camera. Yes, I had voted for John Major and was very happy to do so. No, I did not think at all about voting in any other direction and on any sensible analysis . . . Without an inkling of trouble to come, I continued my walk to the department and got on with my work. The whole incident had taken perhaps two or three minutes.

To my astonishment, I heard the fatal remark repeated on the lunchtime news. I had to drag pretty fast through my mind to remember what I had said, but even as the newscaster regaled the offending words to the nation, I knew that I was in deep. How many ways are there of admitting that you got it horribly wrong? The quote sounded grudging to say the least, and at its most generous was damning with faint praise. As the day went on, it remained the only remarkable quote of the campaign. Of course, once the remark was out, our press office was flooded with requests for me to expand on it. I realised I had to do so quickly, so I accepted several invitations including *Newsnight* which would go out after the result was declared. At least I might be able to repair some of the damage.

Thankfully, Major polled far better than I could ever have hoped, with 218 votes against Redwood and abstentions of 109. Literally a two-thirds majority, and, crucially for the Tories, a better result than Tony Blair had achieved when he had been elected in a similar ballot. Even more to the point it was a better result than John had achieved in 1990. I was massively relieved. This could be presented as a credible, indeed creditable endorsement of a Prime Minister at that time in a parliament. I now had to look after number one, and said my piece as prettily as I could, but I knew that the explanation is never as interesting as the headline.

Most of my colleagues thought I had lost my marbles. Old Jack Page, the now retired member for Harrow, even penned me a note alleging treachery and/or crass stupidity. Dame Elaine Kellett-Bowman screeched at me in the corridor and, given that she had hardly passed a word with me in the twelve years, I imagined I was not her flavour of the month either. To compound my troubles, the Prime Minister would obviously now reshuffle his government. By now I was so wound up at Transport with such an excellent team around me that I really did not relish the prospect of moving. Nonetheless, in the days running up to the election several commentators had assumed I would be in line for promotion. Now, those same commentators wondered whether I would survive.

When George Young arrived as our new Secretary of State he told me that keeping me had not been easy. I hardly blame the Prime Minister; I think if I was in his position I would probably have been rather less charitable. By leaving me where I was, he actually gave me just what I wanted, but I confess to a few uneasy moments during the day. As with every reshuffle, the day started with every Minister being put on call by Number 10. As the news of the changes unfolded, my telephone, thankfully, did not ring. Had it done so, I was pretty clear what the message would have been. The problem was that as day turned to evening, I had heard nothing, good or bad. We were not even clear that the reshuffle was over; there might be more left for the next day. Sitting with Emma in the Vineyard House, an excellent Greek restaurant close to my home in Camberwell, I eventually rang Alex Allen, the Prime Minister's private secretary. 'Am I involved in this?' was my only question. 'No, Steve, I would stop worrying if I were you,' he soothed. 'It's all over.' Thank God for that, I silently retorted. It had been a close call.

When I arrived at Westminster the next day, one journalist asked me whether I was still a Minister. 'Well, the car called this morning, so I take it I am.'

It seemed an appropriate commentary. Regrets? You could say I've had a few.

20

Ersatz Tories

The Conservative Government from 1992 has been to hell and back over Back to Basics, Scott, Greenbury, Nolan, Europe and the rest, but it can take consolation from the inevitable truth that the principal cause of its unpopularity is none of these. In the early sixties, Supermac became a term of derision rather than admiration. Harold Macmillan finally resigned in favour of Alec Douglas-Home, and the slogan Labour deployed in the 1964 general election was 'Thirteen Years of Tory Misrule'. The greatest enemy of all for a government in office for seventeen continuous years is boredom. That, and a whole generation of the electorate who simply have no experience of life under anything other than the government of the day. Neither does that apply only to voters who will be eighteen at the next election. Very few under forty will actually have worried about a mortgage, children's education, job prospects, industrial relations or inflation in the way that those of us who managed businesses in the seventies did. A great bulk of the electorate is, I suspect, all too willing to contemplate change for the sake of it. 'Anything must be better than this lot,' will always earn a round of applause on *Any Questions* or *Question Time*. Commentators are not only cynical about a generation of politicians who are almost too well-known, but desperate to write the story of a new team. If a healthy democracy relies on alternation, as it surely does, then it also demands an electable opposition. Less so in 1983 or 1987, but certainly in 1992 it was not the Tories who won, but Labour who lost. The conventional wisdom is that oppositions do not win elections, government's lose them, but after a generation of one-party government, that proposition is reversed. All expectations are centred on change and it would be remarkable if Labour were not to succeed at their next attempt. What is even more remarkable is that they may not do so.

245

My thesis is simple. Over the last seventeen years, however boring, trite, mendacious, craven or depraved, the Conservatives have been right on every single major issue. That position has not changed. I cannot recall a time when I felt more comfortable about being a Conservative. If imitation is the sincerest form of flattery, then I only have to contemplate the spectacle of Tony Blair desperately attempting to persuade the electorate that they can trust him, honest they can, because in their hearts they know he's a Tory. It is a tribute to the extraordinary confectionary skills of Peter Mandelson and Alastair Campbell that he should have been so successful in this deception, but it is also a remarkably frank admission by the Labour leader that were he to stand on the principles on which his party was founded and which they have promoted for decades, he would simply not be elected. A Labour leader who stood for higher taxes, even partial abolition of trade union reform, the Social Chapter, the minimum wage and the reintroduction of mixed-ability comprehensive teaching controlled by local education authorities, would not have a snowball's chance in hell. This is not Conservative wisdom, it is Labour's own analysis.

It follows that it is necessary to test the proposition that Labour is simply an ersatz Tory party. Mr Blair has certainly learned the lessons of 1992. It will make him an infinitely more difficult opponent simply that he is not Neil Kinnock and that Gordon Brown will never repeat John Smith's fatal error of a detailed shadow budget. Nonetheless, as one who was not born with a silver spoon in his mouth and who has no compunction about the idea of voting Labour if I felt the party genuinely represented the best future for me and for Britain, what I cannot ignore is the clear evidence that the next Labour government will not be composed of a neat set of Blair clones. Were it to be, I could live with it, except that Tony is a shade too right-wing for me on some issues, but when a party decides to hold its nose and think of victory, to allow its leader to mouth whatever platitudes are necessary to obtain power, then beware what will follow.

Negative campaigning, pointing to your opponent's deficiencies as your principal argument may not be attractive. The Big Idea, the New Deal, is no doubt more inspiring, but when we know so much of what a Blair government would be obliged to introduce in practice, I personally have no compunction about pressing the point home at every turn. I also find nothing remarkable in the proposition that after seventeen years, 'steady as she goes' is not only a truly conservative agenda, it is patently sensible. I believe it was H. L. Mencken who asserted, 'No one ever lost money underestimating the taste of the American people.' Nor, I suspect, can an election be lost by underestimating the strategic insight of the British electorate. Whether the temptation to seek greener grass will overwhelm common sense remains to be seen.

A Blair government would be an interesting creature. I have always found Tony himself easy, charming and agreeable. I must be among the very few who also believe that when, as Shadow Home Secretary, he articulated a policy of being tough on crime, and tough on the causes of crime, he had actually hit the nail on the head. He had identified that believing in crime prevention, community-building and inner-city regeneration as the way in which to eradicate criminality did not mean putting the rights of criminals ahead of those of victims. Nor did it mean opening the jails, or being soft on violence. His neat encapsulation expressed my own view better than I could have done, and I have personally been saddened to see the good work which Douglas Hurd began and, to their credit, David Waddington and Ken Baker continued, now being devalued.

There is also a conventional wisdom in Tory circles that a Labour majority would instantly inflict on Blair the fate that befell the hapless John McIntosh, the GLC leader who lasted a matter of hours before being ousted in a left-wing coup by Ken Livingstone. That is to underrate Blair on two counts. First, the power of patronage which a Prime Minister enjoys is so vast, and the number of newly-elected members keen on promotion to government so great that a new Prime Minister who has kissed hands with his sovereign is no pushover, particularly when a whole generation of Labour party members will be desperate to consolidate their new found success and long for the arrival of the red box and the Rover. Second, because Blair is clearly prepared to be ruthless when necessary. Clare Short has suggested that this is somehow an aberration induced by Messrs Mandelson and Campbell, but nothing could be further from the truth. The party leader who was prepared to take on the sterile tokenism of the left over Clause 4 is one determined to allow nothing to stand in the way of success. No, Tony Blair will be a hard nut to crack, both for the Tories and his own left wing. That does not say he is invulnerable; ironically, men think that women think Tony Blair attractive, but in my experience, women of every political opinion and none prefer Major as a man. Tony's toothpaste smile and carefully Folleted wardrobe strikes many as simply smarmy. At least one close friend of mine is convinced he was a body double for Jack Nicholson's Joker. He is also vulnerable in the sense that he literally sits on the fringe of his party. It must be unique in democratic politics for a mass movement to elect its most right-wing member as its leader. Not only will every Labour Member of Parliament stand to the left of Tony Blair, but every paid up member of the Labour Party too.

A prominent Scottish trade unionist was talking to a lobby correspondent at the Glasgow Conference which Tony Blair attended to debate Clause 4. 'We hate him, you know. He's betrayed everything we believe in; he won't increase public spending, he despises us and he's sold out to the Tories on practically everything else.' I doubt his interlocutor was particularly surprised; the private view of Tony Blair within the Labour party is frequently unprintable, even among Labour MPs who have enjoyed a convivial evening in the Commons Kremlin bar. 'But we're going to zip it until he gets us elected.'

That is Tony Blair's greatest weapon, and one he has copied directly from the Conservatives. As Labour tore itself apart with internal divisions for nearly twenty years under Wilson, Callaghan, Foot and Kinnock, it was the Tories who remembered, and now seem to have forgotten, that electors dislike parties at war with themselves. It is also the one weapon which delivers real power to the image-makers and spin-doctors who surround the Labour leader. Most Labour MPs dislike Peter Mandelson more than Norman Tebbit, and they resent the power which he, and Alastair Campbell, Blair's personal press aide, wield. John Major must envy their ability to strike fear into the hearts of even senior members of the Shadow Cabinet, let alone candidates in marginal seats. Woe betide the TV programme that tries to canvass these hopefuls if a hostile word emanates from Walworth Road or the Leader's Office.

Whilst both men are undoubtedly talented (and privately likeable) they do not possess any black magic powers which are likely to survive long after the election of a Labour government. The reality is that Labour at all levels simply wants to win, and will suffer any indignity or humiliation along the way as long as it can convince itself that the end justifies the means. Once the election is over, I suspect the courtiers will find themselves marginalised extraordinarily quickly.

Labour's deputy leader, John Prescott, has been widely credited with having brought a substantial section of the trade union movement and the left to the new Labour Party. He is a genuinely attractive character despite the scowl and the equally balanced chips so evidently borne on both shoulders. There is a sense of real intregrity about the man and I do know from personal experience that when a deal is made with John Prescott, he delivers to the letter. My concern is not, therefore, whether John Prescott is a nice, honest or laudable politician. My personal nightmare is that he should be a heartbeat away from the greatest office in the land. If the United States occasionally agonises over its inability to produce better quality Presidential candidates, then the thought of John Prescott exercising high office truly appals me. I appreciate this will be an unpopular view, for he is an enormously popular man, but I cannot overlook his extraordinarily tangential relationship with the English language, nor the primitive and fallacious arguments on which he bases his no doubt earnest creed. A Prescott government, or one in which he had a significant influence, would be one dedicated to the interests of producers rather than consumers, hostile to business in any form, and incapable of grasping the intricacies of international diplomacy. I wonder when electors in Britain will awaken to that depressingly obvious conclusion. I suspect they will simply do so too late.

Gordon Brown must rue the day he decided not to oppose his friend Tony when John Smith's unexpected death threw both men into a struggle neither had foreseen. Neither Chancellors nor their shadows are ever likely to top party popularity polls, but in Brown's case he has simply disappeared from view. His dispatch box performances have been frankly disappointing whilst television cruelly exposes his disconcerting habit of dropping his jaw several inches two or three times every sentence. He also has the unfortunate task of telling his own side exactly what they do not want to hear. He dare not suggest additional taxes, despite virtually every one of his colleagues demanding them, and Clare Short, at least, indicating a willingness to contribute. Nor can he promise a brass farthing of extra spending for fear of frightening the horses on the international currency markets. He must ask himself daily why he allowed himself so easily to be persuaded to allow Blair a clear run. Their own relationship appears to have deteriorated significantly over recent months. It is hard to see it improving in the run-up to an election.

Although Labour is undeniably short of experience, any objective observer would recognise that there is, nonetheless, some genuine talent in its ranks. Donald Dewar, one of the few to have ever previously held office, is enormously impressive at close quarters and is unlikely to want to remain as a silent Chief Whip in any Labour administration. He would be a major asset, with wise counsel and a generous wit. Robin Cook, too, impresses. His appearance no doubt counts against him, but he is astute, performs extremely well at the dispatch box and is clearly popular with his colleagues. The next Labour government will also need Jack Cunningham, if he can be bothered to turn his mind to it. Jack is as near an elder statesman as the Labour party possesses, and over the years of opposition he has grown sleeker, and some say more cynical by the day. He may offend the left, and the anti-nuclear lobby, but Blair will need him. He oozes reliability, reasonableness and an impression of being in control. In any event, Jack would so much enjoy National Heritage where all the tickets really are free that it seems cruel to deny him the opportunity. At Transport, Michael Meacher succeeded John Prescott, but it is hard to see Meacher playing any significant role after the next election whether Labour win or lose. Not only has he no sense of humour whatever, as demonstrated by his ludicrous and deservedly unsuccessful libel action against a newspaper which had the temerity to question his alleged working-class upbringing, but his Old Labour hard line is anathema to the modern party. He must be enormously frustrated to have tasted office early, as a Minister of State in the Department of Trade and Industry nearly two decades ago, only to then waste twenty years calling for a public inquiry each week. It was predictable that Blair would shuffle him aside.

The Clare Short appointment as his successor demonstrated an almost reckless confidence, given that she had already resigned from two opposition posts under Neil Kinnock. For most observers it was not a question of whether Clare would go, but when. It was no surprise that she could not even contain herself until the election. Her unwillingness to conform to the basic rules of collective decision-making left Blair with no option but to demote her. As one who has long pondered the meaning of a political 'gaffe', I might be tempted to agree that gaffes are utterances by politicians which we all know to be true but we all equally know ought not to be said. I know from my personal postbag that the public often react very differently from newspaper pundits to such remarks, but I am sure that what ditched Clare Short was not her willingness to pay more tax or her perfectly rational assertion that the legalisation of soft drugs deserved serious debate; what buried her was walking out of a television studio in high dudgeon when asked to comment on a strike by London Underground train drivers. For those who would hold high office, it is no use complaining that the questions are unfair. After seventeen years, Conservative Ministers take that as given.

Nonetheless, I declare my life membership of the Clare Short fan club. She herself apparently recognises that when she speaks on television her lip appears to curl. It is a desperately unfortunate mannerism in a politician, but particularly for someone who is privately so warm, generous and decent. We were both members of an all-party delegation to the Middle East which allowed us, as so often happens, to find out how much we enjoyed and respected those on the other side of the political divide. I regard her as a friend, and was delighted when she joined us in the Crypt Chapel for Edward's christening. More than a dozen years later, she remembers both my boys' names, and never fails to ask after them. She may not be a particularly successful politician, but she is a diamond of a human being.

As Labour shuffled transport spokespersons even faster than Margaret, my old sparring partner, Andrew Smith, moved from Gordon Brown's Treasury team to take over the portfolio. Although in the Commons for the best part of a decade, and a front bencher for nearly half that time, he is virtually unknown outside Westminster. He is not a showman, but he is able, articulate and sensible and extremely unlikely to cause his leader any loss of sleep. Whilst we have never discussed it, I am sure he will have mused as I have done on our fate – that although I beat him on that night in 1983, and was first to occupy a Minister's chair, it is he who will reach the Privy Council and a seat around the Cabinet table.

No commentary on the current Labour Party would be complete without a mention of one of the most extraordinary phenomena of modern British politics, David Blunkett. I do not know him, nor claim his friendship. I disagree with virtually everything he says, but in my view too little has been made of his staggering achievement. It would be remarkable for someone suffering the handicap of total blindness to be elected to a local council. To go from there to Westminster and to earn deserved promotion to Labour's Shadow Cabinet is no politically correct tokenism. His command of his brief is as total as any of his colleagues. It is perhaps the greatest tribute of all to him that he receives no special treatment either from his own side or ours. He has achieved the greatest feat of all for a disabled person; he has so overcome his handicap that his opponents are themselves blind to it. I would bitterly regret his ever becoming a Secretary of State because he would be a member of a cabinet which I would not wish to see around the table in Number 10, but there is a part of me that would exult in the triumph of individual perseverance and determination which David's elevation would represent. He is an invaluable standard-bearer for the disabled and a constant reminder to the rest of us that obstacles in any life are there to be overcome.

In every party there are those who through inexperience or lack of exposure are not well-known, but who insiders identify as certain to shine. Several of the new Labour women will clearly do well. Margaret Hodge was successfully shaken off her loony-left days as leader of Islington Council and has now successfully reinvented herself as the quintessential Blairite. She has bags of experience, and is a good television performer. So too is Tessa Jowell who won Dulwich for Labour in 1992 and has impressed by her hard work, intelligence and warmth. Among the men, Alun Michael from Labour's home affairs team and Graham Allen who shadowed me in the transport team will surely do well, as will Geoff Hoon, Jim Dowd and Keith Hill. There are, too, plenty of experienced, longer-serving Labour members such as Stuart Bell, Robin Corbett and Geoffrey Robinson (if he could be enticed away from his millions) who ought to provide much needed experience.

I do not want to see a Labour government elected. On balance I believe it would be bad for Britain in 1997 because that government would inevitably increase public spending, would be obliged to raise taxes even if it were not in any event emotionally disposed to do so, would abandon trade union reforms which have transformed our industrial relations after decades of anarchy, and would throw away vital advantages for Britain in Europe. I have no doubt that in 1992 pencils hovered over ballot papers whilst electors struggled with their Labour hearts and their Tory heads. That time the heads won. Those who believe, as I do, that the Clinton slogan, 'It's the economy, stupid!' still rules, will appreciate that next time the choice may be just as unedifying, but the right decision just as inevitable.

21

It Was Just One of Those Things

As soon as the dust settled on the 1992 general election, I knew that one day soon I was going to have to repair the hole in my personal finances. Whilst losers at Lloyd's, including several MPs, were lobbying for special tax treatment, I had quietly lost more than several of them put together. In its heyday I could have sold my own stake in the car business for well over a million pounds, not to mention the property and investments in which I had a healthy equity. All that had gone, and at the age of forty-eight I was worth less than when I was eighteen.

I make no complaint; I was wholly responsible for whatever transpired, and I have never asked for the rules to be re-written. Transferring the blame to Lawson and Thatcher is an empty cop-out. Although I enjoyed my job as a Minister more than any throughout my life, I also knew that politics would never pay me enough to put back the decent pension I had once accumulated, to give me a home I could enjoy and a comfortable life in work and retirement. When I made the announcement that I would not be seeking re-election, one journalist remarked, 'I suppose you're worried about a Labour win.' My reply was instant. 'It's not a Labour win that worries me, it's the Tories winning I can't afford.' Many a true word is spoken in jest. In government there is absolutely no question of accumulating capital, which is the essential ingredient of any successful business career. In opposition I could in theory take on a new business career, but if I have learned anything from experience it is that no man can serve two mistresses, and whilst an MP can happily take on a couple of non-executive directorships and still discharge his or her constituency duties to the full, what is not possible is to be fully involved in active business and still do justice to a seat at Westminster. I have no desire to be the kind of semi-detached Member who simply uses the best club in the land as an entry ticket to the occasional boardroom. I am also in the fortunate position of being able to earn more outside the House of Commons than in it. That is not true of all MPs, many of whom are paid twice what they are worth, but when the person who runs the Commons catering department earns more than the Prime Minister and First Lord of the Treasury, and similar yawning gaps between private and public sector pay exist in almost every walk of life, my own decision became inevitable.

I shall hate leaving politics, but I have never regretted my decision. Nor have I torn up my party membership card. As I contemplate the party that I have worked in for the last twenty years I am drawn to the inescapable conclusion that the only thing the Tories have to fear at the next election is the Tories. Sadly, policies will not determine the outcome of the next general election. Fear of the unknown on the one hand, and the prospect of eternally greener grass on the other are powerful engines that may well determine the outcome, but if it is clear that the Tories ought to win, it is much less clear that the Parliamentary party, at least, has the will to do so. It was always said that small majorities convey great power to Prime Ministers, for no backbencher would dare rock the boat on a critical issue. That proposition at least has been cruelly disproved in recent years. Conservatives squabble endlessly over Europe without ever seeming to appreciate that the difference between Kenneth Clarke and Bill Cash is substantially less than the difference between the Tories and Labour. Even Tory Europhiles would maintain our opposition to the Social Chapter, and accept the necessity for institutional reform. Mr Blair has said he 'will never allow Britain to be isolated in Europe'. A noble sentiment, but one which is likely to be achieved at the expense of tens of thousands of British jobs.

There is so much in-fighting in the contemporary Conservative party that I can only conclude that many MPs have already given up on the next election and are jockeying for positions in opposition. The fact that this attitude is itself the strongest guarantee of Labour success appears to escape them. There are no prizes for coming second in a general election, nor is there much satisfaction to be had from being right, but not being in power. I find it enormously sad that the inevitable topic of conversation amongst Conservatives is speculation about John Major's successor, much of which assumes that the change will come sooner rather than later. I cannot say that I am any happier at that prospect now than I was in 1995, but no doubt John will one day do precisely what he promised and go in his own time whether in power or in opposition. I very much hope there is no early leadership battle, not least because on almost any analysis, a change would run the risk of fragmenting rather than uniting the party. In 1996 there are certainly many contenders, albeit none who stand head and shoulders above the others. All no doubt nurture ambitions, however unrealistic.

As long as there is breath in Michael Heseltine's body he would lead the party if the opportunity arose. I am sure that his wife Anne regularly tries to dissuade him, and equally sure that he takes not the slightest bit of notice. That scribbled career plan on the back of an envelope which led from university to 10 Downing Street has not been forgotten, and only a fool would write Michael off. Even so, he has aged considerably over the last few years and particularly since his heart attack. There would be real questions about his ability to withstand the sheer physical pressure, but more to the point, there are at least two factions within the party to whom he would simply never be acceptable: those who regard him as dangerously wet on Europe, and those who can never forgive him for having dealt the mortal blow to their beloved St Margaret. Heseltine himself knows this, and it was precisely the recognition that he could not win outright which led him to negotiate the largest office in Whitehall as the price for throwing in his hand with John Major in 1995. There is every reason to believe these negotiations continued until the last minute. It cannot be coincidence that so many of Hezza's supporters voted late in the afternoon.

Michael Heseltine's title of Deputy Prime Minister and First Secretary of State may give the impression that he is the second most important man in government, but this would be misleading. Without any doubt, the biggest gun is strapped snugly around the ample waist of the Chancellor of the Exchequer, Kenneth Clarke. Ken ought on any reckoning to be the candidate to succeed John Major. He has vast ministerial experience, including a spell at Transport. That allows me to confirm first hand impressions from senior civil servants that he stood head and shoulders above the others of his generation, as a minister who effortlessly mastered his brief, who has a brilliant

256

debating style in the House of Commons and an extraordinary talent for being able to develop a cogent argument persuasively.

I offer one small insight. When Ken was Minister of Health he introduced a Limited List of drugs which would no longer be prescribed in their branded form, but would be available on the much cheaper generic basis. One of my constituents ran a pharmaceutical company, one of whose products – a laxative as I recall – was adversely affected. He demanded an urgent meeting with Ken, which I duly arranged. When we met at the Department of Health, Ken was alone except for the Chief Medical Officer who, apart from nodding when Ken introduced him, took no further part in the proceedings. My constituent outlined his problem. It was all deeply technical and I assumed Ken would look to his medical advisor to assist. Far from it; when my man had finished, Ken proceeded to demolish every shred of his argument in turn. Even I could see that it was an enormously impressive tour de force. As we left, my pharmacist turned to me: 'God, he was good, wasn't he?', he whispered. ' 'Fraid so,' I replied. 'I think you just lost.' My man wasn't bitter, he could see he had been rebuffed by a formidable talent.

Ken is an attractive figure, particularly to those who know the man rather than the TV image. He is engagingly normal, genuinely preferring a pint and a small cigar in the local watching Nottingham Forest to more exalted company, yet just as at home in the highest circles of intellectual debate. He conveys a breezy indifference to the opinions of the rest of the world which has earned him the undying hatred of teachers and nurses, both of whom he was quite happy to take on where others would have feared to tread, but which also has allowed him to pursue his own enthusiasm for all things European in a way which has outraged the Tory right. So indifferent is he to the reaction he provokes, to the point of appearing to revel in the discomfiture on his own side, that he has effectively ensured that a great many colleagues who might otherwise be happy to see him take the helm have been deterred. I, for one, would have looked long and hard at Ken Clarke were it not for my conviction that a Clarke premiership would take Britain far too fast down quite the wrong path towards a federal union in Europe.

The other left-of-centre candidate emerging strongly over recent years has been Stephen Dorrell. His longest attachment

257

was as PPS to Peter Walker, in which role he was generally regarded as sopping wet. A spell in the Treasury seems to have had the effect on him which it has on all who pass through its portals. Wet or dry, they appear to undergo a frontal lobotomy which turns them all out uttering arid Treasury-speak, and Steven Dorrell is no exception. He is undoubtedly bright and a smooth television performer, but I doubt whether he has the warmth and ability to project his personality to the party and the wider audience. His pale, generally unsmiling and deceptively young face is somehow emotionless. Logical, yes; unusually prepared to put the facts before the public to allow them to judge for themselves. All this is creditable, but there is a Spock-like aura around him which many find unsettling.

If none of the three candidates perceived as coming from the left of the party are likely to inherit the mantle, what then of the right? Peter Lilley has kept his head down in one of the most difficult jobs for a Tory, that of wrestling with the enormous complexity of the social security budget, which consumes a third of everything we pay in taxes, and it is generally agreed that he has performed miracles there. His civil servants and colleagues both like him, but he too has yet to break through and project an image of himself to the public as anything other than the cabinet minister whose name no one can remember. That used to be a favourite joke of Peter's. I suspect now the humour of it is wearing thin. He will be a valuable member of any Conservative administration over the next twenty years, but I cannot see him persuading the public that he is a natural leader.

John Redwood emerged from the shadows of the Welsh Office to march centre stage during the 1995 leadership election, and he has proved reluctant to leave. He is undoubtedly extremely clever, and rather in the fashion of Nicholas Ridley after John the Baptist, he may well point the party in the direction it ought to pursue, particularly if the Conservatives want to put clear blue water between themselves and Labour. John's problem is not intellect, nor political vision. From where I stand, he would simply be an impossible package to sell to the electorate. Not only would the *Sun* start reissuing those cut-out Vulcan ears, but some unkind soul either in Walworth Road or, dare I suggest, Central Office, would find that video tape of his performance of the Welsh National Anthem, put the tape on a loop and play it over and over. He is a good man, and those who have had the fortune to know him and break through the icy reserve know that he is a warm and genuine individual. Politics, however, is not just about what you are, but what you present. On those grounds, in an age when image is more important than philosophy, John Redwood too fails my acid test.

I first met Michael Portillo when out campaigning for him during his by-election after by Anthony Berry's assassination at Brighton. Then, hair combed forward rather than swept back, he impressed as personable, competent, friendly and self-assured. In those days, his close association with Nigel Lawson, to whom he was a special advisor, did him no harm. Margaret Thatcher liked him and promoted him early. That promotion has continued under John Major, and until the Redwood leadership challenge, he was seen by most commentators as the right-winger most likely to succeed. John Redwood's audacity undoubtedly harmed Portillo, who was seen to have been left flat-footed by a braver rival. Leaked plans to instal war-cabinet style telephone equipment in his house did not help either. When he subsequently confirmed he would not run, in crude terms many on the right believed that he had bottled out. No doubt stung by that, his conference speech that October sounded panicky, and struck a discordant note with too many commentators to have enhanced his prospects. Ever since, the left, who detest his views on Europe, and fear his obvious competence, have launched wave after wave of attack. He has been accused of selling off Admiralty Arch when the property was not even his department's to sell. He was cruelly misrepresented as unpopular with the service chiefs who have actually come to see him as extremely competent, professional and supportive. Constant references to Miguel Xavier Port-ee-o attempt to portray him, absurdly, as somehow not qualified to be British. To me, he nonetheless remains the outstanding candidate. He may need to improve the quality of the advice he is given from those around him. He might do well to reconsider whether the shadowy figure of multi-millionaire David Hart is an asset or a liability, but the talent, the intellect and the personal charisma are all there. During the dozens of cabinet committees I attended, he was consistantly one of the most impressive performers. He is good on television and the radio, but can also reach a wider audience when necessary. He is, in short, a class act.

If Michael Portillo has an Achilles heel it is that there are those on the left of the party who would sooner elect Dame Elaine Kellett-Bowman. There are other candidates who perhaps inspire less passion, but could turn that precisely to their own advantage. By any reckoning, Michael Howard ought to be a strong leadership contender, but somehow, and for reasons I am not totally sure I understand, he has pursued arguably the purest blue-rinse Tory agenda on crime of any Home Secretary since the war, without earning any brownie points from either left or right in doing so. There is a remoteness about him, an iced coating which it is not easy to penetrate, and he has few parliamentary followers.

Malcolm Rifkind has performed well in any job he has undertaken, including Transport, Defence and now the Foreign Office. He is the ultimate safe pair of hands whose party piece is to speak in enormous detail without notes on any subject in his portfolio. Apart from his perilously small majority in his Edinburgh seat, where he suffers the same insecurity as did Christopher Patten in Bath, he has few enemies, but, like Howard, no strong body of support either. He might, *in extremis*, be a compromise candidate if the vital issue were to be Europe, but compromises of that kind, as the Labour party know all too well, seldom work. Brian Mawhinney must be in with a shout, not least because he betrays no allegiance to right or left. He is impossible to pin down, barring a vague presumption that he is sceptical on Europe without ever publicly identifying himself with that cohort. He was greener at Transport than most commentators would have given him credit, and his Health Service performance scored high marks for technical merit. Whilst he is not easy to cast as a conciliator, he might just be the ideal person to persuade the Tories not to waste time fighting amongst themselves instead of tackling Labour.

There are three other individuals who cannot be ignored in any overview of Tory succession prospects. The Prince across the Water, Christopher Patten already has the Pickfords van booked for a return to Britain when the Hong Kong handover is complete. Given that he cannot voluntarily quit his position until 1997, he is guaranteed not to be available to the Conservative party until after the next general election. There are rumours that Sir Nicholas Scott, the fortunate incumbent of one of the safest seats in the country, might consider exchanging it for a peerage to allow his old friend to take over in Chelsea. The trouble with such rumours is that they are based on nonsense. It is not unreasonable to assume that John Major would be happy to help the man widely credited with his 1992 general election success, but constituency associations are notoriously fickle and the faintest whiff of placing by Central Office would be likely to be fatal to Patten's chances. A more plausible scenario is that he does indeed return, picks up a by-election within a year or so, and then is rapidly able to re-establish his credentials as an intellectual heavyweight. Even so, memories die fast. The 1992 Commons intake do not know him; even less so will the new arrivals after 1997. He is also perceived to be firmly of the left and the conventional wisdom is that whoever is the next leader of the Conservative party is likely to take it, to some degree or other, to the right.

One candidate who could do that is the remarkable Michael Forsyth. He arrived at Westminster when I did in 1983, a strong right-winger, arch-advocate of privatisation, deregulation and competitive tendering, scourge of the unions, and cordially loathed by every Labour supporter north of the border. He was an instinctive Thatcherite, a Eurosceptic to his fingertips and a man who takes no prisoners. Given the shortage of Tories who can manage joined-up writing north of the border he was soon in the Scottish Office under Rifkind and Ian Lang. It was he who was seen to take the fight aggressively to Labour during those years, and the very idea of allowing him to take over as Secretary of State was instantly dismissed on the basis that foxes should generally be kept well away from hen coops. There was many a sharp intake of breath when John Major did just that. Incredibly, he has won friends and admiration for his competence, his subtlety and his political touch. The old aggression seems to have given way to a great maturity, and there are an increasing number on the Tory right who rate him highly. His masterstroke in prohibiting the flying of the European flag on government buildings during the beef-war is still the most imaginative, successful and cost-free gesture of that whole unhappy episode, and endeared him to millions. Unfortunately his majority in Stirling is wafer-thin, and whether his appeal would translate south of the border is still an open question.

In my view, however, the outstanding talent of his generation is William Hague. Forgetting the hype around his early conference performance (which was, incidentally, enormously impressive) he has emerged as the brightest rising star on the Tory benches. He is deservedly popular with colleagues, attracting almost no enemies despite his meteoric rise. He is highly regarded by his civil servants as a man who masters his brief and can communicate it forcefully. He is a good television performer with a relaxed, easy style and above all he has managed to avoid being pigeonholed. The general assumption is that he is right-wing without ever straying into disloyalty, and certainly not to the extent of alienating the left, which Portillo and Forsyth have certainly done. I have known him well since he first arrived in the House of Commons as Leon Brittan's successor in Richmond, Yorkshire. We share the dubious distinction of being the last two men to win a by-election for the Conservatives – these days we are virtually an endangered species. Privately, he is as enjoyable as his easy public manner might suggest. Behind that, however, is a fearsome intellect which is capable of articulating a strategy for the Conservative party which is as coherent and believable as any I have heard. William Waldegrave and John Moore can both attest to the lethal disadvantage of being described too early as the next Prime Minister but one. In both cases I could never quite understand the media logic, but if it does not do too much damage to either of their causes, let me record that the next leader of the Conservative party will be either Michael Portillo or William Hague.

Having made my decision to leave Parliament I suggested to John Major that I stand down as a Minister when he next came to reshuffle his government, and did so in July 1996. Although I hated leaving, I knew that my time at the department would inevitably have come to an end when the general election was called, and at least I had the benefit of an orderly exit. We all shed copious tears on the day. The extraordinary pressure of ministerial life meant that Stephen, Heather, Rachel and Angela were much more to me than just civil servants. Fortunately, my successor was the excellent John Bowis, the man who took Battersea from Alf Dubs, and had already served with distinction at Health. I knew the team would warm to him and be as loyal as they had been to me. Re-entry to real life is as difficult for an ex-Minister as it must have been for the crew of Apollo 13.

The day after I left I lunched with John Maples, the former Treasury Minister who was also Deputy Chairman of the party and is now due to replace Alan Howarth as Member for Stratford-on-Avon. It was a long-standing date and I was looking forward to a relaxing gossip. It was raining hard when we left the Caprice and I realised I had no driver or car waiting. For more than four years the last thing I had had to worry about was transport. For that matter, I seldom carried cash. Thank goodness I had a tenner in my pocket. I waved energetically at a passing black cab and in true London fashion he waved back. As I tiptoed past the puddles in Arlington Place I knew that freedom had its price.

In Epping Forest, too, life has moved on. With quite uncharacteristic perspicacity, they chose Eleanor Laing, John MacGregor's special advisor, as the candidate to succeed me and I could not have been more pleased. Eleanor has a great future in the Conservative Party. She is able, hard-working and politically perceptive, but she is also attractive, with a delightful personality and, most important of all, a rich husband. She will be a great asset to the Conservative Party, and will surely one day make the Cabinet.

Valedictories are not my style, but as I look forward to a more lucrative, not to say relaxed life outside Parliament, at least for the next few years, I can also look back on nearly twenty since I first became a county councillor in Berkshire. My motives have never altered. I continue to believe that any democracy suffers the politicians it deserves, and that the price that good men pay for not being involved in politics is to be governed by people less able than themselves. Since I announced that I was standing down, Parliament has voted large salary increases for both Members and Ministers. As ever, my timing was appalling. Predictably, the rises caused outrage in the media, although for once it seemed the public had understood that, as I put it on several occasions when I was asked, if you pay peanuts you get monkeys. Attempting to compare the merits of an MP and a nurse, teacher or accounts clerk is an impossible and essentially futile undertaking. What is important is not whether MPs 'deserve' a large rise. There can be no argument that suggests they are inherently more 'deserving' than any other group in society. The question, however, should be whether our democracy deserves to be served by people who regard £30,000 a year as an adequate reward for their labours. The salary is now £43,000.

Unless we are prepared to pay sufficient to attract candidates of high calibre, we are in real danger of finding ourselves represented increasingly by nobs and nerds. The nobs, almost all of whom by definition serve out of a sense of noblesse oblige, deserve more credit than they get. Most of them could spend their lives quite happily with a strawberry daiquiri on a Caribbean beach. I admire them for their willingness to submit themselves to the daily grind which is an MP's lot, but such men and women, however conscientious, have a view of life which is not shared by the overwhelming majority of the population. Even Margaret Thatcher, wealthy by marriage if not by birth, clearly found it difficult to understand the aspirations and motivations of people who struggle to pay bills, mortgages or school fees. Thanks to Dennis, she never knew the sinking feeling in the pit of the stomach when commitments loom and income vanishes.

At the other end of the scale, all the political parties are increasingly prone to elect young, overwhelmingly male, politics graduates who join Central Office or Walworth Road, direct from university, graduate to a think-tank, move on to be a special advisor to a Minister or Shadow, find themselves on a candidates list, perhaps fight a hopeless seat first time round, and then present themselves in their early thirties for a safe one. They generally have to cast around by this time for a girlfriend, sex previously not having played a prominent role in their lives. If Tory, they live in bedsits in Islington or Kennington to which they retire early and sober to read another chapter of Hayek or the latest offering from the Centre for Policy Studies. They buy their underwear from M & S, and relax watching *Star Trek*. They may not frighten the enemy, but by God, they frighten me.

Money alone is not the answer. These days, when MPs are rated with journalists and estate agents and slightly below solicitors in public esteem, there are many more attractive ways of serving society than in Parliament. The low esteem is not in my view terminal. It owes its currency to that sense of cynicism and boredom which accompanies very long periods of one-party government. It was last prevalent in the early sixties in Britain when the Conservatives had been in office since 1951. As long as politics is not seen as an end in itself, and election is not simply a means of making money, there is hope for the future. Despite all the synthetic furore over alleged sleaze, it is worth recalling that there has not been one criminal charge laid against a single Member of Parliament or Minister. The contrast with other democracies in Japan, Germany, France, and the United States ought to be better appreciated than it is. Nor are our politicians capable of being bracketed as if they were a profession, a breed apart. The best of them – indeed the vast majority – could earn more for themselves in a more secure environment doing other things. They are teachers, lecturers, bankers, doctors, trade union officials and entrepreneurs who are not prepared to stand on the sidelines whilst others, perhaps less well qualified, make the decisions. If politicians were abolished by decree on Sunday, it would be necesary to re-invent them on Monday morning. The prospect of an intrusive press, of having one's entire private life turned over for public inspection, is a massive disincentive to many. 'Who needs it? Why do any of you bother? It simply can't be worth it,' is the typical reaction of intelligent observers who know full well that there is not one of us who does not have a skeleton in his or her cupboard somewhere, and who would not relish the prospect of the kind of unpleasant exposure which has now to be regarded as commonplace.

There is, I fear, no easy solution. A right to privacy is as important as any other of our freedoms. Squaring that right with our equal right to a free press is not easy either. I am strongly in favour of outlawing the tapping of telephone conversations – or at least, their subsequent resale for gain. (It has been a criminal offence to intercept and open a letter for nearly a century – it is high time that newspapers and others were treated as criminals if they condone or actively encourage interceptions of electronic communications in order to market the result.) The Waleses may be their own worst enemies, but neither of them deserved to have their private conversations treated as public property. It is undeniable that a right to privacy should not be allowed to frustrate a matter of genuine public interest. At present, however, it is what interests the public that is so often confused with a public interest in the right to know. Although I would want to see a stronger and more effective mechanism for reining in Fleet Street from its worst excesses, I do not believe a general right to privacy is either practicable or desirable. As far as politicians are concerned, the public is perfectly well able to make up its mind about individuals when presented with the evidence that they say one thing and do another. The unique position which democratically elected representatives occupy in any society does impose on them the need to accept that on occasions the press make life thoroughly unpleasant with little if any justification.

I offer a contrast with our nearest neighbours, the French. I do not believe it is a coincidence that in France a privacy law exists which prevented the ordinary French people from knowing that, for example, President Mitterrand had at least one illegitimate child with whom he was in constant touch, and at the same time, several senior members of his government were either on trial or imprisoned on serious corruption charges. That atmosphere in which politicians are tempted to believe that they are somehow above lesser mortals, and can shield themselves from unwelcome attention, is corrosive and unattractive. On balance, we would do well to leave things as they are.

In any event, for me this particular chapter is over. I look to the future with the same mixture of excitement and apprehension that I have always done. I have no fixed idea of what the future holds, but I can guarantee that the next twenty years will be hard pushed to match the sheer exhilaration of the last. On the day I filled the black bin liner with the contents of my ministerial desk and together with Emma, bade farewell to my second family, Stephen Heard penned this mildly amended version of Cole Porter's immortal verse to a farewell card. I am glad it is how they felt about me. You can write it on my tombstone:

> *So long and amen;*
> *Here's hoping we'll meet now and then.*
> *It was great fun,*
> *But it was just one of those things.*

Index

Agababian, Vahe 38
Aitken, Jonathan 92
Aitken, Lady Violet 32
Ali, Tariq 26
Ali Khan, Jehenbaz 37
Alison, Michael 148
Allen, Graham 252
Allen, Stephen 177
Amess, David 175
Anderson, Clive 23
Arbery, Brian 177
Arbuthnot, James 241
Archer, Jeffrey 174
Ashcroft, John 124
Ashton, Peter 208
Atkins, Robert 58
Attwood, Richard 33
Axon, Jim 128

Baker, Kenneth 58, 71, 98–9,
    115–6, 158–9, 223, 247
  appointed Home Secretary 158
  appointed to Education 109
  as Home Secretary 160–65
  at Education 121–2
  Brixton Prison Breakout 166–8
  Community Charge 107–8
  national lottery 165–6
  on education 108
Baker, Peter 24
Banks, Robert 54
Barrett, Robin 24
Batty, Sir William 31

Bell, Sir Tim 210
Bell, Stuart 252
Bellingham, Henry 2, 204
Bellwin, Irwin 98
Bendell, Bruce 183
Benn, Tony 83
Bentliffe, Donald 14
Benyon, Tom 48–51, 53, 61
Berry, Tony 105, 124–5
Bevins, Antony 140
Biggs-Davison, John 65, 126–7,
    134
Bird, Christopher 180
Blair, Tony 84, 98, 243, 246–8
  ersatz Tory? 246
  formidable adversary 174
Blunkett, David 99, 252
Bond, Dorian St George 180
Booth, Hartley 222
Bossom, Sir Clive 61
Bottomley, Virginia 166, 229,
    230, 239
Bowis, John 262
Bowman-Shaw, Sir Neville 38
Bradman, Godfrey 92, 185
Braine, Bernard 133
Bright, Keith 186
Brittan, Leon 95, 100
Brooke, Peter 166
Brown, A.B. 21–2
Brown, Colin 129
Brown, Gordon 246, 249–50
Brown, Michael 222

Brown, Sir Patrick 181–2, 223, 227, 230
Bruinvels, Peter 127
Buchanan, Elizabeth 210
Burley, David 120
Burns, Simon 128
Burt, Alistair 160
Butler, Sir Robin 197

Caines, Jean 141
Caithness, Malcolm 212, 221–2, 223, 227
Callaghan, James 81, 94
Campbell, Alastair 246, 248
Cash, Bill 255
Channon, Paul 227, 228
Chaplin, Sheila 113, 117
Churchill, Sir Winston 81, 86, 133, 135, 147
Clark, Alan 141, 149, 183
Clarke, Kenneth 239, 240
   future leader? 255–7
Cole, John 143
Condon, Sir Paul 1, 207
Cook, Robin 250
Coombs, Simon 51, 76, 105
Corbett, Robin 252
Cotton, Brian 40
Courtney, Emma 2–3, 204–5, 208, 217, 235, 244, 266
Cowie, Sir Tom 35
Critchley, Julian 96
Crosland, Tony 26
Crossman, Richard 26
Cryer, Bob 82
Cundell, Peggy 44
Cunningham, Jack 250
Currie, Edwina 14
   eggs and salmonella 130–1
   media revelations 214–5
Cutler, Alan 28–30

Davidson, Jim 82
Davidson, Richard 24
Davis, David, 82

Day, Debbie 66, 70, 136
Day, Sir Graham 75
Deacon, Brian 176
Dee, Karen 183, 223
de Sancha, Antonia 3
Dempster, Nigel 200–201
Derbah, Mustaphah 39
Dewar, Donald 250
Dicks, Terry, 106
Dimbleby, David 132
Djanogly, Jonathan 115
Dorrell, Stephen 166
   future leader? 257–8
Dowd, Jim 252
Downie, Paul 178
Dubs, Alf 262
Dunwoody, Gwyneth 236
Durband, Alan 12, 212
Dykes, Hugh 236

Edmondson, Caroline 136–7, 208, 215
Edmondson, Peter 171
Edwardes, Michael 75
Edwards, J.R. (Baz) 11, 13
El Bazi, Eddie 38
England, Rachel 183, 262
Evans, David 81

Faulkner, David 120
Featherstone-Witty, Mark 13
Fennell, Desmond 186
Ferrari, Enzo 33
Field, Barry 81
Flaxman, John 53
Flight, Howard 127
Foot, Michael 26, 52–3, 81, 85
Forsyth, Michael 143, 261
Foster, Derek 88
Foster, Sir Norman 198
Fowler, Norman 4, 85, 193
Fowles, John 31
Fox, Marcus 133
Frankel, Maurice 91–2, 137
Franks, Oliver 20–1

Freeman, John 32, 36
Freeman, Mary 52, 55
Freeman, Roger 82, 212, 223,
    227
Frith, Ken 119
Frost, David 164

Gardiner, George 54
Garel-Jones, Tristan 87, 89, 156
Garrett, Tony 129
Gibson, Michael 28
Gibson, Nick 40
Gibson, Tom 55
Gibson-Jarvie, Bob 33
Godden, Margaret 54, 58
Goodman, Harry 186
Gorman, Teresa 239
Gorst, John 236
Goschen, Giles 228
Gow, Ian 47, 105, 146–9, 151–2
    killed 146
Grimshaw, John 196
Gummer, John 52, 138
Gunn, John 125
Gunn, Sheila 129, 168–9, 201,
    204, 208, 217
Gurnett, Tricia 128, 131, 134,
    175, 208, 211, 215

Haggar, Nick 135
Hague, William 262
Hailsham, Quintin 26, 111
Hall, Joan 48–9
Hamilton, Archie 148
Hampson, Keith 58, 154
Hanley, Jeremy 82
Hannam, John 66
Harris, Robin 51
Harrison, George 10
Hart, David 259
Harvey, Nick 236
Hatton, Derek 99, 123
Hawthorn, Mike 33
Heard, Stephen 183, 262, 266
Heath, Edward 47, 81, 82–3, 94,

95, 158, 235
Helm, Martin 214, 223
Heseltine, Michael 57–8, 84,
    100–101, 125, 151, 173,
    183, 235, 239, 240
    challenge to Thatcher 152–3
    future leader? 256
    leadership election, second
    round 156
    Westland 100, 101
Hickmett, Richard 127
Hill, Graham 33
Hill, Keith 252
Hind, Kenneth 87
Hoare, Ronnie 32–4, 202
Hodge, Margaret 97, 252
Hogg, Douglas 107
Hogg, Paul 178, 183
Homan, Hugh, 2, 24
Hooley, Peter 208
Hoon, Geoff 252
Hougham, John 184
Howard, Michael 143, 260
Howarth, Alan 263
Howe, Geoffrey 39, 95, 99–100,
    111
    resignation speech 151
Howell, David 95
Hughes, Robert 222
Hughes, Simon 74
Hulks, Carole 183
Hunt, David 239
Hunt, James 32, 36
Hurd, Douglas 57, 119–120, 143,
    158, 160, 247
    leadership election 156
    Sunday trading 111, 112

Ince, Anthony 66, 118, 135, 169,
    171
Ingham, Bernard 222
Ireland, Innes 33

Jackson, Robert 53
Jenkin, Patrick 98, 99, 107, 160

Jones, George 129
Jones, Tom 73
Jones, Tudor 11
Joseph, Keith 95, 160
    at Education 101–2, 108–9
Jowell, Tessa 252

Kantor, Ralph 121
Kavanagh, Trevor 209, 211
Keays, Sara 95, 116
Kellett-Bowman, Elaine 81, 243, 260
Kent, Prince Michael 37
Kenwright, Bill 10, 12
Kerpel, Tony 161, 163, 164, 166, 167
Key, Robert 58, 212, 223, 227–8
King, John 186
King, Roger 76
King, Tom 229
Kinnock, Neil 84, 85, 117, 173, 246
Kirkbride, Julie 215
Kirkwood, Archie 92
Knight, Ted 97
Kurtz, Zöe 55

Ladak, Ali 39
Laing, Eleanor 212, 226, 263
Lamont, Norman 53, 110, 143, 145, 158, 166
Lang, Ian 261
Lawson, Dominic 141–2, 144
Lawson, Nigel 95, 99, 108–9, 111, 141, 259
Leigh, Sir Geoffrey 212
Lennox-Boyd, Mark 148–9
Lethbridge, Nemone 25
Lewis, Terry 82
Lightbown, David 98
Lilley, Peter 258
Lithgow, Adrian 208
Littlejohn, Richard 209
Livingstone, Ken 96, 97–9, 188, 247

Lowe, Martin 38–9
Lyons, Sir William 33

MacFarlane, Neil 57
MacGregor, John 82, 177, 178, 181, 192, 195, 208, 212–3, 223, 226–8, 231, 233
MacIntosh, John 96, 247
Mackay, Andrew 221
Mackay, John 227
Major, John 60–1, 107, 110, 124, 136, 140, 143, 144, 173, 192, 210, 222
    'back me or sack me' 235, 238–243
    'Back to Basics' 3, 219
    Chancellor 151
    Chief Secretary to the Treasury 132
    first government 158
    leadership election 156
    leadership victory 157
    leadership vote, 1995 243
    Redwood challenge 239
Mandelson, Peter 246, 248
Maples, John 263
Marlow, Angela 183, 262
Marlow, Tony 135–6, 239
Marx, Clare 202–203, 214
Mason, Tania 40, 127, 129
Masterman, John 20
Mates, Michael 58, 154
Maudling, Reginald 26
Mawhinney, Brian 54, 181, 189
    appointed party chairman 233
    at Transport 226, 229–34
    future leader? 260
Maxwell, Robert 77–8
McCartney, Paul 10, 12–13
McLoughlin, Patrick 58, 178
McNair-Wilson, Michael 50, 63, 147
McNutt, Alasdair 54, 113
Mcacher, Michael 250
Mellor, David 3, 166, 209, 220,

227
Meyer, Anthony 151, 153, 154
Michael, Alun 252
Milier, Fiona 70
Miller, Hal 70, 140
Milligan, Stephen 215, 222
Mitchell, Andrew 111
Mitterrand, François 266
Montagu, Nick 182, 213, 215,
    223, 230
Montgomery, Fergus 153
Moore, John 153, 262
Morrison, Peter 148–9, 153–5,
    241
Morrison, Sarah 125
Moss, Lewis 45
Murray, Stephen 130
Muscat, Jim and Ingrid 135

Neave, Airey 47, 94, 105
Nestor, Magdalene 178, 223
Newlands, Glynn 73
Newton, Wilfrid 186–7, 192, 194
Nicholls, John 1, 83, 207, 216,
    223
Nichols, Patrick 58
Nicholson, Emma 58
Nicholson, Sir John 35
Norris, Edward 129, 135, 200,
    204, 205, 251
Norris, Eileen 6–10, 113, 129,
    175
Norris, John 6–9, 133
Norris, Richard 6
Norris, Tony 66, 200, 202, 204,
    251
Norris, Vicky 2, 31, 52, 55, 78,
    129, 169, 200–1, 202–3, 204,
    205, 216
    as campaigner 55, 113, 175
    née Gibson 28

O'Brien, Fred 35–7
Oldland, Mike 31
Ottaway, Richard 50, 58

Owen, David 85
Owen, Victor, 77, 135

Page, Jack 243
Paisley, Rev. Ian 82
Parkes, Mike 33
Parkinson, Cecil 95, 116, 192,
    227
Parris, Matthew 178
Patten, Chris 30, 58, 117, 141,
    144, 156, 173
    future leader? 260
Patten, John 51, 71–2, 85, 119,
    156
Pickthall, Colin 87
Pilley, Heather 183, 262
Porritt, Jonathon 189
Porter, Vernon 55, 104
Portillo, Michael 173, 190, 239,
    240, 259, 262
Powell, Charles 142
Powell, Enoch 81, 83–4
Power, Jim 28
Prescott, John 249, 250
Prior, James 95, 125
Pym, Francis 94–5, 176

Radford, Mike 25
Redwood, John 53, 136, 233,
    239–40, 258–9
Reece, Sir Gordon 84
Reece, Lesley 66
Reichmann, Paul 190
Reynolds, Francis 24, 26–7
Rhys-Williams, Brandon 126
Richards, Rod 222
Riddell, Peter 114
Ridley, Nicholas 82, 101,
    108–109, 138–144, 153, 188,
    217, 258
Ridley, Tony 185–86
Rifkind, Malcolm 177, 187, 226,
    260
Rippon, Geoffrey 111
Robinson, Geoffrey 252

Robinson, Mark 127
Rogers, Gareth 'Jolly' 12, 16
Rogers, Sir Richard 198
Ryder, Richard 169, 208

Sarrel, Lady Pamela 44
Sayeed, Jonathan 83
Scott, James 118
Scott, Sir Nicholas 260
Scott, Sir Richard 197
Sharp, David 2, 200
Sharp, Jennifer 1–3, 200, 205,
    207, 208, 216
Shattock, Gordon 103
Shaw, Giles 76
Shepherd, Richard 137
Sheppard, Allen 125, 198
Shore, Peter 236
Short, Clare 247, 250–1
Sissons, Peter 10, 12
Skinner, Dennis 21–2, 236
Skinner, Geoff 191
Smart, Victor 129
Smith, Andrew 54, 59–60,
    114–15, 117, 130, 251
Smith, Chris 92
Smith, John 84, 173–4, 246, 249
Smith, Malcolm 42
Soames, Christopher 147
Soames, Nicholas 137–8
Somerson, Hugo 136
Sopel, Jon 242
Sopwith, Tommy 32
Spearing, Nigel 236
Spicer, Jim 126
Spring, Richard 222
St John Stevas, Norman 94
Stanley, Martin 139, 142
Stephens, Philip 191
Stewart, David 214
Stewart, Ian 139
Stirling, James 27
Stradling-Thomas, John 148
Strathclyde, Tom 228
Sugar, Alan 134

Sullivan, David 134
Surtees, John 33
Sutch, David 130
Sweeney, Jack 12

Tatchell, Peter 74
Taylor, Lynn 203–204, 209, 216,
    217
Tebbit, Norman 95, 104
Temple, Anthony 24–5
Thatcher, Margaret 4, 47, 52, 61,
    75, 81, 84, 94–7, 100–101,
    103, 111, 117, 124, 138, 190
  1983 General Election 52
  and ERM 151
  Brighton bomb 103–104
  Bruges speech 151
  Cabinet shuffles 94–5
  growing isolation 149, 155
  Heseltine's challenge 152–3
  Leader of the Opposition 47
  leadership challenge 153–6
  local government finance 107
  memoirs 215
  Meyer's leadership challenge
    151
  out of office 146
  PPSs 148
  refusal to listen 150
  Ridley resignation 143–4
Thomas, George 64
Thompson, Andrew 130
Thompson, Patrick 129
Thorne, Neil 241
Tribe, R. Adm. Raymond 43
Trafford, Tony 48–9
Tumim, Judge Stephen 167–8
Tunnicliffe, Denis 186–7, 198
Turner, Andrew 51, 55, 126
Turner, Derek 193

Underwood, John 183–4

Vaizey, John 21–2
van Straubenzee, Bill 53

Vaughan, Dennis 165–6

Waddington, David 79, 90, 247
Wakeham, John 82, 104, 111
Waldegrave, William 21, 105–7, 262
Walden, Brian 182
Walker, Peter 63, 95, 147, 239, 258
Walters, Simon 208, 209
Ward, Christopher 45
Wastell, David 129
Watts, John 228
Weatherill, Bernard 64–5, 85, 111, 133
Webb, Graham 197
Wells, Sir John 52
Whiskin, Nigel 121, 126
Whitelaw, William 95, 222
Whiteley, Simon 223

Whittingdale, John 153, 177
Widdecombe, Ann 52
Williams, Clive 45
Williams, Shirley 124
Wilson, Des 92, 137, 185
Wilson, Harold 21, 26
Wimpress, Doug 37
Wood, Phillip 182
Wood, Sydney 35–37, 40, 45, 194

X, Malcolm 26

Yardley, Patsy 55
Yeo, Tim 48, 156, 220–1
Young, David 58
Young, George 181, 197, 232, 243
Young, Janet 94
Younger, George 153